ACCOMMODATION
MANAGEMENT

ACCOMMODATION MANAGEMENT

Rosemary Hurst

Heinemann : London

William Heinemann Ltd
10 Upper Grosvenor Street, London W1X 9PA
LONDON MELBOURNE
JOHANNESBURG AUCKLAND

First published 1984
Reprinted 1986

Hurst, Rosemary
    Accommodation management.
    1. Institutional housekeeping
    I. Title
    647'.9   TX321
ISBN 0 434 90794 4

Filmset by
Wilmaset, Birkenhead, Merseyside
Printed in Great Britain by
Redwood Burn Limited, Trowbridge, Wiltshire

Contents

Preface

Whether it be in a Hotel, Hospital, University or other Residential Establishment, the main purpose of the Housekeeping and Accommodation Department is to provide a clean, comfortable and attractive environment for all those who use the premises – and these services must be provided in such a way that they do not lead to any safety, fire or health hazards; hygiene is of particular importance with control of pathogenic organisms and the prevention of cross-infection becoming an important factor.

Every year, considerable sums of money are spent and there is an ever-increasing need for accountable management in which performance and output is measured against cost. This can only be achieved with a constant attention to deail, a logical approach to the assessment of what is actually needed and how this can be accomplished, a definition of standards, the introduction of quality controls and the use of building fabrics and surfaces, furnishings and materials which are not only attractive, but are designed to be functional, easy to clean and maintain and are durable. Many Housekeepers and Managers advise on the choice of floor, wall and ceiling finishes and are actively involved in the buying and replacement of the fabrics used for curtains, upholstery and bedding and it is for this reason that these sections have been included.

Labour is the main cost element in the cleaning budget and accounts for between 90 and 95 per cent of the total amount with the remaining percentage being fairly evenly divided between the cost for equipment and the cost for cleaning materials; it follows, therefore, that the main reduction in expenditure can only come from alterations in staff numbers and hours and in the way they are organized. The first part of the book discusses the general aspects of organization, staffing and planning.

Whereas most of the routine work procedures for cleaning and servicing are similar, each of the main sectors in the Industry has its own specifications and interest and the last part of the book gives job descriptions and describes the work and problem areas for each with, at the end, a brief reminder that the housekeeping requirements for offices, public buildings, art centres, theatres and museums offer work which is equally demanding and which requires as much basic knowledge and expertise.

The management of the housekeeping and accommodation services can be a very interesting and rewarding job, seldom one which is from 'nine to five' but one which offers variety, responsibility and demands good technical knowledge, skill and enthusiasm and the ability to create a team from the very mixed members of staff which are employed.

Included at the end of each section are one or two questions or exercises for discussion and, in some cases, for individual research and observation and the use of manufacturers technical data.

Some Student's Comments

(after practical experience in the Industry)

'Staff should be given the right equipment with which to work; it is no good providing third-rate equipment and expecting a first-class job to result.'

'The Domestic had no set rota for the day and so did what she thought was necessary, having received very little training.'

'The Chambermaid's working methods were particularly poor. At one stage, a chambermaid was seen to clean the washbasin with the W.C. brush and dry it with the guest's soiled towel. This is extremely unhygienic and made the cleaning of the bathroom a waste of time.'

'If the maids required any extra linen, it was too easily obtained from the store; no signature or order form was required.'

'. . . but the Supervisor seemed to spend most of her time compiling duty rosters and the Domestics were left to carry out the job.'

'. . . these problems occurred due to lack of strict supervision and not enough training and also through having very little contact with the Head Housekeeper.'

'. . . more contact with superiors could also solve many problems; the maids had no interest in their job and so did not take care over it. Managers should socialize more with the staff.'

'The management/staff relationship could be a great deal better if both sides would come into closer contact with each other.'

'Communication was the biggest barrier I encountered. In both places, there were groups of people who were governed by position or race and these formed barriers with other members of staff.'

'In my visit, I was interested to see the colour schemes and materials used in decoration and furbishment. It was obvious from the glaring insubtleties and poor fabrics that the hotel was built in the early 1970s and had been a victim of budgetry control!'

'Theft occurs because of the easy access to both hotels and hospitals by the general public.'

'At the hotel, the security on the premises was strict with everybody coming in carefully vetted but in the hospital, the security was very lax which is understandable as any form of security would be almost impossible.'

'A very instructive visit. I can't think how they manage to make a profit.'

1
Staff Planning and Organization

The main costs arising from servicing a building are for labour, cleaning materials and equipment. When budgets are examined, it is found that the cost of labour accounts for between 90 and 95 per cent of the total spent, with only 5 to 10 per cent expended on materials and equipment so that, whilst potential savings on materials and equipment cannot be ignored, it is obvious that the greatest economies can only come from the control of labour – the numbers employed, the grades and categories of the staff and the number of hours worked. This can only be determined by a logical analysis of the needs and function of the department.

1.1 Determination of the work-load – the needs and functions

In most departments the work-load can be divided into two categories. *Fixed* work can be defined as the tasks and duties which have to be completed irrespective of the number of people in the building – such areas as the main entrance, public areas and rooms, corridors and cloakrooms – whether there are ten or a hundred people on the premises these places must be clean. In hospitals, universities and colleges, long-term residences and public buildings most of the work is of the 'fixed' variety with few variations so that the need for staff remains constant.

Flexible work is directly related to a unit or level of activity. In a hotel the occupancy cycle fluctuates weekly and seasonly and with it the subsequent work-load; when a room is not let, there is no need for cleaning and servicing and it takes considerable skill and accurate forecasts of future occupancy on the part of the Housekeeper to maintain practical staff levels (see Chapter 10).

Given similar circumstances, there should be one 'right' way to clean or service any area; this is usually recorded in a *work specification* otherwise known as the *operating or cleaning manual*. This states the order and method of work for each of the jobs to be completed, the equipment and materials needed and the necessary frequency. The specification must cover all the daily, weekly and periodical cleaning schedules so that, from the information it provides, it is possible to estimate the *time* needed to complete the work – and from the total time, the number and category of staff.

Work study techniques are used to determine the specifications and the standards needed and are used both in the setting-up of a new department and as a means of reviewing the work of an existing organization.

Whilst a small firm will have to employ an outside consultancy firm, many large organizations have their own work study departments who are employed to advise on and review work and staff levels as an on-going process. When these services are not available, a house-keeper should be able to use her own experience and practice to set her own specifications and standards.

There are, however, many advantages in introducing outside specifications to a department as it is more likely that practices and traditions, often regarded as sacrosanct, can be viewed impartially. The work study team should:

(1) Review the work in the overall context of the needs of the establishment and take into account that any change of procedure may affect other areas. They should have the authority to re-allocate work between departments.

An example of this occurred some years ago in the Hospital Service when it was found that between 30 and 35 per cent of a ward-maid's time was spent washing-up. Considerable savings were made when this work was transferred to a central washing-up unit; for instance, there was an immediate 30 per cent reduction in the numbers of domestic staff employed on the ward and, against this, only a small increase in staff for the unit and in porters to move trolleys of clean and dirty crockery. Standards of hygiene improved as it becamse easier to control the 'sterilizing' temperatures, there was less noise on the wards, fewer breakages and a reduction in the costs for detergents so that, although initially, there were heavy capital costs for the installation of new machines, for new trolleys and increased china stocks, the overall savings were considerable.

(2) Record and analyse the way in which the department is already operating. They will want to know: what jobs are being done; their frequency; how many people are concerned; how the work is done with what equipment and materials and the average time taken. These can be costed and the information used as a basis for comparison with any different and improved work method.

Rather than rely on the supervisor's opinion of what is or is not done, observations are made during the normal working day. Some of the information gained can be unexpected; for instance, in one establishment it was found that after lunch had been served, the waiting staff cleaned and polished the silver in the time available before they had to serve teas – all were very busy and no time was wasted but, in total, $13\frac{1}{2}$ hours were spent cleaning silver each day on five days a week and the work study team queried whether it was strictly necessary for 67 hours a week to be expended on this task. Shortly after, stainless steel cutlery was bought and the staff were re-allocated to other jobs.

(3) Develop new and improved methods of working. All the information is studied and discussed with those directly concerned, that is, the housekeeper or domestic manager, supervisors and the work study team. Given similar conditions, there should be one agreed method of servicing each area with the panel of experts deciding what should or should not be done so as to arrive at an overall specification and the development of the cleaning manual.

Whereas a high standard should be the aim, it may not always be economically feasible and may not be needed or expected by the customer. The standard should be related to the type and needs of the establishment. All areas must be *socially acceptable*, that is, they should be clean, tidy and free from untoward smells of smoke, drink or stuffiness but a 5-star hotel will aim at perfection at all times whilst a 1-star hotel may decide that having the furniture polished every two weeks and the windows cleaned every two or three months is all that is necessary and commensurate with the cost of the room, whilst a college may do little more than daily clean during term-time but have a thorough turn-out during the vacations.

Sometimes the changes that are made are very obvious and could have been introduced without outside help but most supervisors have a full-time job and become very closely involved with day-to-day routine. They usually do not have the time or the energy to stand apart and really study what is happening; moreover, a supervisor will not always want to make changes which could prove unpopular.

Even what can seem to be a very minor change in standard or

method can make a great difference in costs as is indicated in the following two reports.

Report on the effect of re-sheeting a bed each day instead of the present system of re-sheeting on departure or on every second day – as suggested by the new General Manager.

From: Executive Housekeeper   Date: 31 December
To: General Manager
Subject: Re-sheeting beds

Present position

The hotel has 240 twin-bedded rooms with an average occupancy throughout the year of 75 per cent. The average guest stay is for two nights. This means that approximately 360 beds are in use each night and, with beds re-sheeted on departure or every second day, about 180 beds are changed daily. Maids will, however, re-sheet a bed if it has become stained or dirty. Each maid services 15 rooms a day.

Costs involved in changing

If the changes are implemented, the difference in costs would be:

Capital costs

Linen stocks would have to be increased by:
    960 Sheets
    960 Pillowcases
    480 Hand towels
    480 Bath towels
    480 Bathmats
I am assuming that towels and bathmats will also be changed daily. This increase in stock allows for the periods when occupancy is at 100 per cent and is based on a 24-hour return from the laundry but makes no allowance for the 48-hour return which occurs each week-end.

Revenue costs

Laundry At present, using a commercial laundry costs are 90p per guest/bed. At 75 per cent occupancy, a budget increase of £1080 a week or £56 160 a year will be required. Capital costs would be avoided if the hotel changed over to linen-hire but the cost of hiring would be about 10 per cent higher than the laundry cost.

Labour Costs are based on the difference in time between remaking a bed – about 2 minutes, and re-sheeting – about 5 minutes. The extra labour needed will be 3 minutes × 180 = about 9 hours each day. I would consider that a staff increase of one full-timer and one part-timer at 20 hours a week would be reasonable if existing standards are to be maintained.

The number of rooms serviced by each maid would be reduced from 15 to 14. At present wage levels, this will increase staff costs by £5250.

Additional costs I have not costed these out but there will be some additional costs for administration, handling, repairs and storage.

Customer expectations

It is questionable whether customers expect a higher standard than at present. Guests have made no adverse comments on the frequency of re-sheeting although this may be because maids have instructions to change sheets and towels more often if they see it is necessary.

Recommendation

Because of the need to revise the budget and the expense involved, I would consider that in the present economic climate, it is unnecessary to change from our present standard.

Report on bedmaking made by the assistant housekeeper (training) to the executive housekeeper

From: Assistant Housekeeper (Training)   Date: 25 October
To: Executive Housekeeper
Subject: Review of Bedmaking Procedures
I have tested the 4 methods of bedmaking as suggested. Methods 1, 2, and 3 use the traditional mattress cover, 2 sheets, 2 blankets, 2 pillows and covers and a bedspread. Method 4 uses the mattress cover, valence, 1 sheet, continental quilt and quilt cover.
The results are as follows:

1. Present method

Sheets, blankets, pillows and bedspread placed on bed and tucked in separately.
Appearance: Good
Average Time Taken: 5 minutes.

2. 'American' method

Bed made by the maid standing at the top of the bed and, from that position, placing and tucking in all bedding, turning down, placing bedspread, then pillows and finishing the top part of bed. The maid then moves to the bottom of the bed and, pulling all bedding straight, tucks in both sheets and blankets and arranges the bedspread. When it is not possible to move the bed away from the bedhead, the same principle applies with the maid working from a position at the centre of each side; that side is finished before she moves to the opposite side to pull the bedding straight. By this method, the maid's walking distance is reduced to about 20 feet.

Appearance: Method looks untidy but final result good

Average Time Taken: under 3 minutes

3. Using two maids

Time is wasted by one maid waiting for the other to unfold sheets and pass blankets.

Appearance: Good

Average Time Taken: 6 minutes

4. Using a continental quilt

Appearance: More informal than the other methods but, if bedding is coloured or patterned to match the room decorations, can look very attractive

Average Time Taken: Under $2\frac{1}{2}$ minutes

Conclusions

It will be seen that an alteration from Method 1 to either Method 2 or 4 will provide savings. At present, a maid servicing 15 twin-bedded rooms is spending about 3 hours in bedmaking; if this time is reduced to even 3 minutes for each bed, one hour is saved on each working day and the number of rooms serviced could be increased to 17. We employ 22 maids to service 240 rooms; this number could be reduced to 20 at a saving of £7800.

If Method 2 is adopted, there are no extra costs apart from those connected with retraining staff. Room appearance stays the same.

If Method 4 is adopted, there will be a re-equipping cost of about £120 per bed – for continental quilt (tog value 9), valance, and 3 sets of sheet and quilt covers. Sheets and covers are supplied in either polyester/cotton or viscose/cotton fabric and require a different wash temperature than that for cotton so it could mean that we will have problems with the laundry. I suppose old linen stocks could be sold off to staff? The appearance of the bed is different and may not be in accordance with our guests' expectations – as a 4-star hotel we will still be required to provide traditional bedding if so requested.

Recommendations

It seems to me that, although the younger generation under 25 to 30 years, are well used to using a quilt, most of our guests are considerably older and may not like the alteration. For this reason and because of the additional expense of re-equipping, I would suggest that Method 2 be adopted and time allocated to retrain staff. Staff numbers can be adjusted by 'natural' wastage.

When the work specification has been agreed, *work measurement* techniques are used to determine the *time* needed to complete the work. This is the *basic time* required by an experienced worker using the agreed method of work, the right equipment and materials and working to a predetermined standard. Once the basic time has been agreed, an *allowance* must then be added for *rest* or *relaxation*. This extra time allows the worker to recover the energy which has been expended and also takes into account any environmental difficulties which are inherent in the job such as bad lighting, awkward work positioning or just the need to constantly lift a heavy load or to trail up and down stairs all day. This rest allowance also covers the time needed for coffee breaks and for changing into uniform and visits to the cloakroom. About $12\frac{1}{2}$ per cent is usually added to the basic time for someone doing light, sedentary work and about 15 to 18 per cent for a room-maid who exerts more physical effort (p. 8).

A *contingency allowance* may also be needed to allow for unforeseen interruptions to the work flow; this can happen in a number of jobs such as Domestic Assistant in a hospital or in many supervisory jobs where there is contact with the public.

Basic time plus the percentage *allowance for rest and contingency* result in the *standard time* which is required for each unit of work and it is this time which is used to calculate the time in *hours per week* for the average *work-load* of the department (p. 9).

Obviously, as staff continuously point out, circumstances are not always, or ever, normal and some areas become particularly dirty and need longer cleaning times than have been allowed. This is where the swings and roundabout philosophy comes into force, and time saved on a 'clean area' is carried over to a dirty job. It is only when the abnormal becomes the normal that standard times are revised.

Rest or relaxation allowances (as a percentage of basic times).

Constant allowances	Men %	Women %		Men %	Women %
Personal	5	7	Mental strain – of a fairly		
Basic fatigue	4	4	complex process	1	1
Variable allowances			– of complex, wide span		
depending on the job			of attention	4	4
Standing	2	4	– very complex	8	8
Awkward – bending	2	3	Monotony – low	0	0
Very awkward – lying			– medium	1	1
or stretching	7	7	– high	4	4
Lifting a weight:			*Variable allowances*		
4.5 kg	1	2	depending on the		
11.3 kg	4	6	environment		
18.1 kg	9	13	Bad light		
22.7 kg	13	20	– well below		
Fine or exacting work	2	2	recommended level	2	2
Very exacting work	5	5	– quite inadequate	5	5
			Noise level		
			– continuous	0	0
			– intermittent, loud	2	2
			– high-pitched, loud	5	5

Rest allowance percentages are based on medical research and take into account the energy expended or the strain inherent in a job. They are usually negotiated with the staff or trade union representative. The variation between the allowances for men and women recognize the difference in strength and muscle power. The allowance percentages are not applied to the entire job but only to those parts of it where they are applicable.

A large establishment will have an agreed staff requirement for a certain number of hours each week for the basic cleaning and servicing; in addition, it is usual to add a percentage for *relief staff*, to cover any absenteeism, sickness and holidays. This percentage depends on local circumstances but is often between 15 and 18 per cent.

The work study team should also help to decide which category and grade of staff is necessary for the particular level of work bearing in mind that with careful training basic-grade staff can be very adaptable.

When there is any big alteration in work routines, all staff must be told what is happening and how they could be affected. Any changes made should mean that the department is more economical to run, that the work is easier or that it is more hygienic, that there is less waste or it provides more job satisfaction – the advantages of change should be obvious as should the advantage of new working methods.

Examples of standard times.

	Job No.	Basic Time (min)	Rest Allowance (%)	Contingency Allowance (%)	Standard Time (min)
Re-making a bed	1	1.8	22.0	10	2.38
Re-sheeting a bed	2	3.9	22.5	10	5.17
Cleaning a washbasin	3	1.2	13.0	10	1.48
Cleaning a bath	4	1.92	14.5	10	2.40
Cleaning a shower	5	1.0	13.0	10	1.23
Cleaning a W.C.	6	0.94	16.0	10	1.18
Dusting a dressing-table	7	0.43	11.0	10	0.52
Polishing a dressing-table	8	0.85	13.0	10	1.05
Emptying and cleaning wastepaper bin	9	0.72	11.0	10	0.87
Vacuum cleaning – hard floor per 10 m^2	10	1.8	13.5	10	2.22
Vacuum cleaning – carpet per 10 m^2	11	4.3	16.0	10	5.42
Mop sweeping – hard floor per 10 m^2	12	1.2	13.5	10	1.48
Damp mopping – per 10 m^2	13	2.4	16.0	10	3.02
Scrubbing – manual per 10 m^2	14	3.7	22.0	10	4.88
Scrubbing – machine per 10 m^2	15	2.3	13.0	10	2.83
Polishing – machine per 10 m^2	16	2.1	11.0	10	2.54
Cleaning glass – per m^2	17	0.65	13.5	10	0.8

These work measurement times are based on studies for specific equipment, cleaning agents and methods of work and made in an unobstructed area so can only be used as a guide. They do not include any allowance for getting ready, cleaning and putting away the equipment. The rest allowances vary with the job but an overall allowance of 10 per cent has been added for contingencies.

1.2 Staff organization

The number of staff employed depends entirely on the amount of work to be done and the amount of supervision required to ensure that the work is carried out to the required standard. When there is little variation in the work, an establishment may have a staff level of 2500 hours a week, whilst a hotel may have a fixed staff level of, say, 240 hours a week and a flexible staff requirement of one room-maid for every 75 rooms cleaned each week (p. 206).

It is usual for the Housekeeper to decide whether to employ *full-time staff* or to employ *part-time staff* for a variety of hours to cover awkward work periods, evenings and weekend relief.

The employment of full- or part-time staff

It is usually considered more economical to employ full-time staff than part-timers as fewer people means reduced costs for administration, recruitment, selection and training, supervision and record keeping. All staff have to be provided with a minimum of two uniforms and will need a locker and cloakroom facilities; in many cases they receive 'free' meals on duty and extra equipment may be needed. In some instances, there can also be a security problem by having increased numbers of staff.

Part-timers do, however, offer more flexible staffing arrangements, particularly if a department can only operate at limited times, when there is 'peak' working or when shift hours are needed. It also extends the labour market and makes available wives and mothers who, although having a family to manage, can still offer 20 to 30 hours a week. This group of employees can prove extremely reliable as they are permanently in the area, need the convenience of a job close to home, are usually intelligent and responsible, and able to turn out for work at short notice if needed.

1.2.2 Self-employed staff

There is a growing tendency for a small firm to employ self-employed staff either on a full- or part-time basis for specific work such as cleaning, bar, restaurant work, or cooking. This means that the employee is responsible for paying his own tax and insurances as a self-employed person and the firm will have no insurance or administration costs.

1.2.3 Living-in staff

Most residential establishments and large office buildings want at least one senior member of staff to live on the premises for the general caretaking and oversight of the building and to be available in an emergency, although obviously, as far as possible, all privacy and off-duty periods must be respected. The establishment becomes their home so accommodation should be self-contained; usually basic furniture is provided with the occupant expected to provide linen, china and the smaller furnishings. Any restrictions on the use of the accommodation should have been discussed at the interview as, although much accommodation is suited for a married couple, some is unsuited for children.

Many firms find it necessary to accommodate single staff and seasonal workers either because the establishment is isolated and there is no suitable alternative accommodation, because the employee is new to the district and needs time to arrange lodgings, or because it is felt best for a teenager or trainee to live on the premises.

Living-in staff are available in an emergency but many managers feel that this advantage is outweighed by the difficulties that can occur; permanent staff may not get on well together, there can be sickness and emotional problems, unwelcome visitors, noise, car-parking – the list can be endless and although a deduction is made for accommodation, this does not always cover the cost of heating, laundry and food.

Living-in staff should be encouraged to develop outside interests as many older employees can become isolated and experience great difficulties when they retire and have to create their own homes; because of these problems, many firms offer accommodation for a limited time only or use hostels which are away from the work area.

When money is deducted for board and lodging most staff are, technically, in rented accommodation and as such, are protected by the Rent Act.

1.2.4 Number of staff to employ

Once it is known how many staff are needed on duty each day, the following formula is used to find the number which have to be employed so that days off are covered.

$$\frac{\text{Number required on duty each day} \times \text{Number of days}}{\text{Number of days worked by the employee}} = \text{Number to employ.}$$

So, if 15 staff are needed on each day of the week and they work a five-day week, then:

$$\frac{15 \times 7}{5} = 21 \text{ staff employed.}$$

In the same way, if the numbers required vary each day, the formula still applies. For example:

Mon.	Tues.	Wed.	Thurs.	Fri.	Sat.	Sun.
18	18	18	15	15	6	6

This means that 96 units of work have to be covered so:

$$\frac{96}{5} = 19\frac{1}{5} \text{ or } 19 \text{ full-time staff} + 1 \text{ part-timer at 8 hours.}$$

1.2.5 Spreadover payments or split duties

Spreadover or split duty payments are made when an employee starts work early in the day, goes off duty and then returns in the evening. Although he may not have exceeded 8 hours work, extra payments have to be made to compensate for the inconvenience and extra travelling costs. The amount which has to paid is agreed by the Wages Council or by Union Agreement.

Split duties are normally unpopular and can be avoided by introducing shift working or by using a part-timer for the evening period.

1.2.6 Actual and paid hours

When estimating for the staff budget, allowance must be made to cover the extra payments for Saturday, Sunday, Bank Holiday, Night and other 'unsocial' hours which have to be worked. Depending on the authority, payments can be at time and a fifth, time and a quarter, time and a half or at double time. As an example the *actual hours* worked during the week might be as follows:

Mon.	Tues.	Wed.	Thur.	Fri.	Sat.	Sun.	
8	8	8	Day off	Rest day	8	8	= 40 hours

but this includes weekend working and if Saturday is paid at time and a half and Sunday is paid at double time the employee is credited with an additional 12 hours and receives pay for 52 hours. The estimates must be based on the *paid hours* – and obviously, from a cost point of view, weekend working should be kept to the minimum.

Overtime payments must also be considered when estimating. Overtime should only be paid when it has been agreed that it is necessary by the supervisor – before it is worked. The main exception to this rule applies to maintenance staff who often have to finish work before going off duty or when it is difficult to estimate for a 'one-off' job in an emergency. Overtime is usually paid for both full- and part-time staff after the normal contracted hours for full-time worker – 38 or 40 hours – have been worked, but in a few cases, it is paid after the contracted hours for the individual part-timer has been worked; in which case, it can be cheaper to employ casual labour.

Many firms consider that it is cheaper to pay a limited amount of overtime rather than to engage extra full-time staff as the cost of employing staff is high and this will avoid redundancy payments if staff levels have to be reduced.

1.2.7 Duty rosters

Duty rosters control the hours of work and should be drawn up well in advance so that all staff know when they will or will not be required on duty. As far as possible, the roster should show an equal distribution of weekends off, early and late duty-turns and split shifts. There should be an overlap of duties sufficient to provide for a handover of duties and to ensure that an area is not left unmanned. Relief staff are used to replace absentees or sickness and are not always rostered but have their duties allocated as the need arises.

Records have to be kept of the hours worked, if all staff work straight shifts with no question of extra payments for Saturday or Sunday work, there is a case for taking the hours worked on trust, as happens with most office and management staff, in the hope that not too many people are arriving at 0910 hours instead of 0900 hours and leaving several minutes earlier than the finishing time. Even a slippage of a few minutes a day can lead to a loss of one to two hours a week.

When extra payments are made, however, accurate records of the hours worked must be kept which means, at the very least, a *signing-in and out book*. This book has many disadvantages; it is too easy for staff to sign-in or out for the time they have been rostered and not for the times when they actually arrive and depart, parts of the book can become illegible, and it can be lost. It is also time-consuming as the information has to be transferred, checked and analysed before wage payments can be made.

The *Clock/Punch Card System* is not always acceptable to staff and unions but it does mean that the information is readily available, that it is in a compact form and it ensures that there is no dispute about the hours worked. As with all systems, this method of recording can be abused and there must be a clear understanding that no member of staff punches a card for anyone else – in some firms this can mean dismissal – and it is not unknown for an employee to punch a card and then disappear to go shopping or down to the 'local' and reappear some time later. Before being passed to the Wages Section, all cards and hours are checked in the housekeeping department to ensure that all the hours worked are the same as on the duty roster and that any absenteeism and sickness is entered.

Records must be kept of *sick certificates* showing the cause of absence and the date for the return to work – the signing off date. An employee can not return to work before this date has been given by the doctor as, although he may feel fit, he could still spread infection. Employers are responsible for paying the State Sickness Benefit to their employees for up to 8 weeks of sickness in any tax year. They recover the amounts paid when they make their monthly returns for National Insurance and Income Tax.

All hours worked are transferred to the *Weekly Time Sheet*. This records absenteeism, sickness, Bank Holiday working, days taken in 'lieu', and Annual Holidays (see page 15).

Similar information is also recorded on the individual Employee Record Card.

It is becoming increasingly important that all staff are flexible and able to adapt to changing conditions – particularly in a small establishment; to encourage this *incentive bonus schemes* and *flexible working hours* have been introduced.

1.2.8 Incentive bonus schemes

These are based on work study assessments of what constitutes a 'fair' day's work for either the individual worker or for a group of workers, and are negotiated with the staff and the unions concerned. Incentive bonus payments are made for increased production which is considered additional to the normal work-load and are used to encourage staff to increase their output. In practice, however, some bonus schemes are based and paid from a lower base-level than would be expected from the work study assessment. This is because in past years, many jobs have been filled by a full-time member of staff working an 8-hour day when the job itself provides work for only $5\frac{1}{2}$

Weekly control/time sheet.

Department.................... Date....................

Paid holiday	Sickness	Absence	Actual hours worked	Overtime (× 1¼)	Overtime (× 1½)	Overtime (× 2)	Total hours paid

Name	Pay scale	Hours worked							Total hours	× 1¼	× 1½	× 2	Remarks
		Mon.	Tues.	Wed.	Thur.	Fri.	Sat.	Sun.					

or 6 hours a day with the result that the employee, through no fault of his own, has become used to working at a lower capacity than is judged to be normal; over a period of years the base-level would be gradually increased until productivity comes in line with the average level of work produced across industry.

The schemes are also used when staff are expected to perform different tasks than those for which they were originally employed and to take on extra responsibilities.

The payment of bonuses should only take place when extra output has been achieved which means that the control and supervision of the scheme is important. Once a bonus has been agreed it can only not be paid to an employee after careful investigation (p. 81). This is discussed further in Section 4.2.

1.2.9 Flexible working hours

Flexible working hours or *flexi-time* is a system that was first introduced in West Germany and is based on the precept that, in many cases, it does not matter at what time a job is done during the day – provided it is done – so that in many cases the starting and finishing time can be left to the discretion of the individual. A company will fix a 'core' time, perhaps from 1100–1500 hours, when all staff are expected to be on the premises and may introduce a rota system to provide basic supervisory or office cover but beyond this, staff are free to arrange their own hours. The system has many advantages. Time is not wasted when adjusting to public transport timetables, the rush-hour can be avoided and it becomes very much easier to combine the job with personal commitments. Moreover, it is almost impossible to be late; any slippage in time lost through late arrival or early departure is automatically adjusted and the time lost is made up. Sickness and absenteeism rates are reduced, morale improves and most staff are loath to change jobs to a firm that does not operate the system.

Whereas flexi-time working is not possible for all grades of staff, it should be possible for departmental heads, some supervisory levels, office and store staff. A few hotels allow room-maids to vary their time of arrival between 0800 and 1000 hours provided a minimum of staff are available for early and late duty.

Flexi-hours are controlled by recording arrival and departure times. This is done either by clock-cards or by feeding the information into the computer; at the end of each pay period the employee is given a statement showing details of the hours worked. Most firms allow a credit or debit balance of between 5 and 8 per cent of the contracted hours which can be adjusted within the next pay period. In practice, most employees seem to keep a small credit balance of hours as a reserve to cover any emergency.

1.2.10 Supervisors

The number of supervisors needed depends very much on the type and the work of the establishment. The role of a supervisor covers three areas. There is:

1 The need to control the amount and the quality of the work produced.
2 The need to provide a focal point for authority and responsibility.
3 The ability to undertake a level of work or to use a skill which cannot be provided by an employee of a lower grade.

The ratio of supervisors to workers depends on the complexity of the work and also on the balance between (1), (2), and (3) above. In a hotel, a floor supervisor will be incharge of a section of between fifty and one hundred rooms with responsibility for five to seven room-maids and a houseporter. In a hospital, a Domestic Supervisor will control the work of between twenty and twenty-four domestic staff working on five or six different wards; the supervisory ratio is much lower than in a hotel as there is a certain amount of supervision and liaison exercised by the nursing staff. In staff accommodation or in a students' hall of residence, supervision may be at the ratio of one to ten or twelve.

The ratio is also affected by the length of time which a department is open during the day; frequently an evening supervisor will be on duty, manning an office, with only one or two maids available to complete the day's work.

All supervisors should have their own area of work so that their exact responsibilities and duties are known and they can develop an interest and pride in the job.

1.3 Departmental records

Records form the memory of a department and are essential both for the planning and scheduling of the day's work and to forecast future requirements. Good records provide written evidence and proof of the performance of any one department and make it possible to decide whether efficiency could be improved.

The type of record kept depends, to a certain extent, on the size of the department and on the standard of any 'back-up' facilities available. Whether or not there are Personnel or Accounts departments, basic information must be kept within the Housekeeping Department as staff details and information may be required when these offices are closed at the weekends or in the evening – or it may not be convenient to them to prepare information in the way needed by the Housekeeper.

A large establishment keeps an up-to-date *desk diary* to record information, news and problems which have to be carried over from one duty supervisor to another and which ties up all aspects of the work carried out within the department. This can make interesting reading and also provides cumulative evidence of staff and equipment faults.

When there is no maintenance department, a small establishment must keep *plans of the building* which show the electrical circuits and fuse boxes, gas runs, and water and central heating pipes with the relevant stop-valves; this also applies to the *sprinkler, fire alarm* and any *fire detection systems* which may be installed as staff must know how these are switched off.

Some or all of the following records should be kept.

1.3.1 Personnel

(a) Staff record cards

These state the name, address, telephone number, date of birth, nationality and national insurance number. When foreign staff are employed, the Labour Permit with expiry date must be recorded.

The back of the card lists the attendance showing sickness and absenteeism, bank holidays and annual leave. This information is entered weekly by the Duty Supervisor at the same time as the clock cards or attendance book is checked before they are passed to the wages section to make-up the wage sheets. Sickness and absenteeism may also be recorded in an *employee absence book*. This is only needed when the department produces an *annual report* which includes the total hours lost for such reasons as absence, sickness, maternity leave, etc.

When employees leave they should be interviewed and the staff record card completed by entering the date and reason for the termination and a brief remark as to suitability; this will form the basis for any reference which may be asked for in the future or to their re-employment. This is necessary as memory can prove fickle when there is a large staff. Some record cards have space for a passport-sized photograph (pp. 20 and 21).

(b) Interview records

When the Housekeeper is responsible for engaging staff, *Application Forms* or an *Interview Book* must be kept; this gives a brief summary of the applicant's particulars, the impression gained and whether or not an engagement is recommended. This is essential when several people have the authority to interview and avoids the problems which can arise when an applicant has been rejected by one supervisor and is interviewed some weeks later by a second supervisor.

(c) Staff training

These record that all staff have received *induction and basic training* in their job, fire training and any special or external courses. The employee usually signs that they know and understand what has been taught and a grading is given. Where there is a Training Department, full records would be kept by them – otherwise, departments are responsible for their own induction and training.

(d) Staff appraisals

These are used by some of the larger companies. They are completed yearly to assess how the individual is performing in their job, where the weaknesses and strengths lay and how these can be remedied or extended by further training. Appraisals should be discussed with the individual concerned and should be used constructively – often as a basis for future promotion and training (see Figures 4.3 and 4.4).

(e) Labour turnover

The cost of labour turnover is high and must take into account advertising, selection, training and the intangible cost of poor and lowered work output caused by reduced morale, unskilled perform-ance and insufficient knowledge of the job situation.

Staff record card.

Side 1

Name	Maiden name	First names	Mr/Mrs/Miss
Address			Phone:
Change of address			Phone:
Date of birth	Nationality	Nat. Ins. No.	Labour permit No. Expiry date
Start date	Position and grade		
Leaving date	Reason		
Ability	Attendance	Appraisal	Re-employment?
Comments			
Clock No.	Locker No.	Uniform	

Side 2

Name	Clock No.	Grade	Dept.

Start date   Holiday Entitlement

B=Bank Hol. D/O=Day Off
L=Leave L/D=Day Off 'in lieu'
S=Sickness A=Absent

Month	Year	1	2	3	4	5	6	7	8	9	10	11	12	13	14	15	16	17	18	19	20	21	22	23	24	25	26	27	28	29	30	31	Totals

A straight percentage gives the number of staff that have been recruited in the previous year and indicates how many will need to be recruited in the future. The Housekeeper should aim for a reduction in turnover from one year to the next. A high turnover of staff points either to an unsatisfactory working environment (such as pay, type of work, lack of equipment, excessive split duties or overtime) or to poor selection and training of staff.

The following formula is used to calculate the turnover percentage:

$$\frac{\text{Number of leavers}}{\text{Average number employed during the period}} \times 100.$$

The *stability index* shows how many staff have been with the department for more than a year and should be used in conjunction with the turnover percentage figure. It is found by:

$$\frac{\text{Present number of employees with 1 year's service or more}}{\text{Total number employed 1 year ago}} \times 100.$$

(f) Records

Records must also be kept of *uniforms* issued, *locker keys* and *staff meetings* and of any *grievance* or *disciplinary proceedings* instituted.

1.3.2 Organization

(a) Operating or cleaning manual

The manual shows the breakdown of all the cleaning and servicing required. The following headings are used: method of cleaning, frequencies, special problems, the work-load estimated in hours per week, the number and grade of staff, equipment, cleaning materials and the storage area in which they are to be kept.

(b) Training manual

This is based on the work identified in the Operating Manual.

(c) Duty rosters, weekly time sheets and room-maid's analysis

These show the actual hours worked or number of rooms cleaned relating to the staff employed.

(d) Maid's and floor supervisor's reports, arrival and departure lists

It is usually only considered necessary to keep these for three or four weeks before filing them in the wastepaper basket.

(e) Forecast of occupancy and occupancy percentages

(f) Package passes

1.3.3 Equipment and supplies

Stock records should be kept showing all issues and receipts and stock-taking figures along with the *weekly* or *monthly consumption sheets* for laundry, guest supplies and materials. The following details are also necessary: *prices* and *suppliers*; *contracts* and *contractors*; *servicing agreements* for the equipment; *inventories* for each room showing all furnishings and fittings.

1.3.4 Building and maintenance

Room maintenance requests should be filed together with the dates when the work has been completed. Periodically, these will be analysed to highlight problem areas so that they can be eliminated.
Details of *Damage, repairs and costs.*
Planned maintenance schedules and *re-decoration* cycles.
Insurance inspections for fire extinguishers, lifts, boilers and other heavy equipment.

1.3.5 Finance

Details of *Estimates, Budgets* and of *Financial* and *Operating* statements.

1.3.6 Guest records

Lost Property Book.
   Details of regular *Guest and V.I.P. requirements.*
   Guest *Welfare, sickness* and *Doctor visits.*
   Guest questionnaire Reports for complaints and compliments.

1.3.7 Annual report

Some organizations require an annual report. This is a summary of the
year's events in the Department and shows how closely spending and
performance have met the budget target and the standards expected. It
also shows the staff establishment and the percentages for sickness,
absence, labour turnover and stability in addition to any major re-
decorating or furnishing projects and a general assessment of future
trends.

1.4 Exercise and discussion

1 Complete the clock card to show:
   (a) How many hours have been worked?
   (b) How many hours will be paid?
   (c) What action should be taken for lateness?
   (d) Should a sickness certificate have been received?
   Miss Doital is contracted to work an 8-hour day on a 5-day week
basis. Saturday work is paid at time and a half, Sunday at double time
and the first 6 hours of overtime at time and a quarter.
2 A report in *The Small Firm in the Hotel and Catering Industry*
estimates that between 60 and 70 per cent of all hotel costs are fixed;
the Manager is worried that occupancy figures are beginning to fall
below this point so is actively looking for new business and is hoping
to increase weekend occupancy by offering 'special activity' weekends
for families and to provide conference and meeting accommodation to
local industry.
   How would this affect the normal housekeeping routines?

Name I. DOITAL				W/e 5 March			
No 6872							
Dept H/keeping							
Paid hours					Overtime		
Sick Mon.-Fri.					×1¼		
Sick w/end					×1½		
Night duty					×2		
Mon.	Tues.	Wed.	Thurs.	Fri.	Sat.	Sun.	Total
0800	0808		0802	D/o	R/D	0805	
1204	1200		1205			1200	
1303	1301		1307			1310	
1700	1702		2000			1701	

Remarks Sick - Wed   1/3
             (phone call)
Please pay 1 week's holiday entitlement
on 12/3   RH

2
The Use of Contractors

Why employ a contractor? Surely it is better to employ one's own permanent staff who are known and respected by the management and who will be loyal to the establishment and to its interests rather than an anonymous group of workers who take their instructions from an outside company? Besides, a contracting company is in business to make a profit; if they can tender for a job at an economical price and make a profit of 15–20 percent why is it not possible for the present management to do the same work cheaper since they should, after all, have a better knowledge of the work and its problems? To quote from the Contract Cleaning and Maintenance Association (CCMA) 'the answer is specialization. Time devoted by a businessman to work extraneous to his own specialization or flair, is time dissipated.'

The contractor offers many services over a wide range such as:

(1) Laundry and Linen Supply and the Hire of Uniforms;
(2) Specialist cleaning;
    Carpet shampooing and floor treatments,
    Curtain, venetian blind and upholstery cleaning,
    External and internal window cleaning,
    Cloakroom sanibin services,
    Telephone cleaning and sterilization,
    In-depth cleaning for kitchens and toilets,
    Swimming pools,
    Office cleaning, computer suites,
    Night cleaning;
(3) Service and maintenance of equipment, lifts, boilers and heating apparatus;
(4) Equipment hire;

(5) Pest control;
(6) Security.

A large organization usually has the resources and the scope to employ specialists which would be impossible in a small company. A contractor offers expertise and technological knowledge and has the advantage of greater experience in tackling a limited range of jobs than would have many Housekeepers or Domestic Managers. The contractor can afford to provide up-to-date specialist equipment, as it is in constant use, whereas it might only be economical for a company to update machinery once every ten years. Management know the cost in advance and, unless there is a specific clause written into the agreement, any set-backs or unexpected problems are the responsibility of the contractor. It is for the contractor to worry about staff shortages, sickness, holidays and all recruitment, selection and training costs.

When a task is infrequent (perhaps needed only once or twice a year) it is simpler to bring in contractors than to train staff who cannot be expected to reach the same level of proficiency as an employee who specializes in the work and cheaper than recruiting extra staff for a short time. It is uneconomical to buy specialist equipment if it will not be in regular use although it is always possible to hire.

A few establishments have dealt with the problem of over-manning and out-dated work practices and avoided trade union problems by switching the work to contractors and leaving it to them to completely re-organize the work methods, frequencies and timings. In many cases, the contractor will take over and re-train existing staff. Once work patterns have been broken there is nothing, of course, to stop a return to directly employed staff after the contract has been completed.

2.1 Work specification

Before the contractor can *estimate a price for the job*, the employing company has to prepare a work specification. This specification details:

1 The work to be done, its frequency and the access time available:
2 The plan of the building with
    (a) the size of each area,

(b) surface finishes,

(c) power points, water and drain outlets;

3 The contents, furniture and fittings with the approximate sizes and numbers of each item;

4 Special problems such as: antique furniture, confidential material; dangerous equipment or materials, restricted access for cleaning, noise, and patient or customer contact;

5 The expected duration of the contract.

For a big contract, the Contractor would require a site visit and need information about storage facilities; the work will then be costed, a profit margin and Value Added Tax added, and the tender submitted. Material and equipment costs may well be low as most contractors have the added advantage of bulk buying.

2.2 Tendering

For all big jobs it is usual to consider a minimum of three tenders all of which are compared and discussed. Points which must be considered are:

(1) The reliability of the Contractor, his standards and financial stability.

(2) Insurance cover for employer and public liability, and for theft, damage and accident.

(3) Whether his staff are directly employed or does he, in his turn, use self-employed labour? – Are staff references checked? – Is the uniform and appearance in keeping with the employing company?

(4) Supervision and quality control? – What degree of supervision is intended? – Will there be one person to contact when problems arise? – Is there any provision for a joint quality report at set periods during the contract?

(5) How do prices compare between the tendering companies and with present costs? Is there any provision for inflation and wage increases?

The normal duration of a contract is either for a specific job or for between one to three years. Once the contract is made it is legally binding on both sides so great care must be taken to ensure that all requirements are met as, unless a contingency allowance for extra, *ad hoc* or back-up cleaning has been included, it will not be done by the contractor's staff.

2.3 Supervision of the contract

The contractor's supervisor should be available at set times to discuss problem areas. Written records, perhaps in diary form, should be kept of faulty work so that, when needed, there is tangible evidence of the success, or otherwise, of the contract. The vast majority of contracts operate well. Obviously, when there is a lot of money involved, the contractor will hope that the contract will be renewed.

2.4 Available services

2.4.1 Laundry and linen supply

Most sectors of industry use a commercial laundry or linen-hire company to provide roller towels for kitchens and cloakrooms, 'whites' and basic uniforms for maintenance and cleaning staff and for the thin cotton or nylon dust-control mats. This is dealt with more fully in Section 8.2.

2.4.2 Specialist cleaning services

The most widely used service is that for *external window cleaning* particularly in high-rise buildings when cradles are needed; provided windows are accessible and not too high, the internal work is often undertaken by the domestic staff as, particularly in a hotel, there are security and access problems; in a hospital, window cleaning is usually part of the weekly ward routine.

Unless there is a Night Cleaning Supervisor or Resident Caretaker, many offices use contractors as *office cleaning* is either early or late in the day which makes supervision difficult for the Office Manager.

Many busy *kitchens* are *in-depth cleaned*, usually over-night or at the weekend, four to six times a year to supplement the normal kitchen cleaning and to ensure that hygiene requirements are met. This can also apply to cloakroom cleaning.

A *night-cleaning* contract may not, necessarily be more expensive than having cleaning done during the day as, although wage rates are increased, the work can often be done in less time as there are few interruptions. It can also increase security.

2.4.3 Service and maintenance

Service and maintenance for much equipment must be done by trained operators. Indeed, this may be a requirement of the insurance cover.

2.4.4 Equipment hire

There is very little equipment that cannot be hired – at a price; this includes all cleaning equipment, washing machines and tumbledryers, fire extinguishers, furniture, glass, cutlery and tableware, linen and uniforms. There are several advantages, the greatest being that there is no need to provide capital for expensive equipment as the hiring charge is treated as a revenue charge; it is possible to up-date equipment and furnishings more often with, in most cases, servicing the responsibility of the supplier. Whether or not it is advantageous to hire depends, to a certain extent, on how often the item will be used. For example, if hired furniture is used in a bedroom the charges continue whether the room is occupied or not and, for a seasonal hotel, this could prove expensive in the off-season. Damage or loss has to be paid for but fair wear and tear is included in the hire charge.

At the end of the contract, it is occasionally possible for the items to be purchased at second-hand value or for the contract to be renewed for the same items but at a reduced price.

2.4.5 Pest control

Consultants are necessary when there is a severe outbreak of infestation and are often used, as a precautionary measure, for regular inspections of a building.

2.4.6 Security

Bringing in outside consultants can be beneficial as it introduces an unbiased viewpoint and staff will have been carefully vetted.

2.5 Exercise and discussion

1 It has been decided that part of the cleaning will be contracted out. Draw up a specification for the room in which you are in, the nearest cloakroom or bathroom and the entrance to the building–for daily, weekly and periodical cleaning. It is proposed that the contract will run for one year. Detail any special problem areas.

2 Take the specification prepared by the person sitting in front or beside you and prepare the tender you will submit–taking into account the equipment and cleaning materials needed and a percentage for gross profit.

3 In groups of two or three, discuss the tenders and decide which one will be accepted. What factors have you considered in reaching your decision.

3

Services and Maintenance

3.1 Costs

The cost of servicing and maintaining any building so that it is functional, looks and is clean and retains an acceptable appearance for as long as possible varies considerably from one establishment to another. Costs are very closely related to:

1 Customer expectations;
2 Treatment of the premises by both staff and customers;
3 Size and design of the accommodation;
4 Surface finish of floors, walls and ceilings;
5 Type of furniture;
6 Colours, patterns and textures used in the decorative scheme;

Given similar circumstances and requirements, it should be possible to arrive at a basic and economic cost for providing services to differing groups and types of customer.

3.1.1 Customer expectations

These vary widely and are of most concern in the hotel sector as opposed to hospital, staff or student sectors, where the customers are usually only too glad to have a bed and treatment or to find accommodation. Nevertheless, many staff and students have little idea of the cost of providing accommodation and frequently demand a service which has little relation to the amount which they pay (see section 1.2.3).

In the hotel sector, many guests have a pre-determined idea of what should or should not be provided; some will discuss and offer constructive criticism to management either in person or by completing the guest questionnaire but the majority mentally shrug, do not return and do not recommend the hotel to their associates and friends. A high percentage of returning guests is an indication that expectations are being met.

One big problem is always the amount of money that management is prepared to allocate to the housekeeping services and how successful the Housekeeper is in persuading management that high standards can only be obtained when there is sufficient money to train and retain experienced staff.

3.1.2 Treatment of the premises by both staff and customers

There will always be the few who mistreat other people's property but, in general, if the premises look attractive and well-cared for and all signs of damage, stains or tears are repaired or replaced as soon as possible, there is less chance of misuse. As with all things, guidance must come from management and, if the supervisors are obviously concerned that the premises are maintained in good condition, there is more chance that this will happen.

Housekeepers must have sufficient technical knowledge to maintain the premises in the best way using the correct cleaning agents and ensuring that cleaning is carried out at the correct frequencies.

3.1.3 Size and design of the accommodation

In a purpose-built establishment, the size, shape and the lay-out of the furniture and fittings are decided before a decision is reached on the size and shape of the room and takes into account the various functions and activities which are expected to occur. Allowance must also be made for access and working space, these can often over-lap as is shown on p. 34.

Space allowances are also governed by the Fire Precautions Act of 1971, the Local Council Codes of Practice and the Building Regulations; these stipulate the minimum space necessary for circulation areas and are related to the number of people who will be on the premises at any one time. Regulations govern the width of staircases, corridors and exits so that, in the event of a fire or other disaster, the building can be cleared quickly and safely and restrict the

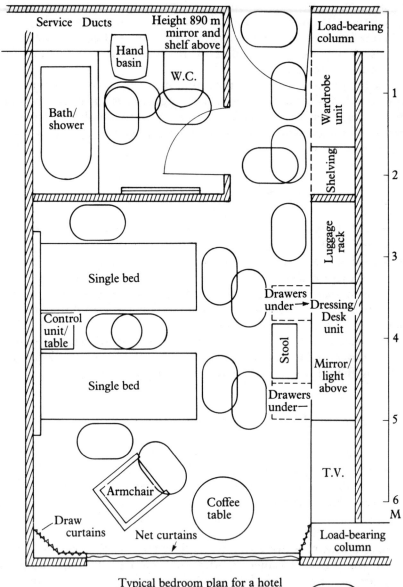

Typical bedroom plan for a hotel
showing overlapping access areas.

number of people who are permitted to be on the premises at any one time. Before there is any change of use or major alteration to the fabric of the building or to the type of furnishings, the Fire Authorities and Planning Officers of the local Councils should be consulted.

The following is an example of how Planning and Fire Regulations affect the width of corridors in a one-staircase and a two-staircase building.

	One-staircase building		Two-staircase building	
Number of people	Evenly distributed (mm)	Concentrated mainly on one floor (mm)	Evenly distributed (mm)	Concentrated mainly on one floor (mm)
Up to: 50	760	760		
100	920	1070		
200	1220	1370	920	1070
300	1520	Not permitted	1070	1220
400	Not permitted	Not permitted	1220	1370
500	Not permitted	Not permitted	1370	1520

For general design purposes, the average space needed for circulation is 0.8 m^2; but where there is constant movement, such as in a hospital casualty unit or a hotel foyer, these allowances increase to between 1.1 and 1.4 m^2. Other minimum space allowances are:

Ballroom: 0.55–0.9 m^2;
Restaurant: 0.9–1.1 m^2;
Seated in a Hall or lecture-room: 0.46–0.6 m^2;
Offices; for each person, 9.3 m^2.

Obviously, circulation space is necessary but it is unproductive and designers go to considerable trouble to reduce it to the minimum and to increase the size of guest, public and function rooms.

3.1.4 Surface finish of floors, walls and ceilings

(a) Floors

The same amount of dust, dirt and stains are deposited on all types of floor surface but some surfaces are able to stand the strain of this rather better than others. For general use, a *carpet* absorbs dust and soiling, does not show every scruff or wheel-mark and retains its appearance better than many other surfaces. A silicone or fluoro-chemical protective film can be sprayed over the carpets and will prevent the fibres absorbing any spillages. Water, oils and dirt will remain on the surface and be easy to wipe off; which means that the frequency of shampooing can be reduced although, as with all other surfaces, dust, grit must be removed and spot-cleaning should be done daily. However, a carpet is unsuitable in an area where there is risk of spilt liquids, grease or chemicals, such as in a service kitchen or a geriatric ward. A damp carpet can take several hours to dry and as long as it is wet will attract and hold the dirt so it should not be walked on for the period; in addition, if the back of a woven carpet becomes wet, shrinkage can occur and there can be water-staining in the pile of a plain carpet. Some types of short-fibred nylon, rubber-backed carpets are non-absorbent and very easy to clean except that the foam-backing can retain moisture and smell.

Long-tufted carpets look very attractive but are difficult to clean and many require raking over to remove all footmarks.

Traditional woven carpets have long been joined by other types of soft floor coverings. These are less expensive as they have been produced by non-woven methods yet they offer similar advantages; there is a softer, more luxurious appearance to a room, they are quiet and make good sound absorbers and thermal insulators, they do not indent easily and are relatively quick to clean. Provided the right grade has been used for the density of traffic expected and provided they have been laid correctly on a dry, even, sub-floor the life expectancy is good. In use, they compare well with the cost of many of the 'hard' floors as they require no polish or buffing.

The 'hard' floors are usually divided into three categories. Wood, cork, magnesite and some of the cements, marbles and terrazzo are *porous* and must be *sealed* before going into use to prevent dirt, grease and liquids sinking into the pores and becoming engrained – in most cases, the seal is protected by polish. How long a seal remains effective depends on the density of both foot and wheeled traffic but it must be replaced as soon as it starts to wear; this is noticable as the floor gradually acquires a grey appearance and becomes progressively more difficult to clean.

A *semi-porous* floor has a much closer texture and is not affected so much by engrained dirt. There are two schools of thought on whether they should be sealed or not but most consider that if the surface is in poor condition, it should be sealed but it is not necessary if it is new and is well looked after. The main semi-porous floors are man-made and include the polyvinylchloride group (P.V.C.), rubber, thermoplastics and linoleum. Linoleum is made from cork granules and oil and can also be treated as a porous floor. These floors are usually protected with water-based polishes as they are damaged by solvents (with the exception of linoleum) but a matt finish can also be obtained without polish simply by the weight and friction of polishing pads and a floor maintenance machine.

An *impervious* floor has a particularly close grain so that all dirt and grease remain on the surface and can be removed quickly by scrubbing or damp-mopping. Quarry and ceramic tiles, most of the terrazzo, granolithic, marble and stone floors fall into this group. Unglazed quarry tiles, marble and terrazzo can be polished if they are used in 'prestige' areas such as a hotel foyers, corridors and heavy-duty areas. These floors are extremely long-lasting and used in areas where damage to most other floors might occur due to chemical spills, excessive heat or heavy machinery.

When cleaning water should be kept to the minimum. This applies to all types of floor, but especially when they are laid in tile form and an adhesive used to fix them to the screed sub-floor as excess water can seep between the cracks and break the adhesive; it can also water mark and may leach out some colour.

To ensure maximum wear from a floor, it must be laid on a completely even sub-floor which is protected by a damp-proof membrane and is dry. Durability is difficult to assess as it depends on how the floor is laid, how carefully it is used by the occupants of the building, the density of the traffic flow and how it is maintained. The grade and thickness of the floor must be suitable for the area. Life expectancy can only be estimated.

There is no single perfect floor surface. In most cases, a floor is chosen for its appearance and the way in which it complements the building and its decorative style and, in too many cases, the functional requirements of the area are forgotten. Functional requirements may include many of the following properties: a floor which is easy and cheap to maintain, is quiet, warm, flame-retardent, has anti-static properties, is hygienic, slip-proof, resists all chemical attack, does not mark, indent or scratch easily and will withstand heavy traffic. Most floors chosen are a compromise.

The following information is required to compare the cost in use of a floor:

(1) The initial cost plus the costs for installation and initial floor treatments;

(2) The cleaning and maintenance costs each year;

(3) Life expectancy.

Dust control mats are the first line of defence for the protection of all types of floor and are designed to remove dust and dirt from shoes before it is carried into the building and to control dust within the building so that it is not transferred from a 'dirty' area such as a kitchen or boiler-house; they are also needed to protect those areas where hygiene and cleanliness are essential such as a hospital operating unit, an intensive care ward or a computer-processing room. Mats should be the width of the entrance or the corridor and of a depth of about 1500 mm to ensure that both shoes are cleaned.

There are several types of mat. Those for external use should be placed at all entrances and are either sunk into a well or 'stepped' so that accidents are avoided. Rubber and aluminium-linked mats are efficient, light and easy to clean; in this type, the rubber flicks dust from the shoe into the cavities between the links which are sufficiently deep to prevent it being blown away and redistributed. Mats with closer strips made from rubber and felt are not so effective as the space for holding dust is more limited. Coconut or coir matting is difficult to clean, particularly heavy when wet and slow to dry.

For internal use, the mats are much lighter and can be made from either nylon, which collects dust by the static electricity built up by the friction of footsteps, from cotton which has been impregnated with a light cleaning oil or by a 'tacky' rubber matting which is effective enough to show every footmark.

Druggets are made from a heavy canvas and are used to protect carpets and floors on wet or snowy days or from damage if furniture or stores are being moved.

(b) Walls

All walls and wall-coverings are usually chosen for their appearance but other properties may also have to be considered.

(1) The Fire Precautions Act stipulates that the wall finish on an escape route should be such that it will not burn easily or create smoke so that only an inorganic material such as plaster, brick or clay tiles are suitable. A thin vinyl or paper may be used as a cover but any thicker papers, wood panels or fabric – even if they are flame-retardent – are not acceptable.

(2) In a kitchen area or in a hospital, hygiene is important and walls should be free from cracks and joins and should be able to withstand regular washing. Usual finishes are a cellulose-based paint, oil paint or ceramic tiles fixed with an impervious grouting.

(3) In kitchen and bathroom areas where there will be condensation and in bars or restaurants where there is smoking, the finish should also be impervious so that water, dirt and grease cannot be absorbed and it is easier to remove nicotine and smoke marks. All surfaces must be washable.

(4) Acoustic properties may be important in busy reception or office areas and low noise levels would be maintained with flock papers or from fabric covers. An underlining of polystyrene is also helpful.

(5) Polystyrene also helps to reduce heat loss. When it is used on an 'escape route' the thickness must not exceed 5 mm for walls, and 12 mm for ceilings where fire is a potential hazard. Polystyrene must not be painted with oil paint as this can cause it to burn fiercely.

(6) A porous finish is used on any newly plastered surface or when there is dampness in the wall so that water vapour can escape into the atmosphere and will not cause damage by blistering the paint or by loosening the adhesive on paper.

(7) To lighten an area mirror or glass bricks can be used.

Walls should protected from damage particularly in public areas and in corridors. The main methods are as follows: to prevent damage from trolleys and wheel-chairs, a metal or wooden rail is fitted at 'strike' level and a metal sheathing fitted to cover corners. Trolleys can be bought with an extra wheel fitted horizontally on each corner so that the trolley will wheel itself along the wall if it is taken too close.

A dado is the Victorian term for covering the lower surface of the wall with a tough material, such as wood-panels, tiles or a dark paint, which will not show dirt or be damaged as easily as a lighter colour or more fragile covering. Door-stops and certain types of hinge prevent doors being swung heavily against the wall. Perspex or a glass panel can be fitted as a surround to light switches to prevent finger-marks. Head-boards or a washable panel should be used anywhere where people can lean against the wall either when they are sitting up in bed or lounging in a chair. Any furniture placed against the wall – tables, chest of drawers or luggage racks should have a short upright section of wood or plastic to prevent damage from rubbing from constant dusting or scratches from the movement of baggage and the lids of cases.

A shelf fitted above a radiator helps to prevent heat convection stains,

There are a number of wall finishes which are commonly used.

Brick and stone Provided a 'warm' colour is used – pinks, apricot or a yellow tone, this finish can look very attractive especially with bright curtains and furniture. The wall should be sprayed with a silicone to prevent dusting but no other decoration is required and little maintenance.

Paint This covers and protects plaster and brick-work.

Emulsion paints are water-based and permeable to water-vapour so should be used on new plaster or anywhere where there is dampness. They have a matt or egg-shell finish which is suitable for bedrooms, corridors and lounge areas and are easy to apply and to touch-up. The walls can be washed – but not too enthusiastically as, being water-based, the paint will be removed gradually.

Oil-based paints are impervious to water so are most suitable to use in bathrooms, service and utility rooms, ward kitchens and sluices as they will be unaffected by steam and condensation. In other areas, the gloss finish can create reflection problems. These paints can be washed regularly but it is not easy to touch-up a damaged area which means that the whole surface usually has to be repainted.

Cellulose paints have the great advantage that they can be applied directly to a brick or stone surface and will cover and hide any irregularities in the wall so they are used extensively in the service areas of a building, in storerooms, cloakroom and locker-rooms kitchens and back corridors. They usually come in a variety of colours and are very difficult (but not impossible) to damage. The walls are easy to clean and can be scrubbed.

All paint surfaces should be washed from the bottom, working up to the top and then rinsed from the top downwards. This is to avoid trickles of dirty water running into an already dirty surface and becoming engrained and almost impossible to remove.

Wallpapers A *plain 'paper' paper* is highly absorbent and difficult to clean but can look very attractive, is cheap and provides a good range of pattern and colour. *Vinyl and washable* papers are more servicable as they can be sponged and are less likely to tear. Many are textured to resemble fabrics, wood or tiles. *Embossed* or textured papers have a pattern profile of several millimetres and need to be vacuumed regularly to stop dust collecting and discolouration. *Flock* papers have the pattern printed onto the paper with an adhesive and are then sprayed with nylon fibres to give a velvet finish. Some can be sponged but, as with the embossed papers, dust must be removed regularly. *Anaglypta* papers are heavily embossed and patterned and are usually painted with an emulsion. They are mainly used for ceilings but are also frequently used as a cheap wall-covering. A *lining paper* is thin and is used under the top paper to give a better finish and to cover any small cracks or irregularities in the wall. Whereas wallpapers are hung vertically, a lining paper is hung horizontally around the room.

Fabrics These should be paper-backed to protect the fabric from shrinkage or staining from the adhesive used for hanging. When it is used in a sunny area it is important that it should be fade-resistent and reach the same specifications as would be needed for curtaining. Cleaning can be a difficulty: vacuum cleaning prevents dust build-up and stains, a few fabrics can be sponged but there is always the risk that tide-marks can be left, even if plain water or a solvent cleaner is used.

Furnishings fabrics to match curtains or the covers are best used when they are fitted to a frame or into tracks as, unless they are backed, any adhesive will mark or shrink the fabric. These fabrics have a selvedge which has to be removed and the width of the material makes it difficult to stretch it level and straight onto the wall.

Ceramic wall tiles These are very serviceable for a heavy-duty area and easy to clean. Problems can be caused by the grouting becoming loose and the growth of mildew between the tiles if they are used in an area with poor ventilation.

Mirrors Mirrors are attractive and very useful to reflect light and to give the illusion of extra space, they do, however, show every mark and have to be cleaned carefully. Condensation and steam can affect the backing causing black spot marks.

Others Most floor finishes, carpets, plastics, cork, wood, marbles, stone and terrezzo can be used for wall coverings but where there is any chance of extra fire-risk, advice should be sought from the Fire Authorities. As in other areas, any material or fabric with a large repeat pattern is expensive as the pattern has to be matched.

(c) Ceilings

In a modern building the void between the ceiling and the room above is often used to house air ducts, pipes, wires, fire sprinklers and fire detectors and the telephone and communication networks with access gained through open grids or panels. An integrated ceiling has grids and panels which incorporate lighting, heating and ventilation circuits – many of these are frequently suspended with tiles, panels or slats fitted to the supports. A suspended ceiling can be used to improve the appearance of an old building and to reduce the area which has to be heated and maintained.

A traditional ceiling is one in which plaster or plaster board is applied to wooden lathes and was then decorated with mouldings and covings. It can be painted or papered.

Acoustic tiles are used to aid sound insulation.

Where there is a strict 'no smoking' policy, ceilings can look fresh and clean for a number of years – but heavy smoking and air pollution soon makes a ceiling look dirty and drab; a ceiling is difficult to wash and is usually redecorated. Many of the acoustic tiles can be painted with an emulsion paint but become highly flammable if an oil-based paint is used. The manufacturer's advice should always be taken. Ceilings may need to be strengthened if a heavy light fitting is used.

3.1.5 Type of furniture

To a certain extent, the type and amount of the furniture depends on what the customer expects, what is needed for the length of stay and on the status and image which the establishment wants to project.

Free-standing furniture, whether it is antique, good reproduction or modern, is used more in luxury class hotels as it offers more variety and interest to a room and gives more flexibility in room arrangement and in its use. Many hotels try to create a country house image and to provide an atmosphere similar to that which the customer might expect at home.

Fitted furniture is more usually found in transient hotels and in staff and student accommodation where space is short. By installing fitted units, a room is made to look bigger with all the available space utilized for storage and living. Savings are made on redecoration costs with less need for carpets and wall finishes. Day-to-day cleaning is simplified as furniture is usually stream-lined with few dust-holding ledges and because it does not have to be moved to clean under or behind. When the furniture can be built-in as the building is being constructed, it is normally less expensive than buying free-standing furniture.

(a) Surface finishes

Antique and reproduction furniture has either a wax or french-polish finish which needs to be re-waxed and polished regularly to preserve the patina of the wood. Care must be taken as furniture can mark easily with heat, water or chemicals.

Most modern and fitted furniture should have a heat-, water- and scratch-resistant finish which will not need waxing. This is usually polyurethane – a synthetic varnish which penetrates the wood and is difficult to remove; a cellulose finish is cheaper but can be scratched.

Both finishes only need to be wiped with a damp cloth and polished with a dry duster.

A synthetic finish should not be applied to antique furniture as it will greatly reduce its value.

Much of the contract furniture is finished with a plastic veneer, such as melamine or formica, and can be patterned and coloured so that it looks like a natural wood and tones with the decorative scheme. The edge of the veneer should be protected with a wooden or metal edging to prevent it lifting or becoming chipped. Again, this type of finish only needs to be polished with a dry duster with smears or finger-marks removed with dilute vinegar and water or a little methylated spirits.

As far as possible furniture should be solid or laminated wood. Chipboard should be avoided as it is not strong enough to withstand heavy wear and constant movement. Moulded plastic used for drawer bases and linings is more hygienic, less likely to stain and has a better appearance than a wooden base. All hinges and handles should be compact to avoid breakage and should be firmly attached with all screws counter-sunk so that they cannot be unscrewed easily.

Upholstered furniture should be protected with arm or head-rests when loose covers are not used; considerable wear is saved when the chair arms are of wood and are not upholstered (Chapter 7).

3.1.6 Colour, pattern and texture

When money is of no concern, it is very attractive to provide off-white carpets and light-coloured upholstery and covers but they can prove very expensive to maintain. Light colours are used, however, in a hospital when it is important to see dust and dirt quickly. Dark colours sound as if they would be a more practical proposition but these too show every speck of fluff or dirt. Dust and footmarks, stains and 'bits' have the most chance of vanishing from sight against a medium-toned, patterned surface composed of two or more different colours. While dust shows at once on dark furniture or dark-coloured paint, it becomes practically invisible on light furniture and cream coloured window-sills and ledges. This should not be taken to mean that the cleaning need not be done thoroughly each day but it is not always economically possible to do it more frequently (Sections 6.3 and 6.4).

Some decorative schemes call for large patterns which can lead to considerable waste as the pattern has to be matched when fabrics are joined together for carpeting, curtains or wall coverings.

Different textures are used to add interest to a room contrasting smooth and roughened surfaces but a rough surfaces holds the dust and dirt and can make cleaning more difficult. Textures are often introduced in floor coverings as a safety measure either to reassure the elderly or to comply with the Health and Safety at Work Act and textured floor vinyls or ridged and embossed quarry tiles are available.

3.2 Cleaning equipment

A sales representative is employed to demonstrate and sell equipment and to stress why it is so much better than that demonstrated by a competitor so everything is made to look easy. The reason why some equipment remains in the cleaner's cupboard and is not used is that it is often difficult and fiddling to clean and to re-assemble, it may be clumsy and too big for the area being cleaned or the cleaner considers that other equipment is more efficient.

All equipment should be designed so that it is easy to use and put together without the need for detailed and complex instructions which normally remain unread.

Cleaning cupboard storage space is always limited, equipment can be expensive so it must be versatile and practical – otherwise, it is money wasted. All equipment must be tough and strongly constructed and of a suitable size for the area being cleaned. Attachment heads should fit easily and be secure.

3.2.1 Selection of equipment

When selecting electrical equipment a number of things must be considered.

(a) Size

Very obviously, the width of a brush head or cleaning nozzle and the diameter of a brush will determine the size of area which can be cleaned in a given time and, provided the cleaning area is unobstructed, it is sensible to buy the largest size available so cutting labour costs. When the area is obstructed with furniture, a large model becomes too clumsy to use and smaller sizes are needed.

(b) Noise

This is very important in hospitals, close to a guest area, and anywhere where cleaning is done during the day. The noise level should be about 5 decibels lower than the average level of noise in that area so that the machine is not noticed by the occupants.

(c) Power rating

The machine should have enough power to be used for long periods during the day without the engine burning out. This precludes the use of many of the machines on the domestic market.

(d) Construction

Stainless steel is almost indestructable although it will dent; it is easy to clean and will resist corrosion. The plastics most used, polyamide and polypropylene, are tough but there is a slight possibility of cracking.

(e) Safety

All equipment must meet the British Electrical safety requirements, the motor fitted with an overheating protector, protected from dust, and completely separated from the water tank when water is being used.

(f) Weight

This can be important if there are no lifts available to move equipment from one floor to another, otherwise use may be restricted.

3.2.2 Dust control

Dust and grit is walked and blown into a building and is also produced by the activities of the occupants and from their skin, hair and clothing.

(a) Dust control mats

These are essential as a passive means of collecting dust and grit before it is walked into a building and to control its movement within the building (see section 11.3.2).

(b) Air conditioning

Air conditioning removes dust and bacteria as the air is filtered before being warmed (or cooled) and recirculated. It makes a great difference to dust levels on floor, furniture and curtains.

(c) Dust control equipment

This consists of vacuum cleaners, carpet sweepers, mop sweepers, high dusters, brooms and brushes, feather dusters and nylon flicks and dusters.

Vacuum cleaners The British Standards 3999 of 1973 measures the performance of household electrical appliances. Part 12 gives the procedures for assessing the performance of commercial vacuum cleaners and takes into account dust removal, thread pick-up, the ability to go under furniture, air flow and suction power and the durability of both brushes and nozzles. A well-designed vacuum cleaner provides the most hygienic method of collecting dust and can be used on all surfaces, hard floors and carpets, staircases, chairs and upholstery, carved furniture, and will collect flies from window sills and dust, cobwebs and spiders from walls and ceilings. An adequate filter and exhaust system will hold the dust within the cleaner and prevent it being redistributed into the room.

The medical Research Council recommends that for hospital use not more than 10 microns of dust and bacteria per cubic foot of air should be blown back through the cleaner into a main hospital theatre or 0.1–2.0 microns into special theatres and intensive care units.

A number of hospitals and a few hotels have a *central vacuum system* which avoids this problem. Cleaning accessories and the flexible hoses are plugged into sockets connected to a powerful motor, usually located in the basement which provides suction. Dust is sucked through the duct pipes to be collected, and disposed of, at one point so there is no need for manual handling of dust on floors and wards. The main problems arise when the central motor either breaks down or is taken out of service for maintenance; provided there are no acute bends on the pipes, it should not be blocked by paper tissues and other large debris which may be picked up.

There are three main types of vacuum – the upright, the cylinder and the tub or canister.

(1) The *upright vacuum* was originally designed to clean carpets

and has a revolving brush which 'lifts and beats' and suction which draws the dust round the motor into the bag. The best-designed have an outer, solid dust-container which is usually made from plastic and is used with an inner paper bag, this along with the filters on the exhaust prevent dust being blown out into the air or into the motor. The brush drive should be protected within the machine so it is not damaged by paperclips and pins. The suction head should be designed so that it can clean to the edges of the carpet.

All can be adapted to use flexible hose, extension tubes and a wide range of attachments but the result is not so compact or easy to use as the cylinder or tub models; it is slower to change from one type of surface to another and the machine can be top-heavy particularly when used for stair-cleaning. The machines themselves are complex with more parts to be maintained.

(2) The *cylinder vacuum* is compact, flexible and easy to use on any surface, with good filtering systems – but is limited in the size of the dust-bag.

(3) The *tub or canister vacuum* is similar to the cylinder but, because the motor is at the top and not placed at the side, has a much greater dust-bag capacity. Most have three or four filters and have the exhaust air diffused from the top of the machine, about 18 in above ground level so that there is less chance of dust becoming air-borne before it can be collected. Along with the usual attachments a lift and beat unit, similar to that on the upright vacuum, can be fitted.

The tub is more versatile than the other two types as it can be fitted with a float-valve and used to pick up water. Experimental tests show that for all types of machine, the dust and grit pick-up from carpets is usually only between 50 and 60 per cent of the amount deposited with the upright machine being more effective on fitted, woven carpets with a deep pile and the cylinder and tub machines better on non-woven carpets and on hard surfaces.

Carpet sweepers These will remove surface dust, crumbs and debris from carpets and are very useful for a fast, quiet, clean-up in a restaurant or foyer. They should, however, be used as an additional aid to the vacuum cleaner. Grit at the base of a carpet tuft causes the greatest amount of damage and can only be removed by suction power.

Mop sweepers They remove dust from hard floor surfaces, are fast, quiet, economical and only slightly less hygienic than a vacuum cleaner. They have swivel heads so it is easy to clean under furniture and around corners and legs. The detachable heads are easy to remove and wash when dirty. Head sizes can be as little as 45 cm up to 80 cm with the large V-sweepers opening out to 180 cm. Mop-heads are made from cotton, nylon or are disposable.

A cotton head is usually impregnated or sprayed with a light cleaning oil; this is not sufficient to make a floor slippery but enough to hold dust in the yarn. Impregnation is not necessary with a nylon head as this attracts and holds the dust through the static build-up of electricity. A disposable head, usually made from cellulose, is used when hygiene requirements are important.

High dusters A vacuum cleaner, using extension tubes, is the most efficient dust collector but it is heavy and can be slow and clumsy to use; by far the quickest and easiest tool is one which is similar, but lighter, than a mop-sweeper. The nylon swivel-head removes dust from the tops of wardrobes, light fittings and ledges and extension tubes enable cleaning up to between 4 and 16 metres without the need for a stepladder.

Some high-dusters are made with a brush-type head which dislodges but does not collect the dust and is stiffer and less flexible.

Brooms and brushes Brush heads are stiff for carpets and soft for a hard surface and are useful for clearing small quantities of dust but are inefficient and not to be recommended for any large area as the sweeping action pushes dust up into the air; this can take up to an hour to resettle on the floor or the furniture so means that the job is only half done. When a brush *has* to be used in a large area, such as a ballroom or gymnasium, it is used in conjunction with a sweeping compound which is slightly oily. This is scattered over the floor and prevents the dust becoming airborne as both are swept up together.

A brush may be necessary when there is a lot of debris on the floor, such as paper, cigarette ends or food remains.

Feather dusters and Nylon flicks Feathers are light and useful for flicking dust from a chandelier or from a sculptured wall surface but the dust is not held and has to be recollected. A nylon flick is more efficient but not as good as a high dusting mop.

Dusters These are usually made from brushed cotton flannelette which is inconvenient to wash if the colour runs. A duster made from a brushed nylon fabric attracts the dust and is easier and quicker to wash and dry.

3.2.3 Dirt removal

Dirt is defined as dust, grit and grease which has become attached to a surface either by water and grease or because the finish is rough or textured. Light soiling is removed by a damp cloth but heavier dirt requires a cleaning agent and a certain amount of friction – usually provided by mops or a scrubbing brush. The resulting sludge has then got to be removed. The removal of dirt is, invariably, a more expensive and laborious process than collecting dust.

Equipment for removing dirt

There is a large variety of equipment available: floor maintenance machines; damp-mops; deck scrubbers; scrubbing brushes and abrasive pads; sponge mops; carpet shampooers; wall and ceiling cleaning machines; high pressure cleaners.

Floor maintenance machines These are used to scrub, scarify to remove the heaviest of grease and oil deposits, spray-clean, polish and shampoo carpets. The machines can be designed with either one, two or three brush or drive-heads although the *two-brush machines* are mainly found on the domestic market. A *three-brush machine* is very stable and easy to operate but could be more expensive due to the cost of the extra brushes. There are more moving parts to go wrong but most makes of three-brush machines are very reliable.

Most machines in use are the *single-brush machines*; some are not so easy to operate as the angle of the handle adjusts the weight on the brush drive and sends the machine either to the right or left depending on the direction in which the brush is rotating; with many machines, this rotation can be altered so that the wear on a brush is even.

A *basic* machine has a brush speed of about 200 r.p.m. (revolutions per minute) and, with a tank fitted, can be used for all cleaning tasks; a central water feed from the tank reduces splashing on skirting boards and furniture to the minimum. These are powerful machines so, for preference, should be fitted with a safety switch and 'deadman's' handle which operates when the handle is left in the neutral position. A 'low profile' with a clearance of 25 cm means that the machine can clean under most furniture and equipment.

In a *high-speed* machine, the brush revolves two to three times faster than in the basic model and, because of this speed, cannot be used for scrubbing or shampooing. All the machines can be used with either brushes or a driving disc which is fitted with nylon or polyester pads. These are graded for abrasiveness and used for scrubbing, spray-cleaning, polishing and buffing.

Brushes are expensive and have to be treated with care as they can be easily damaged. The weight of the machine will flatten the bristles if it is left standing for any length of time or if the brushes are left on during storage; when they are washed, the brushes must be left to dry on their side so that the water does not make the wooden back sodden. Pads are turned and used on both sides and washed when dirty; they are always used for spray-cleaning as the dirt and water is collected in the pads.

The simplest method of removing scrub water from the floor, and which leaves it nearly dry, is to use a *wet pick-up* or *wet vacuum*; these either have a fixed 'outrigger' squeegee head which can be adjusted to suit the floor surface and allows for wear on the blades or a flexible hose to collect water from under pipes or from places inaccessible to a fixed blade. The tank should be easy to empty (it can get very heavy) and rust-proof.

When only one vacuum cleaner can be bought, there is an obvious advantage in buying one which can be used for both dry and wet pick-up. There is also a great advantage in buying a *dual machine* which scrubs and dries in one operation; this reduces labour costs and the need to co-ordinate the work of two separate machines and is safer as the floor is not left wet. The speed of operation depends on the size of the brush or squeegee head, on the amount of dirt and on how much the floor is obstructed and will vary from about 400 m² per hour up to 2500–3000 m² per hour.

When a wet pick-up is not available, a *floor squeegee* is both fast and efficient particularly in an area where the water can be pushed down a floor-drain or gulley.

Damp-mopping systems are used to remove light soiling and water. All mop heads should be detachable so that they can be washed and dried and are not left in a damp, smelly condition to provide a good breeding place for bacteria. A flat 'Kentucky'-type mop-head fits easily into the mopholder and is made with long cotton strands; a 'stay-flat' mop has stitching across the strands so that they cannot become tangled but spread out across the floor making the cleaning much faster. The detachable mop-heads are used with *step-on roller buckets* or with buckets fitted with *gear-operated wringers*, both of which remove a high percentage of water.

A *double-bucket trolley* system is used in hospitals and elsewhere when hygiene is important; one bucket is kept for clean water whilst dirty water from the floor is wrung out into the second bucket so that, as far as possible, only clean water is mopped onto the floor and dirt is not re-distributed. In all mopping systems, the water *must* be changed as soon as it becomes dirty and the mop-heads washed and dried at the end of each shift.

A *deck-scrubber* is almost as efficient as hand-scrubbing when dirt has to be removed manually and is more acceptable to the Cleaner who often prefers this method to getting down on her hands and knees. An *abrasive pad*, either on a hand-holder or long pole, is also effective.

Sponge mops are used for spot-cleaning light dirt and to clean small areas such as a bathroom or service-room floor – provided the surface is not uneven as the sponge tears easily. They are also very useful for wall and window cleaning as is a light-weight Window Squeegee.

Carpet shampooers Most carpets are fitted so must be cleaned *in situ*; by doing so regularly it is estimated that the life of the carpet is extended anything up to 50 per cent, an important factor when one considers how expensive it is to renew the carpeting in a building. Even with the best of vacuums, a heavy-duty, contract carpet can absorb as much as one kilogram of dirt in each square metre.

There are three main methods for cleaning but whichever is used, the carpet is first vacuumed, stains are removed either by using the carpet detergent or a proprietry stain remover and a test is made to ensure that all the colours will remain fast.

(1) *Soil extraction machines* are very simple to use. A cleaning detergent or solvent is mixed with water and is forced, under pressure, into a spray so that a very fine mist penetrates into the carpet fibres. This loosens both the surface and the deep dirt which is then extracted from the pile by means of a powerful vacuum into a recovery tank. Over 90 per cent of the liquid is recovered which means that the carpet is left slightly damp, will dry out within the hour and the room can be re-used the same day. The effectiveness of the machine is always evident by the amount of dirt in the recovery tank. Accessories will convert this type of machine into an upholstery, curtain or a fabric wallcovering cleaner.

(2) A *Roller, rotary brush machine* uses a dry foam detergent which it spreads and works into the carpet pile; this loosens the dirt. The foam evaporates leaving a dirt containing residue which is vacuumed away as soon as the carpet is dry. As the foam contains little moisture, this is usually about an hour later. Both these machines are expensive but can be hired by a small establishment.

(3) A soft, carpet-shampoo brush can be fitted to a *Floor maintenance machine* and used with dry-foam detergent. This is scrubbed into the carpet which is then left to dry before being vacuumed to remove the dirt residue. A wet pick-up can be used, directly after the floor machine to remove some of the water. This method has the disadvantage that more water is used than in the other two methods so that the carpet can take much longer to dry and the

action of the brush can distort the pile; it is, however, quite an economical and viable method for cleaning carpet tiles or needle-punch and bonded-fibre soft floor coverings if there is nothing else available.

When cleaning, great care must be taken that the pile does not become too wet and it is completely dry before it is walked on and furniture replaced; it is equally important that the backing remains dry to avoid shrinkage. If the backing is a plastic foam, this can remain damp for a long time and could smell.

Wall and ceiling cleaning machines These are available for cleaning washable surfaces. There are two types: one operates by releasing detergent into a sponge cleaning pad, the other is a detergent spray which can also be used to clean acoustic tiles, chandeliers and similar objects. The chemical in the spray unites with the dirt and loosens it. In this case, furniture and carpets should be covered as the fine mist could cause damage to polished surfaces.

High pressure cleaners These are used mainly for the hard, impervious surfaces in a kitchen or cloakroom/toilet area. The dirt and grease is removed by a jet of either hot water or steam which can be directed under, over and behind equipment and fittings. Most of the machines operate at a range of pressures and temperatures and have adjustable nozzles for awkward corners. When used, it is important not to concentrate too long on any one area as the grouting between tiles can be damaged or washed out.

3.3 Cleaning materials

Cleaning materials are used to:

1 Make it easy to remove dirt from a surface;
2 Prevent dirt becoming engrained in a surface or fabric;
3 Prevent a surface being damaged by heat, water, chemicals or scratches;
4 Prolong the life of surfaces and fabrics;
5 Enhance the appearance.

Although many of the chemicals used remove dirt and stains quickly and easily, there is always the long-term risk that they will damage the surface so that, as a general rule, the mildest chemicals are used rather than the strongest. A manufacturer's price list groups cleaning materials under the following headings:

1 Primers and sealers;
2 Polishes;
3 Cleaners;
4 Toilet cleaners and deodorizers;
5 Kitchen cleaners;
6 Disinfectants;
7 Air fresheners.

3.3.1 Primers and Sealers

Any floor or surface which is porous, such as wood, wood composition, cork or magnesite must have some sort of protection to prevent dirt and grease becoming engrained or changes in the water content causing the structure to swell or warp. A *seal* is a semi-permanent finish which is designed to sink into the surface, fill the pores in the structure and leave it impervious to all liquids, grease and dirt, which will remain on the surface where they can be wiped off easily.

A *primer* is specially designed to penetrate and to form a strong bond with a seal and, when used, produces a better and longer-lasting result than a seal on its own. Depending on the amount of traffic, two or three coats of seal are applied. There are five types of seal in common use.

(a) Oleo-resinous

These are solvent-based and must *not* be used on asphalt, P.V.C., rubber or thermoplastic as the solvent will soften and crack the surface – nor must they be used on marble, terrazzo, quarry tiles or stone as the oil will not soak in easily and the floor will darken; it is also inadvisable to use on linoleum as, again it will darken the surface and be extremely difficult to remove.

These seals are used on wood, wood composition, cork and magnesite. They are not as durable as the plastic seals but they have the advantage that they are very easy to apply and, when worn, the surface need only be cleaned and a new coat applied which keys into the remaining seal. These seals darken the floor a little so, when colour is important, they should not be used.

The drying time is from eight to ten hours and the seal needs to harden overnight before a second or third coat is applied.

(b) Plastic

The earlier plastic seals were based on urea-formaldehyde; these are still available but those based on polyurethane are increasingly used, because they are more durable and give a better finish.

Plastic seals are also solvent-based so must *not* be used on asphalt, P.V.C., rubber or thermoplastic but are suitable for marble, terrazzo, quarry tiles, stone, linoleum and wood, wood composition, cork and magnesite. These seals are very durable with good resistance to chemicals and give a good gloss finish. A clear seal will not darken wood or other materials. Rather more care has to be used in their application and they have the great disadvantage that, when they become worn, the seal has to be stripped from the entire floor before a new seal can be applied.

A one-pot seal will take between 3 and 4 hours to dry and needs about 8 hours to harden. A two-pot seal consists of one can of the plastic (urea-formaldehyde or polyurethane) and a second pot of a hardener or accelerator – this dries in half the time; the hardening time remains the same.

(c) Pigmented

Again there are two types – one based on synthetic rubber and used for concrete and magnesite and the other, a two-pot polyurethane, which is used on concrete, magnesite and asphalt. There is no need to use polish on either seal.

The synthetic rubber seal can be obtained in various colours and has good durability and resistance. Two coats are necessary; depending on the consistency and temperature, each coat takes between 3 and 8 hours to dry and a further 6 hours to harden before the next coat is applied. The floor can be retouched when necessary with the new coat of seal keying in with the previous coats. The seal should last between one and two years.

A two-pot polyurethane pigmented seal can be obtained in almost any colour and provides very good resistance but, as with the two-pot plastic seal, it is very difficult to recoat when worn and the entire floor has to be treated. The usual way is to roughen the floor by sanding and then to soften the old seal with a solvent and recoat with the new seal as soon as the solvent has evaporated. When applying, each coat takes about two hours to dry and will harden in two to three hours. It will last from eighteen months to two years in a heavy traffic area and longer with light traffic.

(d) Silicate

Silicate is used on cement or a lime-based stone to prevent dusting and water and grease penetration. It is clear, very easy to apply by damp-mopping or using a watering-can and is easy to recoat when needed. Resistence to abrasion and chemicals is limited. Sodium silicate is mixed with additives and water and mopped or watered onto the cement. This reacts with the lime to form calcium silicate which, as the water evaporates, is left as a silicate glass impregnating the surface. Two to three coats are necessary. These dry in an hour—hardening takes 12 to 14 hours.

(e) Water-based seals

These are used on P.V.C., linoleum, rubber, thermoplastic, marble, terrazzo, asphalt, magnesite and stone. The best quality is based on acrylic polymer resin which provides a 'plastic' skin to the floor; it has a clear, light appearance and has good resistance to water, oil and grease and detergents but will not withstand acids and solvents. One to two coats are needed which dry within 20 to 30 minutes with the second coat applied after half an hour. Depending on the wear, it should last from one to three years and is comparatively easy to remove with an alkaline-solvent detergent.

The basic rules for applying primers and seals are as follows:

(1) The surface must be completely clean with no dirt or engrained grease and must be completely dry and dust-free. All traces of cleaning solvents or alkaline detergents should have been rinsed off.

(2) They should be applied with the room temperature at approximately 17–19°C, if the temperature is much higher the seal becomes more fluid and thin and the coverage not sufficient; when the temperature is too low, the reverse occurs with the seal thickening so that it will not penetrate easily into the pores.

(3) A seal must be left to harden before the next application otherwise the seal may 'lift'.

(4) The room must be well ventilated to dispense any fumes which could affect the operator and to speed the drying process.

3.3.2 Polishes

Polishes are used on floors, furniture, metal and windows.

Floor polishes are used to improve the appearance of the floor, to protect it from damage caused by spills and to prevent dirt, grease and liquids soaking into the fabric – so making cleaning much easier. Until the late 1920s, the only polish available was solvent-based but solvent affects many of the man-made floorings, such as P.V.C. and thermoplastics, so it became necessary to introduce a polish which was water-based; since then, the water-based emulsions have become the most widely used.

(a) Solvent-based polishes

The earliest record of floor polishing seems to be from Italy in the thirteenth century when beeswax was dissolved in a solvent, turpentine. Since then other waxes have been used, montan wax from coal, carnauba, palm and cotton oils from plants, shellac from insects and, latterly, the synthetic waxes such as paraffin and resins.

A paste wax has between 25 and 30 per cent wax content and must be applied in a very thin layer to the floor and buffed to harden. The floor must be completely clean as any dirt will become entrapped in the wax and held to the floor. A liquid wax has between 8 and 12 per cent wax content and is much easier to apply, the higher proportion of solvent means it can be sprayed on the floor.

Solvent polishes must only be used on wood, wood composition, cork, linoleum, and magnesite floors; they must not be used on P.V.C., rubber, thermoplastic or asphalt.

(b) Water-based or emulsion polishes

There have been many developments in the make-up of these polishes; originally, carnauba wax, shellac and borax were used to form an emulsion. Later, a synthetic polymer resin was added. They are more versatile than a solvent polish as harder waxes can be used and the proportions of the wax and resin altered to suit requirements. Water-based polish is not used on an unsealed, porous floor as the water would sink into the pores and affect the structure.

The main ingredients are:

(1) Wax – used to give a high gloss achieved by polishing and buffing.

(2) Polymer resin – this 'dries-bright' to give a high, initial gloss. No machine is necessary. It also makes the polish tougher and less likely to mark.

(3) Resin – as a levelling agent and an aid to hardening the polish.

The main reason for its inclusion is that it is alkali-soluble which means that a polished floor can be mopped or scrubbed using a neutral detergent in the water and the polish will not be affected but as soon as an alkaline detergent is used, the alkali combines with the resin, the polish is softened and can then be scrubbed or rinsed away from the floor.

Water-based emulsion polishes fall into three main categories, that is *fully buffable, semi-buffable* and *dry-bright,* the difference between them being in the percentages of wax, resin and polymer.

	Fully buffable	Semi-buffable	Dry-bright
Wax (%)	45–60	25–40	5–15
Polymer (%)	20–40	45–60	50–70
Resin (%)	5–15	5–15	5–15

Both a fully and semi-buffable polish have to be buffed up by a machine so that they become hard and more durable and a good gloss is produced. A dry-bright polish contains so little wax that machine buffing makes no difference to the initial gloss obtained from the polymer.

A *fully buffable* polish dries to a low sheen and must be hardened between applications by buffing. It has good resistance to carbon-black but will mark with water, stains and dirt. Its great advantage is that the gloss can be renewed by buffing for a longer period than the other emulsions so it is used in an area where it is not possible to re-wax frequently.

A *semi-buffable* polish dries to a subdued gloss which is increased by buffing; this also increases durability and gives it better resistance to marking than a fully buffable polish so it is more frequently used.

A *dry-bright* polish requires no buffing so it would be used either when no floor machine is available or when the area is too small to merit the expense of a machine such as in a bathroom with a hard floor or for the skirting to carpet squares or rugs. It can be expensive to use in a heavy-duty area as, once the gloss has been worn, it cannot be renewed and the floor has to be cleaned and re-waxed. A dry-bright is very durable and has good resistance to water, stains and dirt; carbon-black is more difficult to remove.

One of the later developments in emulsion polishes has been the *metallized polish* in which the resin has been removed and replaced with a metal particle, usually zinc or zirconium, which is bonded to the polymer molecule. This gives much greater durability and resistance to marking and, because there is no alkali-soluble resin, means that it can be cleaned with alkaline detergent and is unaffected by the soap-suds in a bathroom. To remove this type of emulsion, an ammonia-based stripping-agent is used. Metallized polishes are buffable, semi-buffable or dry-brights.

With both solvent- or water-based polishes, the initial treatment is to apply two or three very thin layers of polish which are hardened between each application. A *high solids* emulsion is designed to provide a thick film with one application. It takes about 20 minutes to dry and is used in areas where cleaning times are limited.

A *wash and wax* is used as a detergent to remove dirt and to leave a thin layer of polish. It is not suitable for use in a really dirty area.

Provided it has been applied correctly, an application of polish should not make a floor slippery.

Slip resistence depends on the type of polish and the correct application. The degree of slipping is measured as a co-efficient of friction ranging from 1.0 which is very slip-resistent to 0.0 which is extremely slippery. The co-efficient of friction for polishes is:

    0.3 Solvent wax polish (paste);
    0.4 Solvent wax polish (liquid);
    0.5 Water-based polish (fully buffable);
    0.6 Water-based polish (semi-buffable);
    0.7 Water-based polish (dry-bright).

There is a chance of one in a million of slipping on a floor with a co-efficient of 0.4. A floor can become slippery if two different polishes are used, one over the other, or if they have been applied too thickly or not hardened between applications. All floors are extremely slippery and dangerous when wet.

(c) Polish application

As with the application of seals and primers, the basic rule is that the floor must be clean, dust-free, dry and have no trace of cleaning solvents or alkaline detergent. Any trace of these will affect the new polish being laid so that it will not harden and dries to a dull 'bloom' with the only solution being to strip the polish off and start again which is expensive and very tedious. To avoid this problem, vinegar is added to the rinse water to *neutralize* the alkali.

The *traditional method* of maintaining a polished floor is to apply two or three layers of polish with each layer hardened by buffing. The first two layers are applied to within eight or nine inches from the skirting board or any fitted furniture and the last layer taken up to the skirting boards as no-one walks or stands so close to the edge of the room, the polish will not be worn. It is there only for the appearance. The floor is swept or mopped daily and buffed periodically to restore the gloss. When there is insufficient wax left, the floor is swept and damp-mopped to remove dirt and a new coat of polish applied. Eventually, this will not produce a good result as there can be a dirt build-up with dirt trapped between the layers of polish and the polish discolours gradually with time; this means that all the old polish has to be stripped off, the floor rinsed and the process re-started with the basis of another three coats of polish. Usually, this may have to be done once or twice a year; it takes time and puts the area out of action whilst it is being scrubbed and rewaxed.

Spray-cleaning is a cleaning method which removes dirt and leaves a layer of polish. It is much quicker than the traditional method and has the advantage that the floor can be cleaned whilst people are using the area as the only section out of action is the 2 m^2 under the floor machine. A solution of emulsion polish and water, diluted in the ratio of 1:8 or 1:10, is sprayed on to a small section of floor and immediately, whilst still damp, the section is machine buffed using nylon or polyester pads. The pads pick up the dirt, remove scuff marks and the floor is left dry with a gloss which, if needed, can be increased with a softer pad to finish the process.

Spray-cleaning is very effective on a badly maintained wood floor if a liquid, solvent-based polish is used. This can be diluted with white spirit.

A *mopping unit* uses the same water-based solution that is used for spray-cleaning; the floor is damp-mopped, dried and machine-buffed. This method is not suitable for a solvent-based polish as the solvent will merely re-distribute the dirt and evaporate before it can be removed.

The most common faults in polishing are:

(1) Traces of dirt and grease preventing the even coating of emulsion polish;

(2) Alkali left on a floor causing an emulsion polish to 'powder' and 'bloom'.

(3) Dirt build-up as the result of poor maintenance, i.e., polish taken too close to the skirting boards and re-waxing on a dirty or dusty surface.

As a guide to the amount of polish required:

Solvent-based polish on a porous floor – 1 litre : 60 m^2;

Water-based polish on a porous floor – 1 litre : 80 m^2;
Water-based polish on a semi-porous floor – 1 litre : 100 m^2.

(d) Furniture polish

As with a floor, furniture is polished to maintain its appearance and to protect the structure of the wood by filling the pores with wax; this helps to prevent a change in the moisture content and avoids cracks and unevenness caused by the wood drying out or swelling as moisture is absorbed. The wax also prevents engrained dirt and stains; some polishes contain an insecticide which limits the activities of the furniture beetle.

Much of the modern furniture produced for commercial use is given a protective finish which is based on either polyurethane, polyester or melamine and requires no more maintenance than dusting and rubbing up with a dry cloth; older furniture, antiques and good reproductions, do not have this type of finish and must be waxed and polished.

A *furniture paste*, containing 25–30 per cent wax in a solvent-base, gives the soft gloss patina which is the characteristic of antique furniture, unfortunately, it gives little protection against stains, heat and water marks so care must be taken. If the wood becomes badly stained it is best to have it repaired professionally but a smaller stain can be removed by rubbing with a metal polish, silver polish for a very fine-grained wood and brass polish for a heavier grain. The abrasive, helped by the solvent, will remove a very fine layer from the surface of the wood and with it the marks; wax polish or linseed oil is then used to restore the gloss. A proprietary stain remover can also be used.

Furniture creams and *aerosol polishes* contain little natural wax but a high proportion of synthetic polymers and silicone to give a high gloss polish and good protection. They are quick and easy to use. A silicone polish must not be used on a floor as it is slippery.

Teak and afrormosia are not polished but maintained in good condition by *oil*, usually a mixture of linseed and white spirit.

Furniture and fittings must be clean before polish is applied. Grease and stickiness can be removed quickly by wiping over with a solution of vinegar and water, about 2 tablespoons to the pint; this is equally good for cleaning finger marks from the backs of chairs, banisters and the edges of doors, and from ceramic tiles and formica table-tops.

(e) Metal polishes

Most metals require some periodical attention to remove tarnish and scratch marks. Tarnish is caused by the interaction of the metal with sulphur pollutants in the air and with sulphur and acids in some foods. Scratches are caused by the general wear and tear of use.

Whilst tarnish can be removed by either abrasive or chemical means, scratches can only be healed by causing the surface metal to 'flow' into the scratch, this is achieved by rubbing with a fine abrasive and a small proportion of a fatty acid which makes the metal behave like a fluid and fill the scratch. A chemical cleaner gives fast tarnish removal but antique and good quality metals should be cleaned with an abrasive to restore the patina. Hotel-quality 'silver' would be cleaned with an abrasive less frequently.

Cleaning methods are affected by the hardness of the metal and by its finish. Gold, silver and some of the pewter alloys are soft and scratch easily so that only a very fine abrasive, such as iron oxide, and soft cloths can be used. Brass, copper, zinc and some pewter alloys are much harder and coarser abrasives can be used such as powdered whiting or talc. A good cleaner contains a balanced abrasive powder, a fatty acid and a solvent or a small amount of detergent suspended in a water/alcohol or petroleum base.

The original polishes were a mixture of very fine clay and fat; in 1905, the first liquid polishes were introduced.

Silver, E.P.N.S and some pewter alloys These can be cleaned by:

(1) A plate powder or jeweller's rouge; this is iron oxide mixed to a paste with either methylated spirit, which evaporates quickly or with water. This is the best material to clean valuable and antique gold and silver.

(2) Liquid silver polish.

(3) A burnishing machine; this has a rotating drum which is half-filled with stainless steel ball-bearings and an alkaline detergent. The silver is placed in the drum and the rotating ball-bearings act as an abrasive to remove scratches whilst tarnish is removed with the detergent.

(4) A 'silver-dip'; an acid solution which removes tarnish but does not heal scratches. Stainless steel can be badly affected by silver dip, so much so that it may be impossible to remove the discolouration. Care must be taken particularly if work is done on a draining-board or when knife-handles are being cleaned.

(5) Aluminium forms the basis of two different cleaning methods both using a chemical reaction. An aluminium pan, filled with water, is brought to the boil and a little salt added; when silver is held in the water nothing happens, but as soon as it touches the aluminium the tarnish will disappear immediately – with no detriment to the silver. In the other method, aluminium is placed in a plastic bowl and a handful of washing soda and boiling water added; provided the silver is in contact with the aluminium, an electrolytic action is set up and the tarnish removed. Both methods are suitable for cutlery cleaning.

(6) Long-life cleaners leave a protective chemical film on the metal which inhibits tarnish.

All cutlery and plates must be washed after cleaning to remove any trace of the cleaner.

Brass, bronze, copper, and some pewter alloys A 'hard' metal polish is used. *Copper* can also be cleaned with acid, lemon juice or vinegar (acetic acid) used with or without a little salt. Stronger acids, such as hydrochloric acid diluted in the ratio of 1:6, can be used on badly stained copper but great care must be taken to avoid damage to the hands and to other fabrics. *Pewter* develops a patina when it is not polished which is often considered preferable to a polished surface. *Stainless steel* usually only requires washing in hot, detergent water and the infrequent use of a stainless steel cleaner. It can be stained or darkened by salt and vinegar mixtures, silver-dip and undiluted chlorine bleach; stains which are almost impossible to remove, although it is sometimes possible to remove heat stains with methylated spirits and a coarse abrasive. *Aluminium* is damaged by alkali which pits and dissolves the surface. Cleaning is with a neutral detergent. Stains are removed with a weak acid, (apple or rhubarb during cooking) or a coarse abrasive. *Chromium* should not corrode or tarnish, *anodysed metals* are protected by a thin layer of aluminium oxide; both require periodical cleaning with hot detergent and water. *Lacquer* alters the appearance of a metal and does not withstand abrasion. It must never be used on any valuable or antique metal but is useful to prevent tarnishing on many of the door plates and fittings, handles, rails and other fixtures.

(f) Window polishes and cleaners

A *window polish* contains a very fine abrasive such as iron oxide or powdered whiting, a grease solvent or detergent and an emulsifier. A small amount is applied to the glass, left to dry and polished. When windows are cleaned regularly, it seems unnecessary to use an abrasive. A *window cleaner* consists of a grease solvent or ammonia. Vinegar and water also gives a good result. Traditionally, a chamois leather is used to polish windows and mirrors but this is now being replaced with synthetic fabrics and lint-free cloths.

Methylated spirits are used to clean antique or expensive mirrors and the glass protecting paintings as it evaporates quickly and prevents water penetrating into the silver-backing or water-marking a picture. These spirits are flammable and care must be taken with their use.

3.3.3 Detergents

Strictly speaking, a detergent is any substance which can be used to 'wipe off' and cleanse a surface; the simplest detergent is water. To clean efficiently, a detergent should meet the following requirements:

(1) It should be soluble in water;

(2) Be unaffected by either hard or soft water or by the temperature;

(3) Must 'wet' a surface quickly (the surface tension of the water must be reduced);

(4) Loosen the dirt, lift it from the surface and hold it in suspension.

(5) Rinse the dirt away leaving a clean, smear-free finish.

(6) Be non-poisonous, biogradable and non-corrosive.

For most cleaning a *foaming property* is unnecessary and unwanted, particularly when the detergent is used in a washing-up machine or for scrubbing. The *strength* should be variable and related to the amount of dirt which has to be removed and the type of surface. As a general rule, the mildest cleaning agent should be used to remove dirt rather than a strong agent which can damage and pit the surface.

The *pH scale* is used to determine whether a liquid is acid or alkaline and measures its strength. A liquid can be checked by using 'universal' or 'litmus' paper and comparing the colour change.

```
←——— Acid ———→  Neutral ←——— Alkali ———→
|————————————————————————————————————————|
  0  1  2  3  4  5  6  7  8  9 10 11 12 13 14
```

Soap is made from fatty acids and oils which are saponified by boiling with an alkali; it is an expensive and ineffectual cleaning agent as it is affected by the hardness of water and by temperature and forms scum and a greasy film which then has to be removed from a surface. Until the 1940s, hard 'bar' soap was used extensively for cleaning.

Synthetic detergents are a by-product of the petroleum industry: alkyl sulphonates and sodium cetyl sulphonates and are either acid, neutral or alkali. Acid can affect floors and an acid detergent is not normally used for routine cleaning.

A *neutral detergent* has a pH value of 7–7.5 and is used for all general cleaning, floor scrubbing and washing-up. Price depends on the dilution rate; this is usually expressed as being 7, 15 or 30 per cent active for a very concentrated liquid. A neutral detergent should not harm any fabrics or surfaces and, unless being used constantly, should not affect the hands and skin.

An *alkaline detergent* has a pH value of between 9 and 12.5 or 13 and is used to remove heavy dirt and grease deposits and also to remove an emulsion floor polish. An ammonia-free, alkaline detergent is used to remove a metallized emulsion polish. These detergents can be in liquid or powder form. Gloves must be used when handling this type of detergent as it does affect the skin; constant use can affect some fabrics and surfaces.

A *germicidal detergent* is a mixture of a compatible disinfectant with a detergent. These must be specially formulated by the manufacturer and are never mixed haphazardly as many disinfectants are inactivated by a detergent. Research by the Public Health Laboratory Service has shown that the use of disinfectants is unnecessary for routine cleaning except in particularly dirty areas where urine, pus or faeces may be present and in food hygiene areas.

A *dry-foam carpet and upholstery cleaner* is a detergent which has a foam property added. This is because the fabric has to be kept as dry as possible and the detergent is designed to remove dirt in the foam crystals. The water content evaporates and dirt and crystals are vacuumed when the fabric is dry.

A *solvent-based detergent* is used to remove solvent-based polishes by the addition of white spirit and additives to the detergent base. This has the advantage over the use of paraffin or white spirit which evaporates quickly leaving the dirt to reharden on the floor and there is less fire risk because of the water content.

A *gel cleaner* is a specially fortified alkaline detergent; a small amount of a solvent gives extra power and strength to the alkali and quickens the softening of an emulsion polish or of dirt as the gel sticks to the surface so allowing the detergent to be in contact for a longer time. The solvent evaporates before the floor surface is affected.

3.3.4 Toilet cleansers and deodorizers

A toilet cleanser is needed for two entirely different tasks; one task is to kill bacteria and micro-organisms by means of a disinfectant; the other task is to remove encrustations of calcium and magnesium salt deposits from the water forming the trap in the 'U'-bend. For this an acid cleaner is needed. When a toilet is being used and flushed constantly the water is not standing sufficiently long for these deposits to occur and there is no need to use this type of cleaner.

An *acid cleaner* can be in either powder or liquid form, the lattter being best for commercial use as the acid can be sprayed where it is needed. It is based on compounds of phosphoric acid, sodium bisulphate, oxalic acid, gluconic acid and hydrochloric acid which become active when in contact with water. These acids require a minimum period of two to three hours to remove the deposits so are usually put into the toilet at night or when it will not be used for some time. It is usually only necessary to use this type of cleaner once a week.

The *disinfectant* used in the toilet is sodium hypochlorite. This must never be used at the same time as an acid cleaner as the two combine to produce a highly toxic gas which can be very unpleasant and dangerous in a confined space such as a toilet. For this reason, disinfectants and acid cleaners should not be issued to staff at the same time, disinfectant can be used daily whilst a supervisor would use the acid cleaner only when it is considered necessary.

Many cleansers are formulated to combine the acid with a disinfectant; this is safe although it is more expensive than using the disinfectant on its own.

Channel Blocks combine a certain amount of disinfection with a deodoriser and are placed in urinals and under the rim of the toilet, to disguise any smells. Provided the cleaning is done correctly and the toilet is well ventilated, any smell should be quickly dispersed so that, in many cases these blocks should not be necessary.

3.3.5 Kitchen cleaners

These are issued for oven cleaning to remove heavy, baked-on, deposits of food and grease. They are made either from potassium and sodium hydroxides or from caustic soda and a fat solvent. They can give off toxic fumes and if used on a hot surface, great care must be taken to ensure that they do not come in contact with clothes, the skin, aluminium, zinc or paint. Gloves must be worn.

3.3.6 Disinfectants

In routine cleaning, a disinfectant is normally only used when adequate cleaning cannot be done by any other means or when advised to do so by the Medical Authorities (see section 11.3.4).

For general use, a disinfectant should not be strong-smelling, particularly when used in a food area, be non-corrosive and should have a long shelf-life. It must be remembered that bacteria will only be killed when they are in contact with the disinfectant for sufficient time; sodium hypochlorite used in the toilet needs a minimum of seven minutes contact before it is effective.

3.3.7 Air fresheners

These are usually in aerosol form and used to disguise other penetrating smells which cling such as tobacco smoke, beer and general stuffiness. The smell of sickness in a lift or a toilet smell can be difficult to eradicate by the more normal means of good ventilation and sufficient air changes.

3.4 Planned preventive maintenance

About 40 per cent of all building work is concerned with the maintenance of a building and the amount spent is an important feature in the overall running costs. Regular inspection and attention to minor faults does much to minimize heavy expenditure.

The main aim of preventive maintenance is to:

(1) Limit the deterioration of a building in order to eliminate costly emergency repairs.

(2) Reduce wear and replacement costs and day-to-day main-tenance requirements.

(3) Keep the building and its contents in a safe condition.

(4) Analyse building and equipment faults so that better designs or systems can be introduced.

(5) Use the maintenance staff efficiently and economically with a planned work-load in such a way that they are not constantly taken off a major job to cope with small repairs.

The building inspection is usually at three levels: (1) day-to-day supervision by the housekeeping staff and the reporting of all defects for repair; (2) regular inspections by the management, particularly when estimates are being prepared for future budgets and (3) periodic inspections, often every two to three years, by a professional surveyor or an estates manager who has the technical knowledge to make a thorough examination of the physical condition of the building and assess the standard of maintenance and who will take into account all the requirements of the Building and Water Regulations, the Fire Precautions Act and the Health and Safety at Work Act.

Dampness causes major problems; it can affect the condition of wall finishes, floors and furniture with an extreme penetration leading to dry and wet rot. Dampness can arise for a number of reasons: a *faulty or non-existent damp-course*; *subsidence*; by *rain penetration* caused by faults in the mortar and pointing; damage caused by climbing plants such as ivy, leaking or blocked gutters and downpipes, flashings and joints around windows and doors and bridging across cavity walls; by *broken or loose tiles* and by damage to flat roofs; by *breaks* in paintwork caused by blistering and flaking.

Electrical wiring should be inspected regularly for any signs of a breakdown in the insulation and for damage to plugs and sockets. The Electricity Board recommends a thorough check every fifteen years.

Any projection, protruding handle or fitting is always liable to be damaged as are walls and corners. Much can be done to reduce the need for maintenance by providing finishes which require little or no re-decoration and are designed to be vandal-proof.

One type of damage, often overlooked until too late, is that caused by rats, mice, insects, beetles and fungi – all of which are only too ready to take advantage of lax management and are happy to gnaw, eat or digest their way through the building fabric.

A large establishment will have a Maintenance Department which will employ fully qualified electricians, plumbers, carpenters, boiler operators and interior decorators whilst a smaller establishment will often make do with a handyman porter who also keeps an eye on the central heating boiler.

Redecoration schemes can be organized in two ways. In the first scheme, the programme of work is scheduled to be completed over several years and uses directly employed staff. This means that 20 or

25 per cent of the building is redecorated each year and the work completed during a slack period. In the second method, the entire building is redecorated once every three, four or five years; this method is more suitable when the building closes for a time and contractors are employed although if the establishment is part of a group, the decorators may be permanently employed and move from one unit to another.

The *frequency* of redecoration depends on the standard of the accommodation with, in some instances, the work being completed every year or eighteen months or, in a 4 or 5-star hotel as soon as the guest room shows any signs of wear or staining which cannot be removed by routine cleaning. Most smaller establishments will plan to redecorate bedrooms and corridors every four or five years and the public areas more frequently depending on their usage.

3.5 Pest control

Good housekeeping plays an important part in the control of pests. The Prevention of Damage by Pests Act of 1949 makes it obligatory for owners to report a serious infestation of rats or mice to the local authorities. The Food and Drugs Act of 1955 makes it an offence to sell food which has been contaminated and this was re-inforced by the Food Hygiene Regulations of 1970 which made it clear that premises, where there are catering facilities, must be kept free from pests. In 1976, the Food and Drugs (Control of Food on Premises) Act gave local authorities the power to close dirty food premises within 72 hours and considered that evidence of pests on the premises was sufficient evidence of unhygienic conditions.

There are many problems caused by infestation. At the very worst, for a catering business, there is closure, but all firms run the risk of losing customers when they see evidence of infestation or if they read reports in the press of the details of any prosecutions. There are health risks and loss caused by the damage to food and stores and the damage caused to the fabric of the building and its safety by rodents gnawing through electric cables and gas pipes, wood and skirting boards. There is also the problem of reduced staff morale which, in extreme cases, may mean that it is difficult to recruit labour.

Research shows that most damage is done by the furniture beetle, this is closely followed by the destruction and contamination caused by rats, mice, flies and ants. The increasing use of fitted carpets has led to greater damage by the carpet beetle who can live, reasonably undisturbed, at the base of a tuft and wreck havoc, causing bald patches to appear in the carpet pile. Moths have become less of a problem with the increasing use of man-made fibres and fewer woollen materials, although these fabrics can still be bitten or cut by the insect even though they are not eaten.

All pests need warmth and a place to breed, food and water, and like to be undisturbed. *Control* depends mainly on a frequent and regular cleaning programme which goes behind and underneath furniture and fittings, and ensures that premises are clean with no food debris left available for feeding. Unless there is a very large infestation, pests are not usually seen during the day-time but are nocturnal and scavenge at night so that it is important that any signs, droppings, damage or trails are reported. Rubbish must be carefully controlled and kept in covered containers, tied into rubbish bags or compacted. The rubbish area should be cleaned regularly and kept tidy.

Cats and dogs, living wild, are a constant source of trouble particularly when the premises are spread over a big area and many staff members have to be discouraged from putting out saucers of milk and food and can become very emotional when there is any suggestion of removing them from the premises by poisoning or by the local R.S.P.C.A. Birds can also be a problem, although this is rather more easily solved by using netting, removing perch sites (when possible) or by narcotics.

Many pests arrive in a building by means of delivery vans where they may be found hidden amongst sacks and boxes or in the supply of clean linen from the laundry. This has resulted in some large firms asking for a certificate from their suppliers to show that both premises and delivery vans are kept clear of infestation by regular servicing from a specialist pesticide company. Many large companies cannot afford any risk of bad publicity. A small firm may be prepared to cope with infestation as and when it occurs; one of the first things to do is to contact the local authority as an infestation may be affecting other buildings in the neighbourhood and the Health Inspectors are often able to pin-point the source of the infestation and inspect other buildings and locations in the area. They will also be in a position to know which are the most effective pesticides to use as over the years, many pests have developed an immunity to some of the more common poisons; a large or persistent infestation usually means, however, that a specialist firm is contracted.

Improved standards and methods of control have reduced infestations but have gone nowhere near eliminating them, so it is necessary to be aware of the problem and take immediate action as soon as there are signs that unwelcome visitors have arrived.

3.6 Flowers and plants

Flowers are almost a necessity to provide freshness, interest and a touch of colour and individuality to an establishment and need not be too expensive if they are combined with leaves, foliage and twigs which give bulk and background to an arrangement.

Flowers are usually placed in the foyer and reception, in restaurants as a large centre piece and as smaller arrangements on the individual tables, in the bars and in V.I.P. rooms. Many large, city establishments have a contract with a florist to provide and check all floral arrangements regularly but this sort of contract can be expensive and many smaller hotels and residences buy and arrange their own flowers or may be lucky enough to grow and cut flowers and foliage in their own grounds.

Flowers and plants are fragile and prefer to have a regular supply of fresh water, a cool, smoke-free atmosphere and will last much longer if they can be transferred from the public rooms and restaurants at night and refreshed in a cool room until needed.

Flowers should always be bought or picked in the bud and can be kept for several days before use if they are rolled carefully in dampened paper and stored in a cool room. For preference, there should be a small *Flower-room* which has work tables, a sink and sufficient storage for the equipment.

Keen arrangers collect a vast assortment of bits and pieces, the basic requirements are:

(1) A supply of containers in all shapes and sizes in china and porcelain, metal, glass or basket;

(2) A plentiful supply of chicken-wire which is crumpled and fixed in the container so that the arrangements are held firmly in place;

(3) Pin-holders used, either on their own in a small arrangement or with the chicken-wire and plasticine to hold the pin-holders in place;

(4) A porous material, such as *Oasis*, is often used for the smaller delicate arrangements, but it is broken and crumbles quickly when used with heavy, woody stemmed blooms; and sand makes a good alternative.

(5) Secateurs and a sharp knife;

(6) Lemonade straws and fine wire;

(7) Buckets for storage and a supply of newspapers;

All flowers and foliage should be conditioned before being used so that they last longer. This is done by:

(1) Removing all leaves from the bottom of the stem so none will be

below the water line as these wilt or will make the water discoloured and smelly;

(2) All flowers and leaves should be refreshed by plunging into water and leaving them, preferably overnight, in a cool, draught-free place. Further treatment depends on the type of flower and:

(*a*) All non-woody stems are cut at an angle to avoid starving them of water;

(*b*) All woody stems, such as those of roses or chrysanthemums, are crushed and bruised;

(*c*) Hollow stems, as of lupins or delphiniums, are filled with water which is retained in the stem by a small piece of cotton wool;

(*d*) The stems of carnations and pinks are cut between the joints;

(*e*) The stems of poppies, euphorbias, or other plants with a milky sap, are singed;

(*f*) A few plants, such as the dahlia or the Christmas rose do best when placed in very hot water;

A good, floral centre-piece should have a definite shape, the most usual being a triangle or a large oval with the shape, size and container used dependent on where it is going to be placed. To obtain reasonable proportions and balance, the height of the finished arrangement should be a minimum of $1\frac{1}{2}$ times the depth of the container or $1\frac{1}{2}$ times its width for a low, table setting.

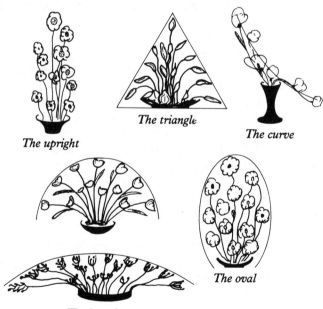

The upright

The triangle

The curve

The long fan

The oval

The arrangement is started by cutting the stem of the tallest bloom and placing it in the central position and the other blooms are then cut with shorter stems and placed so that they radiate from the centre; this displays each bloom to advantage and ensures that none will be masked by another.

When the flowers are to be viewed from all sides for a table or counter decoration, the design is divided into thirds or quarters and the blooms placed symmetrically. Leaves and foliage are used to balance and fill out the design and as a background to the colours and shapes of the flowers. As a general rule, the larger and brighter blooms are placed in the centre, towards the base and the light, smaller flowers kept to the outside of the arrangement.

The flowers used for banquets and formal occasions are set pieces and kept low so that guests can talk to each other in comfort across the table; at other times, restaurant flowers can be more informal with one or two flowers and leaves arranged in a finger bowl or with a single flower in a small vase.

When flowers are arranged and placed in position, the water should be checked and topped-up daily and wilting or dead flowers carefully removed or replaced. A little sugar or aspirin is often added to the water as a 'pick-them-up' and a drop or two of bleach to keep the water fresh. Care must be taken to prevent water being spilt on a wooden surface or a starched tablecloth and most big arrangements should be set on a protective mat.

A formal arrangement is usually placed in V.I.P. rooms with a single rose or carnation in the bathroom.

Many flowers dry well to make attractive arrangements for the winter. Artificial flowers can be very exotic and decorative in their own right but must be kept dust and smoke-free.

House plants make an attractive alternative to cut flowers and, if treated well, last very much longer. They should be kept out of direct sunlight and draughts but they do need some light, otherwise they become elongated and will not produce good flowers. Pots should be watered when the soil is a little dry but not completely dried out; a daily dribble of water usually has the effect of turning the soil into an airless, soggy mass in which few plants survive. Some plants, such as the African violet and cyclamens, are watered from the base; most plants appreciate a daily spray which moistens the leaves and removes dust whilst a little liquid fertiliser is essential if the plants are to remain healthy for any length of time. Ferns and cactus are very accommodating for use in the darker areas.

3.7 Exercise and discussion

1 Floor coverings require many of the following characteristics:
   (a) Long life expectancy.
   (b) Heavy duty – to resist abrasion and spillages from water, chemicals, grease and oil.
   (c) Economic cleaning costs.
   (d) Stability – resistance to cracking and indentation, stretching, shrinking and fading.
   (e) Appearance and wide range of colour and pattern.
   (f) Comfort – resilience, warmth, quietness.
   (g) Safety – slip-resistant, anti-static, flame-retardent, hygienic.
   (h) Vermin-proof.
Which floor coverings are most suitable for each of the above requirements?
Is there one perfect floor?
Floor maintenance accounts for approximately 40 per cent of the time spent in general cleaning – how could this time be reduced?
   What are the advantages of having a floor laid in tiles as opposed to one which is laid in sheets?
2 An Estates Manager has been appointed who will be responsible for planning and controlling all maintenance needs of a group of Hotels. It is a newly created post. How would you organize a maintenance and redecoration programme? What information and records would you need? What arrangements would you make to service and maintain lifts, window cleaning cradles and heavy cleaning equipment.
3 It is policy that 20 per cent of all rooms are redecorated and updated every year. How would the Housekeeper plan that the work is carried out as smoothly as possible? By what means would she keep herself informed of modern trends?
4 Many of the Catering Exhibitions include Trade Stands for Manufacturers of industrial cleaning equipment and materials and you are able to look at, operate and compare several floor machines. After studying the specifications for each, how would you decide which is the best machine to buy?
5 You are going to order new cleaning trolleys for the room-maids. Prepare a specification of the type of trolley you feel you need, taking into account that each maid is servicing 15 twin-bedded rooms and bathrooms.
   What equipment and materials would she need to have with her?

4

Quality Control

To be effective, any system for the control of standards and quality must involve all supervisors but in addition, all staff must know the standards expected and the ways in which they are reached.

The setting of standards starts when the work specification is being defined by the work study team in conjunction with housekeeping and management. This is important as an alteration in standards can affect staff requirements and the costs of running the department (see Chapter 1).

There must always be a balance between costs and results. It is unnecessary to set a higher standard than that justified by the type of establishment and the needs of the user; as has been mentioned elsewhere, there should be no difference in cleanliness but there is often a difference in the frequency with which a task is done – are beds resheeted daily or weekly? How often are the windows cleaned? And the curtains? And what about polishing the furniture?

Work can be graded. This is not always easy but usually some consensus of opinion will produce a workable system. For instance:

A bedroom – Grade 5. No faults found; appearance good.
4. Minimum faults only; i.e. hook off curtain, covers not quite straight, matches missing.
3. Faults; i.e. dust under bed, bathroom floor with dirt in corners and behind door, waste bins not washed.
2. Unsatisfactory; i.e. room looks untidy, bathroom floor not washed, smears on mirrors and tiles, waste bins not emptied, 'bits' on upholstery.

      1. Minimum work done; i.e. bed changed and bath cleaned. No other work done.

      0. No work done.

For a polished floor – Grade 5. High, even polish. No dust, smears or scuff marks.

      4. Good polish but with slight smearing.

      3. Uneven polish. Some dust, smears and scuff marks.

      2. Poor polish, scuff marks. Dust in corners.

      1. Floor roughly swept and badly marked. Little evidence of polish.

      0. No work done.

The aim of quality control is to produce work from all members of staff which is of an overall, consistent standard and which uses all resources, staff, equipment and materials, as efficiently as possible. Control is achieved by:

1 Training staff;
2 Inspecting and measuring the results achieved;
3 Correcting all faults and re-training where necessary.

All standards are dependent on the staff abilities so it is essential that they should understand the necessity for maintaining the quality of their work and the way in which they will be assessed.

4.1 Training staff

Newly appointed staff, whether experienced or not, must be trained to the standards required as no-one can be expected to know automatically what has to be done. The length of time needed for training will be dependent on the amount of previous experience.

A *training manual* is developed from the *job specification* and *task breakdown* and is a logical description of what has to be known in order to get the work completed to a satisfactory standard in the time allocated. Chapter 10 gives the job specification for cleaning a guestroom and bathroom. These are two stages in training staff:

1 *Induction training* is essential to make sure that the new employee feels a welcomed and valued member of the organization as

soon as possible. The training gives basic information which is applicable to all staff. It should take place on the first day of employment. Usually, an *induction checklist* includes the following information:

The Organization – what it is, its aims, objectives and standards. The layout and geography of the building and information on specific work areas. The staff structure and the most important 'who's who'. This is often accompanied by a plan and organization chart for each person and re-inforced by a tour of the building.

Personal requirements – procedures for payment of wages, sickness and absenteeism, days off and holidays, welfare, grievances, locker, cloakroom and canteen facilities. Uniform and dress requirements. Importance of good appearance.

Social skills – importance of good liaison with all other staff and between departments. Customer contacts. Handling complaints.

Safety – safety and accident prevention to meet the requirements of the Health and Safety at Work Act, 1974. Fire precautions to meet the requirements of the Fire Precautions Act, 1971. Hygiene standards to meet the requirements of the Hygiene regulations. Security and the action to take to safeguard both customer's and establishment's property. Lost property and package passes.

Introduction to the employee's immediate supervisor and arrangements made to ensure that the new employee is accompanied to coffee and meal-breaks and has someone who is responsible for them during the first few days.

There should always be a 'follow-up' three to four weeks after the induction to find out how the newcomer is settling into the job and whether there are any problems or difficulties.

2 *Job instruction* should include all details needed to produce a good standard. Information must be given on: the order and method of work, the frequencies, the time allotted to the task, equipment and cleaning agents, safe methods of working, any problem areas. The aim is to make the employee as efficient as possible in the shortest time.

Staff appraisals are carried out in many large organizations and are designed to assess how an employee is performing in the job, where the strength and weaknesses are and to give some indication of the attitude and motivation of the individual. They must always be seen and discussed constructively with the employee. Appraisals are used as a basis to decide future training needs – either for retraining or training to a higher level, perhaps in supervisory skills, and to indicate any potential for promotion. Examples of two different types of appraisal forms are shown on pp. 77 and 78.

Checklist for the assessment of staff.

Name ....

Grade ....

Date of appointment to grade ....

	Good	Average	Poor
Punctuality			
Appearance – general impression care of uniform			

Manner and attitude to:
    guests
    supervisor
    other staff			

Ability to organize work and adjust to flexible working			

The standard of work achieved:
    guest rooms
    cleaning trolley
    service room			

Understanding of the following controls on:
    keys
    security
    lost property
    package passes			

Knowledge of hygiene standards required			

Knowledge of work routines:
    departure room
    occupied room
    vacant room
    periodical cleaning			

Assessment discussed with employee on ....

        Employee's signature ....

        Executive Housekeeper ....

Alternative staff appraisal form.

Name: Department:

Job knowledge and experience: how efficient is the employee?

Little experience or knowledge of job.	Needs guidance	Gets on with job, knows require-ments. Limited guidance.	In full control of job-suggests improvements.

Organizational and supervisory ability: consider whether promotion is possible?

Cannot organize work or be responsible for others	Some organizing ability, usually works well with others.	Organizes and copes well with problems. Works well with colleagues	Flexible and organizes well. Respected by subordinates. Good level of work.

Standard of work, speed and accuracy: consider safety, noise?

Slow, makes mistakes and needs constant checking.	Slow but thorough or quick but makes mistakes.	Good speed and standard of work.	Able to work fast and accurately under pressure.

Supervision required: how far can the employee be left without checking work?

Close supervision needed. No initiative.	Supervision needed to get job done. Will make no decisions.	Competent, needs little supervision.	Very competent. Will sum up a situation and make a decision.

Attitude: to the job, the organization and to colleagues and management?

No interest. Little co-operation.	Makes little effort unless interested. Own problems take priority.	Easy to work with, takes an interest.	Very helpful and co-operative.

Remarks: Date: ....

                                               Assessed by: ....

                                               Agreed by: ....

4.2 Inspection

All work must be inspected regularly by the immediate supervisor who should be responsible for correcting any fault as and when it occurs. Examples of checklists are shown below and on p. 80.

Quality control (hotel floor supervisors checklist).

Date .... Time .... Room number ....

	Yes	No			Yes	No
Door light			Plugs – electric			
Do not disturb			Shaving socket			
Fire notice			Shower fitting			
Door closer			Shower curtain			
Radio			W.C.			
Telephone			W.C. flush			
Telephone directories			Toilet rolls			
Headboards			Soap			
Gideon's bible			Glasses			
Ashtrays and matches			Sanibin			
Bedspread – clean			Washbasin			
Windows			Bath			
Net curtains			Plugs			
Heavy curtains			Towels			
Wardrobe			Towel rail			
Hangers (12)			Bath mat			
Chairs			Mirror			
Drawers and shelves			Tiles and bath panels			
Wastepaper bins			Light fittings			
Portable lights			Heating			
T.V.			Luggage rack			
Special promotions and guest supplies						

General – give your own opinion of the standard of the following:

	Good	Average	Poor		Good	Average	Poor
Carpet				Curtains			
Painted surfaces				Walls			
Wood surfaces				Lights			
Upholstery/covers				Literature			
General impression				Smell			

Please complete the maintenance docket for all defects.

Signed ....

Quality control (Hospital domestic services).

Ward/department ....

Week ending ....

Supervisor ....

Domestic assistants ....

....

....

....

....

Location	Floors							Furniture and fittings							High dusting						
	M	T	W	Th	F	S	Su	M	T	W	Th	F	S	Su	M	T	W	Th	F	S	Su

Points rating

Exceptional	5	Below average	2
Very good	4	Bad	1
Good	3	Not cleaned	0

Signed ....

When staff are paid incentive bonuses it is essential that the quality of the work is maintained. When it is not, staff should be warned that the bonus could be withdrawn.

Policy statement for loss of bonus.

The Management reserves the right to withhold payment of bonus for .... (state how long) from workers who persistently produce sub-standard work, provided that at least two authenticated complaints have been made in any period of three months.

The procedure shall be as follows:

1. Details of the causes of the complaint and the failure to meet the agreed quality standards shall be made in writing and signed by the person making the complaint. (A copy must be given to the member of staff concerned and the local T.U. representative notified.)

2. An independent assessor, who holds a managerial position and has knowledge of the work and of the quality standards, should investigate and consider the complaint.

3. If the complaint is considered justified, the member of staff must receive a written notification of the failure to meet the required standard and, if it is the first justified complaint within any period of three months, warning given that any further failure will result in the withdrawal of bonus for a period of .... months.

To ensure that the overall standard of the supervisors is the same, spot-checks should be carried out periodically by the Executive Housekeeper, Domestic Services Manager or the Manager. In many hotels, it is the custom for the General Manager to take whichever room is available at Reception, sleep in it and to produce a report for the Housekeeper on its comfort, appearance and cleanliness the following morning. Many of the Hotel Groups have a Head Office Inspection Team employed to maintain the standards between all hotels.

Other checks on standards are by means of guest questionnaires and the analysis of guest's complaints. Guests, of course, do not always bother to complain but may take their business elsewhere. An instance of this was given by a businessman who usually spends two or three nights in London each week. He decided to change his hotel when, as he explained, 'it was not at the same standard as it was when he first stayed there. It was using third class linen which was threadbare and darned in places, the bath towel was so thin that he could not dry properly and Room Service only provided enough coffee for two cups at breakfast whilst the new hotel had comfortable linen, provided him with a towelling dressing-gown and he always had three cups of coffee from Room Service. The price was the same. No, he had not mentioned it to the Management.'

Standards in hotels are also monitored by the Automobile Associations whose Inspectors make regular, unannounced visits. After the account has been paid, they will ask to see the Manager and discuss with him the good and bad points of the hotel.

Unfortunately, in many establishments, maintaining standards is left as part of the responsibility of the department head and is dependent solely on his professional pride and interest. Apathy and lack of enthusiasm will lead to low standards.

A very few Hospitals use a questionnaire for patients (p. 83).

4.3 Correcting faults

There is no point in putting in quality controls and setting standards if no action is taken to correct and improve.

Many firms run retraining and refresher courses and train when new equipment and methods are introduced. Training half-hours are useful if they are held regularly as it gives the opportunity for all staff to meet and discuss work problems and to communicate as, so often, supervisors and staff never get together and talk about what they are trying to do. These sessions frequently produce ideas and suggestions which may not have been thought of by the management. They also give an easy opportunity for all staff to get to know each other and to iron out any problems before they become major issues.

4.4 Exercise and discussion

1 You are either the Housekeeper of a hotel with 420 rooms or the Domestic Services Manager in a provincial General Hospital and have been in post for about 6 months. You feel that the standard of work is uneven and, as a means to improve and to increase enthusiasm, you would like to introduce some sort of incentive scheme with a small cash prize at the end of each month for the maid and the supervisor who has gained the most points.

Write the memorandum you send to the Manager or the Regional Domestic Services Manager explaining what you have in mind with reasons and how you propose to administer the scheme.

Hospital questionnaire.

	Excellent	Good	Average	Poor
General impression of the hospital				
Admission				
Reporting instructions				
Courtesy				
Promptness				
Introduction to the ward				
The ward				
Comfort				
Cleanliness				
Quietness				
Lighting				
Temperature				
T.V.				
Radio				
The nursing staff				
Cheerfulness				
Caring ability				
Efficiency				
Promptness				
Information on condition				
Other personnel				
Catering staff and Dietician				
Housekeeping				
Pathology staff				
Physiotherapy staff				
Radiography staff				
Food				
Hot food hot				
Cold food cold				
Appetising				
Looked attractive				
Sufficient				
Services				
Telephone				
Newspapers				
Library				
Shopping facilities				
Visiting arrangements				
Times available				
Privacy				

Do you have any suggestions or comments you would like to make which could improve the service? ....
....
....

5

Fire, Safety and Security

5.1 Fire

'Poor maintenance or misuse of the building by the occupants was shown to nullify fire protection measures completely.'

from a report by the Fire Research Establishment.

Following several disastrous hotel fires, the Fire Precautions Act was introduced in 1971. At present, this Act only applies to hotels, guest houses and other residential establishments which offer and sell accommodation for a profit; eventually, the provisions of the Act will apply to all premises to which the public have access whether or not they are operated for profit – to hospitals, schools and colleges, clubs, entertainment and recreational centres. This does not mean that there are no regulations to govern safety in these areas; the Factory Acts, the Office, Shops and Railway Premises Act, the Licensing laws and many local bye-laws have laid down minimum standards for fire precautions for many years.

Once the required level of fire protection has been installed in a hotel, the Fire Authorities issue the fire certificate. The Authorities are concerned with:

(1) The use and the activities which take place within the building;
(2) The number of people who can be on the premises at any one time;
(3) The lay-out of the building and the escape routes;
(4) The alarm and detection systems;
(5) Suitable methods of fighting fire;
(6) Training of staff;

Any change in the use, structure or a radical change in the type of furnishing and fittings should be reported to the Fire Authorities who will then decide whether the existing fire protection is sufficient or will need extending.

Even though an establishment is not covered by the Act, all managements should take responsibility for ensuring that premises are safe in the event of fire. They should:

(1) Plan to install and maintain precautions to prevent fires starting and to prevent the spread of fire and smoke;

(2) Ensure fires are detected quickly and that adequate alarm systems are installed;

(3) Have plans for the evacuation of staff, guests, patients and visitors;

(4) Have fire fighting arrangements;

(5) Train staff.

There are many causes of fire, a lot are caused through carelessness and ignorance which results in overheating of electrical circuits, fires caused through smoker's materials or fat fires due to overheating. Arson is now a major cause of fire in large public buildings so it is important that all possible prevention procedures are introduced.

5.1.1 Prevention of fire and prevention of fire-spread

(a) Security

Regular security patrols of the building should be undertaken, especially during the night, to check that equipment is turned off and disconnected and also to check for any suspicious happening. Armchairs should be inspected to make sure that there are no smouldering cigarette ends down the sides and hidden by the cushions.

(b) Flame-retardent materials

As far as possible, all fabrics and fittings should be flame-retardent. This is essential for curtains and upholstery covers (see Section 7.3.2).

(c) Flame-retardent finishes

The Fire Precautions Act requires that the surface finish of walls and ceilings on an escape route must be non-flammable as 'the personal hazard to occupants can be severely affected by internal linings and finishes', in the Act, materials are classified into eight groups which indicate where they can be used. Inorganic materials such as, brick, plaster, woodwool slab, ceramic tiles and and concrete are acceptable everywhere; these can be covered by paint or by a thin vinyl or paper covering but not by a heavy flock paper or by fabric – whether these are flame-retardant or not.

(d) Combustible rubbish

All rubbish such as paper and combustible materials should be removed from the premises as soon as possible and not left in cupboards or odd corners; if there is not a daily collection the rubbish should be stored in a safe place or compacted for easy handling. Waste-paper baskets should be made from a non-flammable material. The contents of *ash-trays* should be emptied into a separate metal container and not mixed with the contents of wastepaper baskets.

(e) Electrical wiring

Many fires are caused by the break-down of electrical insulation. The wiring of a building should be checked every fifteen to twenty years. *Overloading* can easily occur when adaptor plugs are used, particularly where there are long-term residents in staff or student accommodation; most rooms have a single power socket and there is a strong temptation for the occupant to run a television, bedside lamp and an electric fire from the same socket. Whether a single socket is overloaded or not depends on the power-rating of each appliance being used; an over-loaded circuit may still operate but heat is produced which will cause the insulation to break-down and, perhaps six or nine months later, result in fire behind a skirting-board or in a loft. To find out whether there is over-loading, the following formula is used: the power-rating of the appliances (measured in *watts*, W), divided by the *voltage*, V, of the electricity gives the resistance of the *wire* which carries the current (measured in *amperes* or *amps*, A).

For example, a 2-bar electric fire has a rating of 2000 watts, a hair-dryer requires 420 watts and a colour television, 150 watts. The three total:

$$\frac{2570 \text{ W}}{240 \text{ V}} = 10^+ \text{ A}.$$

This would be safe to use on a modern power circuit which is installed with sockets which can carry up to 13 amps. It would be unsafe if a 3-bar fire were used, which required 3000 watts. The combination would then need a current of 14.8 A – above the capacity of the circuit.

The same formula is used to determine the correct fuse for each plug which should be related to the power rating of the appliance; if a larger fuse than that recommended is used, it means that the safety factor has been lost and a faulty piece of equipment may still operate with the possibility of it becoming 'live' or causing a fire.

All electrical equipment should be checked regularly for safety and should be approved by the British Electrotechnical Approvals Board.

(f) Storage of flammable materials

Care must be taken when using and storing any flammable materials. This includes some cleaning materials such as solvent-based polishes, methylated spirits and paraffin as well as bar stocks or gas cylinders which should be kept in locked storerooms.

(g) Fireguards

It is illegal to sell a gas, electric or oil-burning fire without a fireguard and an offence, under the Young Persons Act of 1963, to expose children under the age of 12 years (7 years in Scotland) to the risk of burning. This ruling also applies to open wood or coal fires in both hotels and in the home.

(h) Position of fires

Any portable fire should be fixed to the wall at such a height that it cannot cause damage by being too close to curtains, upholstery or opened cupboard doors.

(i) Spontaneous combustion

Spontaneous combustion can occur in greasy cleaning rags or kitchen cloths if they are left piled together in a warm atmosphere or if oil has leaked into the lagging surrounding heated pipes.

(j) Fire-resisting doors

The Fire Authority will try to confine a fire to one area by dividing a building into compartments so stopping the spread of flame and smoke. This is done by fitting *fire-resisting doors* which isolate lift and stair shafts and divide corridors so that there is no more than 18 m of corridor between each door. These doors should 'resist the passage of flame for not less than 20 minutes' and should not collapse under 30 minutes and *must be kept shut* and not wedged open whilst work is in progress. They should be self-closing and marked 'Fire Door – keep shut'. A fire-resisting door which closes automatically when the fire alarm system operates is permissible, however.

As far as possible all doors within the building should be kept shut, particularly at night; even a solidly constructed bedroom door which is shut could save a life; when it is left open, smoke and heat can penetrate into a room and kill.

5.1.2 Fire detectors and alarm systems

Fire detectors are designed to detect either smoke, heat or flame and are wired to an automatic alarm system. There are several principles involved.

There are two types of *smoke detectors*. An *optical detector* relies on smoke particles obscuring a beam of light which is focussed on or near to a photo-electric cell. The particles interfere with the output from the photocell which operates the alarm. An *ionization detector* has a chamber containing two electrodes, across which a potential difference is maintained, and a radioactive source. The radio-activity produces positive and negative gas ions from the air and a current flows between the two electrodes. Smoke particles become attached to the gas ions and the combined weight has the effect of reducing the speed at which the ions are attracted to the electrode. The reduction in the flow of current activates the alarm.

A *heat detector* operates either when a pre-determined temperature has been reached or when there has been an abnormal increase in temperature. There are several methods of operation which use either metals, liquids, gas or changes in the electrical resistance. Metals which melt at a given temperature or expand are used to make or break a circuit. Alternatively, the insulation covering two conductors will melt at a given temperature, so causing the wires to come into contact and activate the alarm. Liquids and gases also expand on heating and are used in a similar way to metals. A change in temperature can be used to alter the electrical resistence of materials used to operate a relay.

Flame detectors work by either detecting ultra-violet or infra-red radiations from heat and flames; these activate a photo-cell and the alarm system.

A *sprinkler system* is installed when the main fire risk is from fabrics, paper or cellulose; metal in the nozzle will melt at a pre-determined temperature and over-lapping sprays of water should contain the fire. It is, however, essential that staff know where the control valve is situated so that the system can be turned off once the danger has passed otherwise much unnecessary damage can be done by the water.

It is unfortunate that many detectors are subject to the false alarms caused by such environmental problems as smoking, vibrations or mechanical faults. Detectors should be situated in all high risk areas such as kitchens, boiler-houses, bars, restaurants, public areas, corridors and in the ventilating and air-conditioning ducts. Most modern hotels will also have a detector fitted into the bed-head in the guest-rooms. The type of detector selected will depend on the probable fire risk and the structure of the building.

An *alarm system* should be linked to an *indicator panel* so that it is possible to check quickly in which part of the building the alarm has been given. This panel should be centrally situated. In a prestige building there is usually a direct link with the Fire Brigade but, in many smaller buildings, it still remains for the switchboard operator to telephone through to the Emergency Services giving details of the fire. The operator will then contact key members of staff.

5.1.3 Evacuation of staff, guests, patients and visitors

The Fire Precautions Act lays down criteria for the distance that has to be travelled from any point within a room to the door and the distances from a room to a stairway or to the final exit. It also stipulates the width of the doorways and corridors which depends on the number of people expected to be using the area. All escape routes and doors must be unobstructed and furniture, staff lockers or equipment should not be left or stored in these areas even for a short time as they would make evacuation difficult. *Emergency lighting* is required for all escape routes, and to illuminate *directional* and *fire exit signs*. It must operate for a minimum period of three hours. All directional arrows and signs are now coloured green on white.

Fire exit doors must never be locked. This, obviously, means that there can be a security problem as access can easily be gained to a building by these means. The most usual fastening is by a push or panic bar which can only be opened from the inside but is considered impractical for most residential buildings and is being replaced by a spring-bolt held in place by either a glass bar or panel which has to be broken to release the bolt. This has the advantage that the Management knows when there has been an unauthorized use of the exit.

An alarm system or closed circuit T.V. can be wired to fire doors and will alert the security staff when the door is opened.

A hospital, large hotel or college will have two alarm warning systems to avoid unnecessary inconvenience to patients or guests. The first alarm will act as a general warning and tell everyone that there is an emergency, the second signal will be to evacuate. Signals may either be continuous or intermittent. When the first alarm is sounded, the supervisor in charge of each section reports for further instructions. A modern building is designed to confine fire to each floor and section area so a building will usually only require partial evacuation; this also helps to solve the problem of what to do with the very large number of people who may be resident each day in a hotel or hospital. Reciprocal arrangements are usually made with a neighbouring establishment to look after guests and staff if evacuation becomes necessary. In a smaller building it is important to evacuate as soon as the alarm is raised.

Clear fire instructions must be placed in each guest room and in all public areas stating the action to be taken, the nearest escape route and the assembly point. This notice is often in several languages. Information must be given to both portering and housekeeping staff if any guest is handicapped.

Once a building has been evacuated, no-one should re-enter it without permission. All occupants must be checked off against staff, guest or patient lists.

5.1.4 Fire fighting arrangements

Fire is a chemical reaction between oxygen, fuel and heat; remove one of these parts of the 'fire triangle' and the fire will go out. There are three main categories of fire.

Class A Fires involving *wood, paper* and *textiles*. These are extinguished by removing the heat using water from hose reels, buckets or water-gas extinguishers. The extinguishers are red.
Class B Fires involving *oils* and *flammable liquids*. These fires are extinguished by removing air or oxygen with either carbon dioxide,

foam dry powder, BCF extinguishers or fibreglass fire-blankets. A carbon dioxide extinguisher is black, foam is cream, dry powder is blue and a BCF (vaporizing liquid) extinguisher is green. This last extinguisher is used mainly on vehicles and should not be used in a confined space, as the fumes can be poisonous, after use the area must be well-ventilated.

Class C Fires which involve *gases*. These are dealt with by removing the fuel, usually by turning off at the mains or by disconnecting a gas cylinder. Any remaining fire is dealt with according to whether it is a class A or B fire.

When a fire has arisen from faulty electrical wiring or appliances, the electricity should be switched off immediately either by removing the plug or, at the mains. Carbon dioxide and dry powder extinguishers are used whenever electricity is involved; any exting-uisher which is water- or foam-based must not be used as there is the possibility of electrocution.

Extinguishers are often supplied on hire by a specialist firm who is also responsible for regular maintenance checks and for re-charging when necessary. For normal risks, the fire authorities consider that a 9-litre water-type extinguisher is sufficient for each 209 m² of floor area with a minimum of two for each floor.

Fire hoses should be located centrally on escape routes and close to staircase enclosures. These are connected to either a wet rising main or to a dry riser. A dry riser is a pipe which runs up the entire height of a building; water is fed into the bottom by the fire brigade hoses and this water can then be taken off the riser at each floor level as it is needed.

Fire fighting equipment must be tested regularly and staff trained in its use but fire fighting should not be undertaken if staff are put at risk; the Fire Brigade are the experts and have considerable experience in judging how a fire will react.

5.1.5 Staff training

The Fire Precautions Act stipulates that all new employees must receive two periods of at least half an hour fire training within the first month of employment, thereafter, all daytime staff must have a further training period of half an hour every six months and staff who work at night, a period of half an hour every three months. Training must be given by a competent person and take the form of a talk, discussion, film; in addition written instructions must be given to each person.

These instructions will be different for each category of staff as some staff members will be needed to help clear the building whilst others will be deployed on fire fighting. Records must be kept, detailing dates, the type of instruction and the names of staff being trained. Some of the training should be in the form of evacuation exercises, preferably with some of the guests or residents involved as it is only then that problem areas can be identified.

All staff should know how to handle an extinguisher and the nearest alarm points and escape routes from each of the work areas.

5.2 Safety and accident prevention

Even though the Health and Safety at Work Act was passed in 1974, a very large number of accidents still occur. Over 13 million working days were lost through industrial accidents between June 1979 and May 1980. Accidents are only reported to the Health or Factory Inspectors if they are fatal, involve a serious injury such as the loss of an eye or a limb or when the employee is away from work for more than three days; the fact that an employee is absent from work for one or two days would not be included in the statistics so, obviously, the situation is even graver than it appears. The aim of the Act is to:

(1) Secure the health, safety and welfare of persons at work.
(2) Protect others from risks arising from the work premises or activities.
(3) Control the storage and use of dangerous materials.
(4) Control the emission of noxious or offensive substances into the atmosphere.

The Act places responsibilities on both the employer and on the employee. The employer is required, as far as is reasonably practicable, to ensure the health, safety and welfare of all employees and to comply with the Act whilst the employee is also required, when at work, to take reasonable care of the health and safety of himself and of other people – guests, patients, students or visitors, who may be affected by the way in which he works.

Employers are expected to implement the Act by issuing a written statement of general policy with respect to health and safety within the company and to state the arrangements made for carrying out this policy. Safety Committees should be set up with either staff representatives from each department or, where there is a Trade

Union, representatives from the Union. The employer's responsibilities are extensive. They have to:

(1) Ensure that all plant and equipment is safe to use and any dangerous parts are fenced and guarded, e.g. food slicing machines, guillotines and all floor machines left in the upward, 'safe' position.

(2) Ensure that all employees know the correct systems of work. Systems must be developed to ensure safe order and methods of working, the type of equipment and materials to use and the safety precautions which should be taken.

(3) Consider the use, storage and movement of materials and equipment. This encompasses such activities as – how to carry pots of boiling water, how to lift heavy weights, how to transport materials and equipment or which cleaning materials are unsafe if used together.

(4) Instruct and train. They must ensure that staff know the correct systems of work and all safety rules. Most employers keep training records and staff are required to sign that they know and understand the equipment and work methods used, this safeguards the employer against any possible claims for compensation following an accident. Staff should understand the reasons why tidiness is essential and know how to report faulty equipment or other hazards.

(5) Supervise. Even though training has been given, supervisors must ensure that staff are carrying out instructions and correct when necessary. A fault in safety procedures cannot be overlooked or condoned.

(6) Maintain the work place in good condition; in particular, floors must be clean, slip-free, kept in good repair and unobstructed.

(7) Provide good working environments and welfare facilities. This applies to the overall cleanliness of the building, the state of decorations, the temperature, light levels, the control of dust and debris, smoking area, seating arrangements and cloakroom, locker and canteen facilities.

The Health and Safety (First Aid) Regulations came into force in 1982 and place a general duty on employers to provide adequate First Aid. As a rough guide, when there are premises with low accident potential, it is only necessary to provide a First Aider when more than 150 people are employed; in a greater hazard area, there should be one when there are between 50 and 150 staff. In other cases, one person should be appointed to take charge when needed and to look after the First Aid Equipment.

There should be at least one *First Aid Box* clearly marked with a white cross on a green background and kept somewhere central with extra boxes kept in 'hazard areas' such as kitchens, boiler houses or laundries. Minimum contents should consist of: a card giving basic advice, individually wrapped adhesive dressings, sterile eye pads with attachment, triangular bandages, safety pins and a selection of sterile, unmedicated, wound dressings in medium, large and extra large sizes. Soap and water or sterile water should be available. Nothing else should be kept in the boxes but a residential establishment will usually have available a thermometer, cotton wool and anti-septic. A First Aid room should be provided when there are more than 400 employees or where there are special or unusual hazards.

A *breach of the regulations* can mean prosecution with the possibility of a £400 fine being imposed by a Magistrate's Court or an unlimited fine being imposed by a Crown Court; if an individual manager or member of staff is found guilty he can face the same fines or could be imprisoned for up to two years. This means that an individual must be careful that he is not put in a position in which he could be blamed for an accident. All hazards and unsafe practices must be reported in writing and copies kept; if an employee is known to be ignoring safety instructions this should be documented and he should receive a copy of the complaint and his signature obtained. This should be kept in staff records.

An *accident book* must be kept when there are more than 10 employees and must be readily accessible at all reasonable times. An entry in the book is sufficient notice of the accident and can be made either by the injured person or by someone acting on his behalf. Obviously, the employer must investigate all accidents and if any difference is found in the accounts of what happened, he should then record this discrepancy. The results of an accident can be immediate or take time to develop so that, as an employee is able to claim compensation up to three years from the date of the accident, the accident book must be kept for three years from the date of the last entry. The information required is the full name, address and occupation of the injured person and also of the person making the entry in the book; when the accident is serious it is helpful to record the names and addresses of any witness. All details of the accident must be taken and should include any relevant information such as lighting, the condition of the floor or stairs or any obstructions.

In addition to the accident book, many companies use their own forms for accident reporting.

From the Housekeeping point of view, care must be taken in the following areas.

(a) Hazard reporting

An easily accessible form or book should be used which can be completed at any time as soon as a potential hazard is noticed or there should be a clear reporting system. Any faulty equipment must be removed from the work area and locked away so that it cannot possibly be used; warning notices must be placed to warn all staff and customers if a fault develops in the building.

(c) Safe working methods

Staff must be tidy and not leave equipment or materials strewn across entrances or in corridors where they can be tripped over. Lids must always be replaced on containers. When using electrical equipment, the operator must always work back towards the plug socket so as to avoid running over the cable. No plug or equipment should be touched with wet hands.

(c) Floors

There is no such thing as a non-slip floor although some are much more slip-resistent than others. Statistics show that 30 per cent of all industrial accidents result from falling, tripping or slipping on floors which are either cracked, uneven, obstructed or are not sufficiently slip-resistent. Any floor which is wet is dangerous so that wet cleaning methods should be undertaken only when few people are about and warning notices must be displayed. Spillages and pools of water left from dripping umbrellas or snow must be wiped up as soon as possible. Accidents are often caused by unsuitable shoes.

Polish, applied correctly, should not be a slip hazard (p. 58). There can be a problem, however, with elderly people who assume that, because a floor has a high polish, it will be slippery. When this is the case, quite a good matt finish can be obtained on a vinyl floor by damp-mopping with soap (not a synthetic detergent) and then buffing with a floor machine. The weight and friction produces a low sheen from the residue of the soap left on the floor.

Where there is a slope on the floor extra slip-resistance should be given. Carborundum or aluminium oxide can be added to concrete to make it less slippery whilst an abrasive vinyl can be used in main corridor areas. This is a pure vinyl mixed with aluminium oxide grains and is suitable for heavy duty areas; under pressure from the weight of a shoe, the softer vinyl recedes leaving the aluminium grains to take the wear and to grip – when the weight is removed, the floor returns to normal and has a smooth, even finish which is easy to clean.

Many Safety Officers recommend that the colour of the floor is changed when different surfaces are used so that the user is more aware that extra care may have to be taken.

The nosing or edge of *stairs* should also be of a different colour.

(d) Lifting

Staff must be taught how to lift or move heavy items or equipment to avoid back injuries. In a survey in the National Health Service it was found that only 50 per cent of patient handlers received training in how to lift, one employee was found to have lifted two and a half tons in under an hour when patient handling. Those at risk included ward staff, hospitals porters, laundry workers and linen and storekeepers.

How to lift and carry.

(1) Do not attempt to lift any object if it is too heavy – get help.

(2) Make sure there are no obstructions and there is a clear space where the load can be placed.

(3) The feet should be between 200–300 mm apart with one foot in advance of the other – this ensures good balance.

(4) Bend the knees to a crouching position. The back should be kept straight although not necessarily vertical. The chin should be kept in so avoiding the head dropping forward or back.

(5) Get a firm grip at opposite corners of the load and keep the arms pressed close to the body so that the body takes the weight instead of the hand and arm muscles. Wear gloves if necessary.

(6) Lift by straightening the legs, using the thigh muscles. The lifting of a heavy object should be done by stages, i.e. from floor to knee, or from knee to the carrying position. Do not try to change the grip when carrying – put the load down first.

(7) The lifting procedure is reversed to set the load down.

(e) Dangerous cleaning (and other) agents

A large number of the agents in common use contain ingredients which are corrosive or toxic if swallowed or splashed on the eyes or skin. Very few of these agents carry instructions on the container to say what to do if they have been misused. On average, 20 children under five die each year from accidental poisoning and many thousands need hospital treatment. Disinfectants and bleach can be lethal, many cleaning agents contain ammonia, white spirit or turpentine or strong alkalis and should be kept locked in cleaning cupboards so that young children or anyone confused cannot harm themselves. Special care should be taken with: oven cleaners, window cleaners, insecticides and rodenticides, bleach and disinfectants, all alkali cleaners, turpentine and all agents containing white spirit, acid cleaners and descalers, and most of the stain removers.

Many agents are bought in bulk and are often in the same type of container which is used in the food industry; when bulk stores are broken up for distribution, the new containers must be clearly labelled and should not have been used for food or drink. Young people, foreigners or those with poor eyesight cannot always read a label and too easily assume that a whisky or squash bottle containing straw-coloured or orange liquid will be drinkable.

(f) Steps and ladders

In many cases, when the right equipment is used, there should be no need to climb up to clean, but in very high areas or when taking down curtains, etc. platform steps should be used. No one should be allowed to climb on chairs or furniture. All steps and ladders should be used on a solid, firm floor and must be strongly constructed; wooden, painted steps should be avoided as the paint can hide worn and rotten wood. When a ladder is used, both the top and bottom must be secured and it should be placed at an angle so that for every four feet it extends up the wall, the foot of the ladder is one foot from the wall – this makes for safer working. For safety, the use of steps, more than three or four feet high, and of ladders should be a two-person operation.

(g) Protective clothing

Most staff understand the importance of wearing protective overalls and headcoverings but do not always appreciate the importance of hand and foot protection. Recent statistics show that there are nearly 54 000 hand accidents a year and nearly 20 000 foot injuries. Gloves must be provided when handling acid or alkali materials or when doing rough work and also when an employee's hands are in and out of detergent. Rubber gloves with an inner glove of cotton should be provided; dermatitis is caused by condensation softening of the skin and can occur if a rubber glove is used on its own. Goggles may be needed for some maintenance work (see also Section 7.6).

(h) Lighting

This should always be at such a level that steps, furniture and all hazards are clearly seen (see section 6.3).

(i) Special provisions

It is useful to install hand rails and grab handles when there are elderly people using a building on the corners of stairs and in bathrooms and by toilets. All premises should be critically inspected regularly with the aim of making them safer for all those who use it. Good housekeeping is essential.

5.3 Security

Unfortunately, the problems of security are becoming ever more important. Better security may not always bring in extra business but it can prevent the loss of profit; the head of London's Police Collation and Intelligence Unit estimated recently that "staff were responsible for 30 per cent of hotel crime and that fiddles deprived hotels of 10 per cent of their gross turnover", and an official of the International Association for Hospital Security is reported as saying that "thefts of hospital linen – from sheets to nappies – are costing the National Health Service more than £3 million a year". Even the Inner London Educational Authority quotes reported losses in excess of £250 000 each year from their schools and colleges. The need is to:

(1) Safeguard both guest and company property from theft and damage.

(2) Prevent assault and attack on guests and staff.

(3) Prevent the disclosure of confidential information concerning guest's movements and property and the trading position and plans of the company.

Whilst it is impossible to deter a persistent thief or a well-planned crime, by introducing security checks and controls it should be possible to stop casual and opportunist crime. For insurance purposes, a company has to take 'reasonable care' to prevent loss. The areas where action should be taken are:

1 Staff;
2 Premises;

3 Stock control;
4 Keys;
5 Security lighting.

5.3.1 Staff

On engagement all staff should be vetted and all *references checked*; the need for this often prevents a large firm taking on casual or temporary staff unless they have been engaged through an agency which has already vetted all applicants. When cash handling is involved, many firms now require an Honesty or Fidelity Bond; this is arranged through an Insurance Company and means that the Insurers will check on the applicant's background more thoroughly than a hotel or hospital would be able to do.

As far as possible, staff cloakrooms and lockers should be away from the work area and no-one should be allowed to take bags or coats to these areas. Uniforms and identity badges are important where there are large numbers and management and security cannot be expected to know all staff members.

A *right of search* may be one of the conditions of the contract of employment. This means that management have the right to stop and search any member of staff at any time; this is important in discouraging petty theft but means that staff have to obtain a *package pass* (Figure 10.7) if they wish to remove any personal gift given to them by a guest. When there is no right of search in the contract, all that management can do if they suspect theft is to say – 'we want to eliminate you from the enquiries, do you mind if we check through your bag?' – and staff are quite entitled to refuse. Obviously, there must always be a witness if any search is made and body searches must always be made by a member of the same sex. Great care must be taken not to accuse a person of theft if there is the slightest doubt that the accusation cannot be proved; privacy is all important when dealing with such matters for both staff and guests.

Staff must be *trained* to be security-conscious and told what action they must take if they see any person acting suspiciously. Room-maids in a hotel must be instructed in the usual 'con' tricks, that is they must not unlock rooms for guests or allow them to remove property from a room while it is being cleaned until they have first checked the guest's room card; if there are any doubts they should notify the housekeeper or security. They must also be taught not to gossip about any valuable property left in a room or about a guest's whereabouts.

5.3.2 Premises

The *entrances* to a building should be restricted; ideally, there should
be one for guests and one for staff and the receipt of stores. These
entrances should be manned; the front hall by the Head Porter and his
staff and re-inforced by the Receptionists and a porter or lodgekeeper
for the staff entrance. *Fire exits* must not be for everyday use; many of
these are controlled by a spring bolt held in place by a glass panel
which is broken to release the door, this, at least, indicates
unauthorized use even if it is after the event. In a large building, fire
exits are wired to an alarm system or are covered by closed circuit
television.

All windows in the basement, on the ground-floor or close to an
outside fire escape, staircase or drain-pipes should either be non-
opening or fitted with a lock. Sky-lights should be barred or made
from toughened glass. It is difficult to climb through a broken
window-pane if it is smaller than 0.05 m^2.

Security paint, metal spikes and broken glass on the tops of walls all
deter would-be climbers.

Internally, it is wise to fit all guest bedroom doors with a chain and a
lensed spy-hole. Luggage rooms must be kept locked with left luggage
being retrieved only on the production of an identitag number.

5.3.3 Stock control

Neither stock-rooms nor store cupboards should be left unlocked at
any time; the stock must be checked regularly and reasons sought for
any discrepancy. As far as possible, all stock and property should be
clearly marked so that it can be easily identified; for instance, cutlery
can be engraved by the supplier or by maintenance, when china is
bought in bulk the pottery can add the name of the firm on the base
under the glaze, stores are often of a brand or from a supplier which
cannot be obtained locally in the shops.

5.3.4 Keys

The control of all keys is essential, particularly the master and grand
master keys, and care must be taken with their distribution and use.
Keys should be checked back at the end of each shift (section 10.2.1).

To increase security standards, many hotels have introduced a keyless lock system using computer-encoded cards; these systems are programmed so that each new customer will be given a card-key to their room with a code number different from that of the previous occupant. As soon as the new card has been processed, it automatically cancels all other cards for that room so there is no fear of cards falling into the wrong hands (section 10.2.3).

Few accommodation departments handle money, if they do, it should be used discreetly, kept locked and transferred to a safe or the bank as soon as possible.

5.3.5 Security lighting

Lighting in corridors and in rooms indicates that there are people on the premises so it is wise, even if part of a building is not in use, to keep some lights on; this can be done by means of time-switches programmed so that as one light is turned off, another is turned on.

The risk of vandalism, theft or assault is much greater at night so it is commonsense to ensure that all outside areas, entrances, car-parks, fire-escapes and the perimeter of the building are illuminated. The level of lighting need only be sufficient to see and deter a would-be wrong-doer and to ensure that both staff and guests can move in safety. The average street lighting is at a level of about 5 lux; it is seldom considered necessary to install security lighting at a higher level than 20 lux particularly when the background colouring of the external walls is pale making it that much easier to see an intruder.

Light fittings should be vandal-proof with either a mesh-guard or plastic enclosure and with each fitting connected to a spur outlet of a ring-circuit electricity supply with all wiring concealed. This prevents the light system being put out of action by cutting the wires. It is possible to connect the system to the emergency lighting supply in case of failure of the mains supply.

Some years ago, the Police started to collate information on hotel crime in London through the *Collation and Intelligence Unit* and to circulate Management and Security Officers with details and descriptions of confidence tricksters and their activities so that many have, subsequently, been identified by hotel staff. The information is also circulated in trade magazines and papers so that hotels, out of the London area, will also obtain details.

The type of information given is as follows 'two confidence men wanted who leave a hotel owing large sums of money, £1,000 or more. One is heavily built, age 32, 1.9 m, plump with black hair, the other is aged about 35, height 1.7 m, blond hair and wears gold-rimmed glasses'; or 'a hotel porter whom police want to see about a £900 safe loss. His description is aged 50, height 5 ft 5 in, grey hair, pale complexion, scar on left palm.'

One problem many hotels face is that of the prostitute. It is often difficult to keep them from using hotel lobbies or being taken to rooms by a guest. Many steal from rooms.

All sectors face the problems caused when building contractors are brought in for decorating or building extensions and there is the constant movement of materials in and out of the building and all have the constant problem of office and staff 'perks' – the use of the telephone for personal calls, of stationery and biros and the tea-bag because one is short at home.

5.4 Vandalism

Vandalism in this country is reputed to cost over £100 million a year and, retrograde as it may seem, it is sensible to take precautions to prevent wanton damage.

It is usually found that there is less vandalism in premises which are well maintained and look attractive than in those which appear uncared for and need decoration, so it is important to repair defects as soon as possible as obvious damage frequently seems to attract other damage.

The main areas which are vandalized are:

(1) Walls.
(2) Windows.
(3) Fittings and fixtures.

5.4.1 Walls

It has been found that murals, designed and painted by the occupants can be a great source of pride and all forms of vandalism are fiercely resisted. Where this type of decoration is unsuitable, graffitti can be prevented by:

(1) The use of specially formulated polyurethane paints which incorporate plastic and provide a tough, impervious surface which will not absorb graffitti paints and can be wiped clean with a solvent – ordinary paint has a slightly porous surface which does absorb graffitti making it difficult to remove;

(2) The design of wall finishes and decorative effects with glazed surfaces providing graffitti-proof walls;

(3) Metal kick-panels which save considerable damage.

5.4.2 Windows

A landscape window is expensive to replace and must be, psychologically, satisfying and easy to break. A small, glazed area does not break so easily, and does not create quite the same effect so may not be worth the effort.

5.4.3 Fittings and fixtures

The tendency is for these to be dismantled, broken or removed. It is possible to use vandal-proof screws, nuts and bolts which are easy to fit but almost impossible to remove. Some have a shaped head that requires its own shaped screw-driver, some have a special head and are used with an ordinary screwdriver but cannot be loosened, others are counter-sunk with the screw-in cover, flush with the surrounds. Another solution is a bolt with a head which is broken off after tightening to leave a smooth, tamper-resistant top.

In cloakroom areas, all pipes, cisterns and fittings should be hidden behind wall panels or in ducts and handles, which provide leverage, replaced by push buttons. Heavy-gauge steel is expensive for lavatory fittings but is extremely difficult to break so can prove cheaper than porcelain. Toilets can be moulded in one piece.

Lift control buttons which are flush with the surrounding panel are less prone to damage than those with protruding buttons.

Light fittings can be fitted with a heavy wire guard, many are designed to be vandal-proof.

As with other security areas, the use of lighting and regular patrols around a building will deter even if they do not always prevent vandalism.

5.5 Bomb scares and bomb attacks

The warning that a bomb has been left on the premises and will explode in half an hour is becoming all too common and it will depend entirely on local circumstances and Police advice whether a building is completely evacuated or a detailed search is made. When a building has to be cleared, staff and guests are usually asked to take their bags with them so reducing the amount of searching required. Evacuation should not be through the foyer and front entrances as this is an obvious place to hide a bomb.

If a bomb has been detonated, even while rescue attempts are being carried out, it must be remembered that there could be a second unexploded bomb.

Staff must always be trained to look out for any cases or bags which have been left unattended and, if they seem suspicious, to notify the Security Officer or the Manager. Petrol or a marzipan smell could mean some type of bomb; no-one should attempt to move a suspicious object or to attempt to neutralize it or use any sort of extinguisher but they should make sure that the area is isolated until the Police or Bomb Disposal experts have checked the area. When an area has to be cleared, staff and customers should collect their belongings, leave the building and assemble at the fire point.

5.6 Exercise and discussion

1 At what point do staff 'perks' become an unacceptable drain on costs?
2 You are the Domestic Bursar in charge of a Hall of Residence for 250 students. It has been brought to your notice that several of the students have brought in cooking equipment and are preparing food in their rooms. You know no names and have no direct proof that this is happening as the equipment is reported as being hidden in the wardrobes when the maids have access for cleaning, you have, however, no reason to disbelieve the report. You are concerned because there is increased risk of fire from over-heating and burning the cooking materials and from over-loading the electrical installation – not to mention the danger of mice and other infestations caused by food being kept in the rooms.

What action will you take through the Student's Committee? Draft the letter that you will send to the Student's Representative. What is the best way to enforce a prohibition of cooking in rooms?

Write the report you make to the Principal.

3 On checking through monthly consumption figures for the past 18 months you find that stock issues have been gradually increasing and you suspect that some members of staff are 'fiddling'. What action would you take?

4 You have just been appointed Domestic Bursar in a Hall of Residence and find that there is no safety policy in force or a procedure laid down on 'what to do if there is an accident.' Prepare the Safety Policy which can be given to both students and staff.

6

Energy & Water Conservation, Light, Colour and Sound

6.1 Energy conservation

All energy is expensive and its use should be monitored carefully to prevent wastage and indiscriminate use. Equipment and lights should always be switched off when they are not required.

6.1.1 Heat conservation

Heat should not be wasted through open doors and windows. When an outside door has to be left open or is in constant use, a heavy polythene strip-barrier curtain placed within a metre of the door is easy to push through and prevents both heat loss and the entrance of cold air. This is not suitable for the foyer of a large hotel but is very practical for staff, student or back entrances into hospitals, colleges or hotels. Natural ventilation through cracks around windows and under doors and the movement of people within the building usually means that there will be about $1\frac{1}{2}$ air changes each hour in a room and there should be little need to open a window in the winter – unless a room has become stuffy with tobacco smoke, people or beer.

More heat should not be provided in a room than is necessary and the level of heating should take into account the activity within the area and the weight and type of clothing usually worn by the occupants. A person sitting, reading or doing light clerical work produces about 475 Btu an hour, heavier work produces about 900 Btu an hour whilst strenuous activity such as dancing in a ballroom can produce over 1500 Btu which means that heating systems must be flexible – an area should be comfortably warm when first entered but the heat reduced or turned off once the heat produced by people and any of the equipment being used starts to take effect. This can be controlled automatically by room thermostats and micro-switches.

A temperature of 13°C is considered suitable when a moderately strenuous activity is being undertaken. The same temperature is also recommended by the National Health Service for staff accommodation where the staff quarters may be occupied for only eight or ten hours a day. This will be sufficient to keep the room aired and free from dampness and is supplemented by secondary heating when the room is occupied by using a gas or electric fire operated on a time-switch or a pay-meter. This practice also extends to many of the student Halls of Residence.

What is considered to be a reasonable temperature varies from one person to another but, generally, temperature requirements seem to become progressively higher with, in Britain, some form of heating needed for about 33 weeks of the year. It is not, however, necessary to heat all rooms to the same temperature if some rooms are out of use, so staff should know the temperatures at which each room thermometer is set and the times at which a time-switch will operate.

In a hotel, individual room temperatures can be controlled by a micro-switch which can be controlled by the key-hook for each of the guest rooms in Reception. When the key is handed in, the weight on the hook automatically switches off the room heating – and by the time the guest returns to his room having collected his key, the heat will be back on; in times of extreme cold, the key can be placed in the guest pigeon-hole and the heating not turned off. An alternative is for the maid to switch the heating down or off when the room is cleaned on a 'departure' and for the porter or receptionist to turn it on when the guest is shown to the room.

In the Office, Shops and Railway Premises Act of 1963, it states that an office should be heated to 16°C after the first hour of work and that a thermometer should be available so that the temperature can be checked by staff.

Living and public rooms, where thicker clothing is worn, should be at a recommended temperature of between 18°C and 21°C whilst bedrooms, bathrooms and hospital patient-care areas, where lighter clothing is worn, at a temperature of between 20°C and 22°C. In order to save fuel, a recent Ministry regulation restricts the heating of public buildings to 20°C.

The main methods of providing heat are as follows.

6.1.2 Central heating

Hot water, steam or air is circulated around a building from a central boiler or heat source. Most systems are designed to produce heat over a range of 18°C to 20°C, that is, if the outside temperature is at −1°C, the internal temperature can be raised to 18 or 19°C. Problems arise when the outside temperature drops below the average as a boiler will not be able to operate beyond its capacity. Some form of secondary heating in the form of portable fires then becomes essential. A sudden drop in temperature to −15 or −20°C does occur but it is so exceptional that it would be uneconomical to install central heating to cope with such extremes.

Hot water central heating systems circulate the water through pipes, panels and radiators. The older method is by means of 'gravity feed', based on the principle that hot water rises, and uses circulation pipes with a diameter of about 6.25 cm; because this is a slow method of circulating, there is a temperature drop of between 18 and 24°C before the water returns to the boiler for reheating. 'Small bore' or 'forced gravity circulation' uses pipes with a diameter of 12–19 mm with the water circulated by means of an electric pump; this is considerably faster than for 'gravity feed' with a temperature drop of about 5 to 6°C and, as there is also less volume of water, means that the boiler capacity is smaller. It is a much neater and more efficient installation − provided there is no electrical failure.

A *reflector panel* fitted behind the radiators will stop heat being absorbed into the walls and reflect it back into the room. The tops of the radiators should be kept clear with nothing allowed to block the outlet grilles.

Warm air heating (or plenum ventilation) is the system whereby air from a central air intake is filtered to remove dust and pollution and is then warmed and distributed by intake fans through ducts. Extraction fans may also be fitted.

Air conditioning is an adaptation of warm air heating and meets more specific requirements in that air can be both heated or cooled and can be passed through a humidifier to control the moisture content before being recirculated. The heat source for warm air heating and air conditioning can be a central boiler but can also be from a *heat recovery unit* which is able to recycle the heat which has been generated within the building by people, lights or equipment. The heat is usually withdrawn by means of extractor fans built into the light fitments. This produces a *controlled environment* and needs a high standard of insulation and double-glazing to be effective.

Another energy saver used for central heating is the *heat pump*. This extracts heat either from air, water or from the ground and, using the same type of component as in a vapour compression refrigeration unit, can increase the temperature. A heat pump has a two-way valve so it can be used to either condense or evaporate depending on whether the unit is being used for heating or cooling. The pump produces more usable energy than it consumes and uses electricity much more efficiently than any other method of heating.

Underfloor heating and *night storage heaters* are also used for background heating.

As far as possible, all methods should be controlled by a thermostat both at the heat source and in the individual room outlet.

6.1.3 Solar heating

This is similar to a refrigeration system. A refrigerant is circulated through collector panels fixed to the roof of a building or on open ground. The refrigerant absorbs the heat from the sun and is then piped to a compressor, which produces an additional rise in temperature, and then to a condenser where the energy is released in the form of heat and the refrigerant recycled to the collecting panels. Water is pumped through the condenser where it collects the heat which can then be used for the hot water supply, central heating or air conditioning. The operation is fully automatic. One system, developed in the U.S.A., can operate for twenty-four hours a day at temperatures well below freezing point.

6.1.4 Fuel and fuel costs

The calorific value of a fuel is defined as the amount of heat energy released when the fuel is burnt. This is measured in *British thermal units* (Btu) with the commercial unit of heat, the *therm* being equal to 100 000 Btu. A Btu is the amount of heat required to raise the temperature of one pound of water through 1°F.

The cost per therm for each fuel is calculated as follows:

Electricity There are 3412 Btu in one unit of electricity so —

$$\frac{\text{cost per unit (in pence)} \times 100\,000}{3412} = \text{cost of 1 therm (in pence)}.$$

Electricity is 100 per cent efficient with no wastage. The amount of energy needed to operate a piece of equipment is measured in watts and is recorded on the rating panel attached to the appliance. There are 1000 watts or 1 kilowatt in one unit of electricity so that the cost of operation is calculated by:

$$\frac{\text{Wattage of appliance}}{1000} \times \text{cost per unit.}$$

Gas A gas installation operates at about 80 per cent efficiency so the cost of a useful therm is

$$\text{cost per therm} \times \frac{100}{80}$$

Energy consumption, whether it is electricity, oil, gas or solid fuel should be monitored monthly and the results plotted either on a graph or a bar chart so that any changes are obvious. In a large building, it is helpful if this information is displayed so that staff are kept informed of the totals used – and the cost.

6.2 Water conservation

Staff, being used to a domestic flat charge for an unlimited supply of water, often find it difficult to appreciate that a commercial concern pay a higher rate and that many have a metered supply and pay for the amount of water which is used. The main wastage comes from:

(1) *Dripping taps* The amount of water lost from a tap dripping at the rate of 2 drops a second is about 378 litres a month and if the drops are breaking into a stream, it can amount to 2600 litres. Extra losses on fuel are incurred if the tap contains hot water and there is frequent damage to porcelain and enamel from iron and copper stains which are difficult to remove.

(2) *The length of the 'dead-leg'* or the length of the pipe from the hot-water supply to the tap – much water can be wasted before the hot water arrives and, in many cases, it is cheaper to install a hot-water heater at an outlet.

Water can be conserved by:

(1) Installing showers rather than baths – more possible in staff, student and hostel accommodation than in a hotel. A shower uses between 23–26 litres of water whilst a bath needs up to 160 litres. There are also other advantages in using showers. Less space is needed and two can be installed in place of one bath, it is quicker to take a shower than a bath so there is less congestion and they are

considerably easier to clean. There is, however, a problem in hard-water districts as, unless a water-softener is in use, the shower-head will need regular descaling or replacement to remove the chalky calcium and magnesium deposits from the water.

(2) Altering the size of the bath, washbasin and the outlet size of the taps. A small standard bath or basin may hold 10 per cent less water than a standard size and about 15 per cent less than a large fitment – and not be considered noticeably smaller by the user. A tap with a smaller outlet means that a basin or bath will take longer to fill – and many people will not wait and will use less water. A *spring-return valve* on the tap ensures that the water is turned off after a fixed period or a press-valve tap will stop working once the pressure is removed.

(3) The *flush* in the W.C. This uses about 20 per cent of all water supplied. At present, most W.C. pans in use in the U.K. have a 9-litre flush and, to quote from the Building Research Establishment's recent publication on Water Research, 'the development of W.C.s with reduced flush volumes could prove to be one of the most effective ways of reducing water consumption within buildings. The alternative is to give the user the opportunity to economize, by installing dual flush cisterns or by converting existing cisterns to controlled flush operation. The new Water Byelaws now require new W.C. cisterns to be of the dual-flush type.' With the dual-flush system, the user can choose between a flush of 4 litres or a full flush of 9 litres, depending on the need. In Europe, many pans are in use with a full flush of 6 litres and there are several which need only 3 litres of water. These are being tested at the Building Research Establishment with results indicating that 'it ought to be possible to produce a suite that will perform to an acceptable standard at 3 litres or a little more, and that such suites can be used in most drainage installations, subject to certain restrictions.'

Research is also continuing on the need for providing flush water in urinals with evidence showing that a waterless urinal does not develop more smells than the conventional type and the ceramic bowl 'requires probably less attention in its weekly regime of cleaning than other urinals.' When plastic traps and waste pipes are used there is no problem from urine attack on copper pipes.

6.3 Lighting

Achieving the correct light levels in a building is very important as, although designs should aim for energy saving, lighting plays a major part in the efficient operation of an establishment.

The main use of a lighting system is:

(1) *To provide good working conditions* and prevent strain and fatigue by the use of the correct light level for the work to be done.

Light levels are measured in *lumens* and *lux*. The amount of light given out by a light source, such as the sun, fire or a lamp bulb, is measured in *lumens* but some of this light is lost as it becomes absorbed by clouds and mist, dirty fittings, coloured shades, dark-coloured furnishings and textiles and by distance. All these factors mean that the amount of usable light which reaches the working surface is often very different from that which leaves the light source. In 1968, the *lux per square metre* was adopted which measures the usuable light as it falls on a horizontal surface and is measured at table height.

On a bright sunny day the level of natural light will be about 50 000 lux; when there is cloud the level is reduced to 5000 lux; when bad light stops play at cricket there is between 500 and 1000 lux. Moonlight produces about ⅕th of a lux. The Illuminating Engineering Society had made recommendations for:

Entrances and Reception areas:	200–300 lux
Bedrooms – general:	100 lux
bedhead and mirrors:	150 lux
Bathroom:	100 lux
Kitchens and offices:	500 lux
Corridors:	100 lux
Restaurants, bars and coffeeshops:	50–150 lux
For detailed and close work:	1000–1500 lux.

Different light levels are often required during the day for such areas as the bar or restaurant with brighter lights in the daytime and more subdued, relaxed lighting in the evenings. Lower wattage bulbs save energy but should not be used at the expense of a gloomy atmosphere.

(2) *To create atmosphere.* Requirements will vary depending on whether it is for business, recreation and relaxation or mystery and romance. Lighting is very closely linked with decorative schemes and does much to attract a particular segment of the public to a hotel and indicates the type of business which the hotel wishes to encourage; bright colours and lights for the younger generation but more mellow tones and softer lights for the more advanced years.

(3) *To provide focal points.* There is a phototropic attraction which draws the eye towards a brighter light and will attract the attention

towards the display of goods that one hopes the customer will buy, the buffet in the restaurant or the bottles of expensive liqueurs and spirits in the bar. Highlighting an important painting or floral display provides a centre of attraction and often draws the attention away from less attractive areas. The level of lighting at the 'focal' point should be kept close to the overall levels as the eye cannot adapt to two distinct levels at the same time without discomfort.

(4) *To guide people around a building* by the use of clear, directional signs.

(5) *To help maintain safety standards.* Corridors, stairways and all main rooms and public areas must be well-lit so that any potential hazard can be clearly seen. Although it is unsafe to turn lights off late at night, energy can be saved by reducing the level either by using sectional light systems or dimmer switches.

Emergency lighting is required on all escape routes and must operate for a minimum period of three hours; it should be automatic and cut in as soon as the main power fails.

(6) *To increase security* particularly in car-parks, on paths leading to buildings and by all entrances; the system should be so designed that as far as possible, shadows are eliminated. When a building is left empty at weekends or during a vacation, a time-switch can regulate corridor and room lights and indicate to an outsider that the building is occupied.

Light fittings are designed to take either an incandescent filament lamp bulb or a fluorscent tube. A filament lamp should meet the requirements of BS 161 and have a burning life of 1000 hours. Long-life, tungsten halide lamps are available but the extended life is achieved with a loss in light output. A heavy-duty lamp can be obtained for use in lifts or any area where there is vibration. The light output for filament lamps is as follows: 40 W gives 420 lumens; 60 W gives 710 lumens; 75 W gives 940 lumens; 100 W gives 1360 lumens. These outputs do, however, decrease with the age of the lamp.

In contrast, a fluorescent tube will last five to six times as long and is cheaper in use as the light output is greater and varies from 35 to 80 lumens for each watt, depending on the type of tube. Fluorescent tubes are filled with mercury vapour through which an electric current is arced between the electrodes. This produces ultra-violet radiation which becomes visible as it strikes the inner, chemical coating of the tube. A high-efficiency tube produces a hard, cold light and between 50 and 80 lumens for each watt; a warmer light is obtained at the cost of efficiency with the output in lumens decreasing to between 35 and 55 for each watt.

A recent development has been the introduction of an energy-saving replacement for the filament lamp. The fluorescent tube can now be made very much smaller and folded so that it is compact and can be fitted into a glass cover and used in the conventional filament lampholder. The new lamp is heavier and a little larger than a filament lamp so that the size of the fitting and the shade or cover must be checked before it is used, as should the condition of the wiring and any frayed or old wires replaced. As the lamps produce less heat they can be used in most lamp fittings provided the temperature of the air within the fitting does not exceed 75°C. Some makes of this lamp have the control gear fitted into the base, others need to be connected with an external, conventional ballast by means of the lampholder. The advantage of this new development is that, although the lamp is more expensive, it lasts about five times as long as a filament lamp and uses about one quarter of the electricity, yielding about 48 lumens for each watt.

A filament lamp gives a warm light which will enhance the yellow, orange and red bands of the spectrum, but care must be taken when selecting a fluorescent tube as the colour rendering can be quite different. Artificial light does not reproduce exactly the same wavelengths of light that we receive from the sun. When light falls on a surface, some of the wavelengths are absorbed in the material and some are reflected back and it is these reflected wavelengths which are seen as colour; because most decorative schemes are seen under both daylight and artificial light conditions, it follows that fabrics must be chosen under both light sources as there can be a distinct colour change with colours which match exactly during the day clashing or becoming 'dead' at night.

When tubes have to be replaced, it is important that the same coloured tube and wattage are used to prevent a subtle difference in the appearance of the room. Conversely, a room which looks dull and uninviting may only need a change in the colour rendering of the lights and in the wattage. The *colour rendering* for lamps is given in the table below.

A room which is decorated in pinks and red will appear dull if a daylight lamp is used but will come alive if the lamp is changed to natural. Restaurants and food displays should be illuminated by light which brings out the red and green tones.

For general use, most light fittings are designed to reflect light down from the ceiling. This helps to brighten the room as the light is diffused and shadows reduced; direct lighting is used to highlight work areas or to spot-light focal areas.

Name	Lumens per watt	Blue/violet	Green	Yellow	Orange/red
Fluorescent lamps					
Northlight					
Colour matching	35–40	Very bright	Bright	Bright	Moderately bright
Artificial daylight	25–35				
Natural	45–65	Turns blue to violet	Makes green yellower	Bright	Fairly bright, reds seem more orange
White and warm white	60–80 35–55	Fairly dull, blues turn violet	Bright but greens more yellow	Very bright	Medium
Daylight	55–80	Fairly bright	Bright	Very bright	Dull
Filament lamps					
Tungsten	8–18	Dull	Bright,	Very bright	Very bright
Tungsten halogen	17–22		greens more yellow		

Light Output and Colour Rendering for Fluorescent/Filament Lamps

Light fittings should be installed so that glare is avoided; a common reason for discomfort is when the lamp or fluorescent tube is in the direct view of the room's occupant and is not shielded by a shade. The normal range of sight is taken to be not more than 30° above the horizontal when standing and up to 55° when sitting, but in bedrooms and bathrooms extra care must be taken and many bedrooms have the central pendant light fitted with a diffuser to protect the sight of anyone laying bed. Uncomfortable glare also occurs when there is too much light contrast and and when light is reflected from a polished or shiny surface such as a mirror or gloss-painted wall.

The British Zonal Classification is used to define the light distribution from the fitting and shade and ranges from BZ 1 to BZ 10. The highest number, BZ 10, refers to a fitting from which the majority of the light is dispersed at the angle made by the ceiling and 45° and provides an indirect, soft illumination with few shadows. BZ 1 has the light distributed between the angles formed by a vertical line and 45° on either side so that direct light is concentrated on to a focal point. The other BZ numbers come between these two extremes. BZ 3 is considered satisfactory for most office and general work.

Light fittings are designed for a specific wattage of lamp; if a lamp with too high a wattage is used it can result in overheating of the holder and wires and damage to the shade.

The cost of electricity is high and as much advantage as possible should be taken of daylight. Studies made by the Building Research Establishment show that, when there is traditional manual switching of lights, much electricity is wasted as lights are switched on at the beginning of the working day but are seldom switched off later during the morning even though the daylight levels have increased as the sun climbs higher and cloud cover varies. When lights were switched off at lunch-time, it was found that they were not usually switched on again until it became dusk – with a saving of 15–20 per cent. When designing a building, the recommended level of light penetration is calculated on the *daylight factor* which takes into account both direct and indirect light from internal and external sources and is measured at average natural light levels when the sky is overcast at about 5000 lumens. In kitchens and offices, the level is taken as 5 per cent of this to give an internal natural light level up to 250 lumens; a living-room is at 1 per cent or 50 lumens and a bedroom as little as 0.5 per cent or 25 lumens. Many buildings are designed to give much greater light.

Automatic photo-electric sensors can be installed to adjust artificial light levels as the natural light varies through the day with an over-rider for manual switching if it is required.

In guest rooms, an electronic control system can be installed with the individual lights operated by a rocker switch and the door switch programmed to switch off all room lights as the guest leaves.

6.4 Colour

Colour, as we know it, originates in the white light radiated from the sun which is transmitted through the atmosphere in a range of wavelengths. Individual colours are seen when light passes through a drop of water or through a glass prism, both of which separate white light into its component parts. The wavelengths are also separated when light falls onto a solid substance such as the earth, a building, furniture or a textile when some of the wavelengths are absorbed by the material – what we see as colour are the wavelengths which have not been absorbed and which are reflected back into the retina of the eye.

A number of colour guides have been introduced as colours are difficult to describe and a bright red, violet or lime-green can mean different things to different people. The Munsell Book of Colour arranges more than 1450 shades and identifies them by numbers which relate to their lightness, hue and chroma or intensity. The ICI Colour Atlas displays over 1300 colours which can be covered with any one of twenty different grey filters so producing a range of over 27 000 identifiable shades.

All the colours of the spectrum are made by combining different amounts of red, green and blue light; the science of colour physics has now produced equipment which is able to measure the colour of a shade by its reflectance at each wavelength and means that colours can now be matched exactly.

6.4.1 Factors which affect colour

(a) The light source

Artificial light does not reproduce exactly the same wavelengths as sunlight so there is often some colour change (p. 115); it follows that a colour scheme with a selection of carpets, wallcoverings and textiles must be chosen under both artificial and natural light conditions. It can be difficult to obtain an exact colour match when using different fabrics.

(b) The intensity of the light

A room which faces south receives both reflected light and direct light whilst the light in a north-facing room is less intense as it has passed over the building and is reflected back into the room from the ground, neighbouring buildings or from the clouds. To compensate for this and to give the impression of extra light and of warmth the more reflective colours are used in decorating – oranges, yellows and some of the reds whilst cooler, more absorbent colours, blues, greens and greys are used in south-facing rooms, which are often over-light, particularly in the summer.

(c) Many colours are affected by a background colour

No colour is seen in isolation and the appearance of many colours is influenced by the adjacent or surrounding colours; for instance, blue against orange or yellow will have a greenish tone whilst the same blue with a violet or deeper blue background will become darker; such colour changes are also affected by the intensity of the light. Problems arise if this is forgotten and a sample from a carpet or curtain matched with a different fabric without taking into account that it is away from the background against which it is normally seen.

(d) Individual personal differences

We know what we see but we do not know what the other person is seeing. Many people are highly conscious of colour and uncomfortable if the background colour of the room does not show them off to advantage and if it is clashing with the colours which they are wearing. For this reason, many hotels have a very conservative colour scheme which will not distract from the customers or from exhibition displays.

(e) Fashion

This varies considerably over the years and is affected by designers and much of the writing in the media. When decorations have to last a considerable time, extremes of fashion should be avoided.

6.4.2 What colours do

There is an *emotional response* – most people consider that red is exciting, dangerous and will attract attention, yellow is bright, fresh and represents spring, orange is warm and comfortable, blues and greens are restful; a light colour gives the impression of space whilst dark blues, reds and greens can be gloomy and overpowering.

Colours are used to *create illusion*. Light colours recede and are used to make a room look larger whilst dark colours advance and make a room appear small and cramped. This principle is used extensively – a high ceiling seems lower if painted in a dark colour but higher if left white or a light colour is used and a long, narrow room appears to be squarer when the short walls are painted white and the longer walls are dark.

Colour also gives the illusion of warmth and there is the story of some office staff who found that they did not need to wear a jacket at work when the blue walls were repainted in a burnt-orange tone. Dark painted articles seem heavier and larger than if they are painted white.

Colour is used to *emphasize* and *contrast* different features or can be used to hide a door or fittings which are required to be unobtrusive; it will direct a customer's attention and guide him towards the bar; it can indicate a danger zone; it conveys information by colour-coding uniforms, equipment, stationery and official forms and cleaning cloths and rubbish containers. It can have a therapeutic value or the reverse;

blues and greens are used in many hospitals as they are considered restful whilst a bright yellow is avoided in the interior of aircraft and ships as it is considered to predispose passengers to nausea.

Some colours are considered lucky or unlucky and this varies from country to country; a problem which can affect international hoteliers.

For practical purposes, a medium-toned colour, preferably with a pattern, will not show dirt and stains as easily as other colours. Dust shows up clearly on a dark surface whilst it can be (almost) invisible on cream paint.

6.4.3 Colour schemes

There are four main colour schemes which are based on the colour circle – these should be used with a neutral colour that is, any shade between white and black; strictly speaking, cream, buff and magnolia are not neutral but are usually considered as such for decoration purposes.

(1) *Monochromatic*. This scheme uses one colour but in different tones and intensities.

(2) *Complementary*. Two colours which are taken from opposite sides of the colour circle with the colours complementing each other so blue and yellow, green and red or orange and violet would be used together.

(3) *Harmonious or Analogous*. Colours which are taken from the same segment of the circle so a room would be decorated in yellow, orange and red or in blues and greens.

(4) *Triad*. Three colours which are selected at equal distances apart on the circle.

In any scheme, if it is to be successful, one colour should be predominant with the other colours used as a contrast and to provide focal points in the cushions, covers or in a special painting. Different tones should be used with the secondary colours either darker or lighter to provide greater interest.

A uniform colour scheme used throughout an establishment conveys the impression of thought and care and is more restful than one where there are abrupt changes. A complete scheme includes not only the furnishings but also includes staff uniforms, the china in the restaurant, the logo on the stationery and the guest supplies used by housekeeping.

When a *pattern* is used it must relate to the size of the room – a large pattern in a large room and a smaller design in a small room otherwise it can be overpowering. Most good schemes rely on one pattern only; if there is more than this, there should be some contrast in size in the design and they should not be too similar. Pattern is desirable in a carpet, upholstery and in the covers as it will hide small stains and blemishes which would be noticed in a plain fabric.

Stripes are also used to create interest and illusion; long corridors appear shorter when stripes run across particularly when there is an assortment of wide and narrow stripes in different colours, a room seems higher with vertical stripes but wider if they are horizontal.

6.5 Sound and acoustics

There are two problems with the transmission of sound. One is to prevent sound penetration from one room to another so that other users in the building are not disturbed and the other is to provide good listening conditions in rooms and conference halls.

What we hear as sound is always caused by some type of vibration which travels in wavelengths and can be transmitted through the air, through or along a sold material or through water. The frequency of the vibrations is measured in Hertz (Hz) with the wavelength being the distance the sound is carried by one complete vibration. The magnitude or level of sound is measured in decibels (dB).

Exposure to 150 dB will cause almost instant deafness as will a level of 140 dB if this continues for more than a minute. A level of 120 dB is unpleasant and causes pain. What level of sound is acceptable depends on the location and on the amount of background noise; in the country this can be as low as 15–20 dB, in the suburbs about 30 dB whilst in a city anywhere between 35 and 45 dB depending on how close one is to a busy main road.

The recommended noise rating (NR) for a bedroom is 25 dB, for a lounge 30 dB and for a restaurant 45 dB; although, as it can be difficult to obtain these ratings economically in a city area, a slightly higher level is often considered acceptable. A hospital ward should have a low noise level but this is also difficult to obtain during the day, as it is very much a work area, so that levels of between 45 and 50 dB are usually accepted. A general office, with typewriters and machinery, will frequently have a background noise level up to 55 dB.

Sound is transmitted by impact and vibration through solid surfaces

Example of the sound absorbency characteristics of fabrics
(When no sound is absorbed, the sound absorption coefficient is 0.0, when all
sound is absorbed it is 1.0.)

	Sound absorption coefficient		
	Low frequency (125 Hz)	Medium frequency (500 Hz)	High frequency (2000 Hz)
Floor finishes			
Concrete, granolithic, stone, marble	0.01	0.02	0.02
Linoleum, thin cork tiles, wood blocks, or rubber – on a solid floor	0.02	0.05	0.01
Foamed vinyl	0.00	0.00	0.15
Vinyl	0.00	0.00	0.05
Carpets			
Axminster – luxury with felt underlay	0.40	0.70	0.87
Wilton – nylon dense short pile with felt underlay	0.25	0.70	0.90
Wilton – wool, dense short pile with felt underlay	0.40	0.70	0.87
Tufted – fine gauge nylon, with high density foam back	0.10	0.30	0.70
Needle loom – nylon surface without underlay	0.05	0.05	0.40
Curtains			
Medium weight, lined, hung straight	0.05	0.15	0.25
Medium weight, lined, hung in folds	0.05	0.35	0.50
Wall coverings			
Paper – conventional	0.00	0.00	0.05
Hessian fabric	0.02	0.10	0.15
Ceiling/wall panels			
P.V.C. acoustic panels $\frac{5}{8}$ in thick	0.30	0.70	0.85

such as walls, floors and ceiling. It is seldom that a sound consists of
only one wavelength, most are very complex and a mixture of low,
medium and high frequencies. The table above gives some indication of
the sound absorbency characteristics of some building materials and
furnishing fabrics. A porous material absorbs sound by converting it
into heat through a network of interlocking pores but a material such
as plastic foam is less successful as the cells are closed and not
connected.

Impact and vibration noise can be reduced by:

(1) The use of sound absorbent materials;
(2) A sound barrier or break, such as double glazing with a
minimum distance of 150 mm between each pane, doors which isolate
one area from another, cavity walls and floors;

(3) The isolation of ventilation ducts and heating and water pipes, ducts can be lined with an absorbent material;

(4) Zoning all noisy areas together and keeping the quiet areas apart from them;

(5) The alignment of a building is important, as far as possible it should be at right angles to a busy road. Some noise protection is obtained by using balconies and angled windows and planting shrubs and trees to provide a sound barrier.

The best *listening conditions* depend on what is being heard and is related to the size, shape and volume of the room. When sound strikes a wall or ceiling, some of the wave is absorbed but some is reflected back and will reverberate around the room until it is finally lost in the furnishings. The waves are reflected at the same angle as they hit the surface so a concave surface will have the effect of focussing sound whilst a convex surface will diffuse it so that, in a conference hall for instance, the curve of a ceiling or an end wall will make an important contribution to the uniform distribution of sound. For a conference hall where it is important that undistorted speech can be heard at the back of the room, the best volume per person has been found to be about 2.8 m^3; when music is played, this volume increases to between 7 and 11 m^3 as an appreciation of music depends on the fullness and reverberation of the sound; singing and opera require conditions which are intermediate with a volume ratio of about 4 to 5.5 m^3 per person.

6.6 Exercise and discussion

1 With the latest increase in prices for fuel and electricity, the Administrator has called for a review of costs and the introduction of an effective control system. Write your reply to him detailing what action you are taking and putting forward any suggestions to improve the situation and prevent an increase in costs.

2 It has been agreed that a basement area can be redecorated and turned into a relaxation and games area. What stipulations would you make regarding the lighting and decorations. Would it be necessary to apply for planning permission or to contact the local Fire Authorities as no building alterations are to be made? What could be done to prevent disturbance to the residents who want to work or sleep?

7

Textiles and Furnishing Fabrics

7.1 Natural and man-made fibres

Some basic knowledge is necessary to understand why fabrics differ from each other in their appearance, texture and characteristics. The two basic forms of textile fibres are the *filament* and the *staple*. A filament is a fibre of a continuous length, that is, it is long enough to use in weaving without having to increase its length by twisting or spinning other fibres to it – an example is silk. Staple is the name given to fibres of limited length which must be spun together before they are long enough to use – such as cotton or wool. *Yarn* is the thread which is produced when either staple or filament fibres are spun together to produce a greater thread diameter. Generally, a filament yarn is thin, smooth and has a sheen whilst a staple yarn is thicker and is less lustrous, but even staple yarns differ depending on the length of the staple – flax, which has a fibre of about 900 mm, is much more silky and finer than the yarn produced from a merino sheep fleece with a fibre of between 50 and 100 mm long; the woollen yarn is bulkier, looser and much warmer than the linen.

The main natural fibres are:

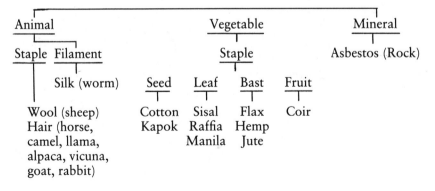

Animal		Vegetable				Mineral
Staple	Filament		Staple			Asbestos (Rock)
	Silk (worm)	Seed	Leaf	Bast	Fruit	
Wool (sheep)		Cotton	Sisal	Flax	Coir	
Hair (horse, camel, llama, alpaca, vicuna, goat, rabbit)		Kapok	Raffia Manila	Hemp Jute		

Cotton is still the most widely used fibre and has many properties which have not yet been reproduced in a man-made fibre. It has a high absorbency and so is particularly suitable for towels or clothing, it feels warm and is heat-resistant, and can be washed and ironed at high temperatures so that the fabric can be sterilized. It is not so strong as linen or silk, but it bleaches well for white goods and dyes easily so it is very suitable for both bedding and for furnishings. The main disadvantage is that cotton may need pre-shrinking or a shrink-resistant finish before it is made up as some fabrics can shrink up to 8 or 9 per cent. It is not flame-retardent but is still a safer fabric for clothing and uniforms than most others as, although it burns, it will not bead and cling to the skin.

The finest and silkiest fabric is made from *Sea Island and Egyptian cotton*; this has a staple of about 55 mm in length and can, in consequence, be spun into a very fine yarn. *American cotton* has a medium-length staple of about 25 mm which produces a coarser fabric and is used extensively for sheets and pillowcases. These are one third of the price of those made from Egyptian cotton. A short staple cotton, under 25 mm, comes from India and Asia.

Linen is made from the bast of the flax plant which produces fibres of about 900 mm, in length so that a very fine thread and cloth can be produced. It has very similar attributes to cotton except that it is colder to the touch, creases more easily and has the reputation for being stronger, especially when wet, so there is less chance of the material being damaged during the wash process. It bleaches well and the appearance is smoother and more lustrous than cotton. Linen, in a damask weave, is the traditional fabric for tablecloths and serviettes and, although now extremely expensive, is still the preferred fabric in the restaurant for its appearance, crispness and starching qualities – and for the fact that it is a material from which it is easy to remove stains. Very few hotels still use linen for sheets and pillowcases as the cost is four or five times as much as for the price of an American cotton sheet but linen is still used for the waiter's and glass cloths for polishing cutlery and glass as, unlike cotton, they leave no lint on the surface.

A *Union* fabric is a mixture of linen and cotton; this produces a material about two-thirds the price of linen and with characteristics midway between the two although, when a linen, a union or a cotton tablecloth are seen side by side, it is easy to see the difference in quality – in the feel, silkiness and the fineness of the weave.

Wool is used to provide warmth in bedding, clothing and as a furnishing fabric. It produces a naturally flame-retardent fabric which has good thermal and acoustic properties; it is resilient and keeps its appearance well and does not soil quickly. However, when used as a fabric, it can be more difficult to clean than other materials as the fibre is scaled and will felt and shrink under the influence of heat, moisture and movement so it is usually dry-cleaned rather than washed. *Merino or botany wool* has a staple of between 50–100 mm in length and is particularly fine, soft and warm and is used for the best, luxury quality blankets – it is not, however, the strongest or the most durable. *Cross-bred* wool has a staple range from 75–200 mm and is used for furnishing fabrics and blankets; as the staple gets longer in length, strength and resilience increase but the lightness, softness and warmth decrease. Carpets are made from long, coarse staples, 150–400 mm in length, which lack softness but are much stronger.

Wool can be re-cycled. Shoddy is obtained by shredding 'soft' rags and using them in knitted or loosely woven fabrics. Mungo is used for closely woven fabrics and comes from the shredding of 'hard' rags.

Silk is woven from very fine filaments into a soft, lustrous cloth which handles and drapes well and can be dyed easily. It is expensive but is still used for many furnishings and covers in a luxury hotel.

Since the 1960s, world production in the manufacture of textiles has more than doubled and with it has come a vast increase in the use of man-made and synthetic fibres which now complement and compete with the natural fibres. Synthetic fibres, either used on their own or mixed or blended with a natural fibre, have gained universal acceptance as their use has meant not only a reduction in the cost of the material but has led to greatly improved performance as the main characteristics of these fibres are to increase durability and comfort. They are generally much easier to clean.

The first development in man-made fibres started in the early 1900s when *viscose* and *acetate* fibres were manufactured from a cellulose base – mainly wood-pulp. Both are still widely used.

Viscose has a soft, hairy texture which adds bulk to a material so that it is frequently blended with more expensive fibres such as wool and cotton. It is highly absorbent which means that it soils easily but it has the advantage of being moth-proof and is slow to build-up static electricity charges. It is not very resilient and, when used on its own, will flatten and lose its appearance quickly; when wet, there is a tendency for it to stretch and to lose strength, both problems which can be avoided when it is blended with nylon or polyester. A blend of cotton and viscose is used for sheets, pillowcases and covers; a blend of $42\frac{1}{2}$ per cent viscose : $42\frac{1}{2}$ per cent wool : 15 per cent nylon is used in the pile of cheaper carpets. Viscose can be modified and made inherently flame-retardent.

Cellulose acetate or artificial silk has a soft, silk-like feel and is used extensively for both dress and furnishing fabrics. It is dimensionally stable and can be heat-set, that is, the material can be permanently pleated.

Man-made synthetic fibres, *polyamide, polyester* and *acrylic* were developed from chemicals in the late 1930s and early 1940s. All are extremely hard-wearing and tough, producing material which has a high resistence to abrasion under both wet and dry conditions. However, all three fibres are poor conductors of electricity and build-up static electricity charges – particularly in a centrally heated building with low humidity; a problem which causes difficulties especially when the fibres are used in carpets, blankets and upholstery.

Polyamide or nylon is made from benzine, oxygen, nitrogen and hydrogen and was the first real synthetic fibre which could be used either as a filament or textured. Texturing is the process which puts a crimp or corrugatation into the filament and gives it the bulk and resilience which is normally associated with a natural fibre such as cotton or wool. Nylon has a low absorption rate of about 4 per cent which means it will soil easily but also washes and dries more quickly than a natural fibre. Most nylons require no ironing.

Nylon is now one of the more important fibres used in carpet manufacture either on its own or blended with wool, polyester, acrylic or polypropylene. It is also used extensively for furnishing fabrics and uniforms.

Polyester can also be used as a filament or textured. It has a very low absorbency rate of 0.4 per cent and is much used for its anti-crease and crease-shedding properties. When blended with cotton, wool or viscose, it produces a fabric which has the characteristics of the natural fibre but with greatly increased durability. Used for sheeting in a 50 : 50 blend with cotton it increases the potential life of the sheet by three- or four-fold.

Polyester is made from ethylene glycol and terephthalic acid which is derived from petroleum. Both nylon and polyester are thermoplastic and can be permanently pleated and shaped.

Acrylic is a bulky fibre producing a yarn not unlike wool but with a slight metallic feel and is rapidly replacing wool in the manufacture of blankets, carpets and furnishing fabrics. Again, it has a low absorbency rate of $1\frac{1}{2}$–2 per cent.

Polypropylene was developed in the early 1950s and is now frequently blended with wool or used on its own in carpeting, it is particularly suitable for out-door use, 'grass' or door-mats as the fibre is non-absorbent and has very good resistance to moulds, fungi and mild chemicals. It makes a tough fabric with good abrasive properties – not quite as good as nylon but better than polyester and has the added advantage that it does not build-up static electricity charges to the same extent.

7.2 Methods of production

Traditionally, textiles have been produced by methods which require much time and skill and the use of long fibres spun into yarn.

(a) Weaving

This is on a loom with the long warp threads interlaced by crossing with a weft thread in a wide variety of designs, texture and colours. The surface can be either smooth, looped or a cut-pile. Damask weave is traditional for table-linen and is a variation of a twill weave with the woven pattern in the design reflected by the light.

(b) Felting

This is a cloth made from wools by pressing and kneading, and causes wool fibres to matt by over-lapping the fibre scales.

(c) Knitting

This is produced by interlocking loops – a method often used for nylon sheeting.

(d) Laces and nets

A very open structure with the threads twisted around each other – they are mainly used for net curtains, table-mats and bedcovers.

(e) Braids and cords

The threads are plaited and intertwined to form a narrow fabric and are now used for edgings and finishes for curtains, covers and upholstery.

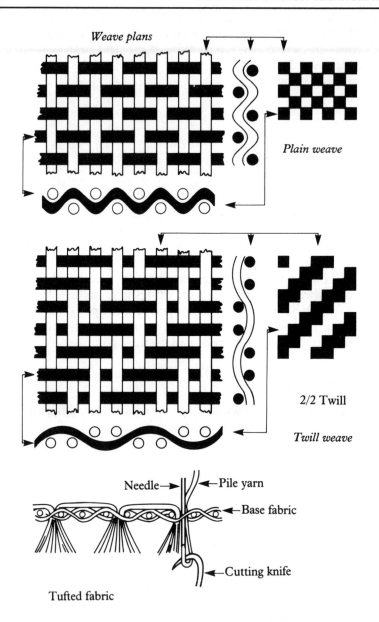

Weave plans

Plain weave

2/2 Twill

Twill weave

Needle→ ←Pile yarn

←Base fabric

←Cutting knife

Tufted fabric

These traditional methods are being overtaken by a number of systems developed to produce fabrics by less conventional means. The weaving loom is becoming outdated in the need to quicken the manufacturing process and to reduce costs; an added impetus has come from the need to find a use for the very short fibres which cannot be spun into yarn.

(f) Tufting

This is the traditional way of making the candlewick fabrics used for bedspreads. More recently the tufting process has become the foremost method for producing carpets and accounts for over 75 per cent of those produced in the U.K. and over 96 per cent in the U.S.A. In this process, the yarn is punched into a base cloth and held in position on the reverse side by a coating of adhesive. The yarn can be left uncut as a cord or can be cut into tufts. An additional backing of foam rubber or felt provides extra thickness and resilience and removes the need for an underlay which is essential in a woven carpet; as the tufts are held in position by the backing, there is no need for the edges to be oversewn or bound so further reducing the cost. Tufting is a very fast process which has opened the way to a much wider use of carpeting in buildings where formerly they would have been considered a luxury and too expensive.

(g) Needle-punching

This process relies on the entanglement of a thick layer of fibres into a cohesive web by means of barbed needles. The process is very rapid and simple and is used extensively for needled carpet tiles which are becoming popular on the contract market for corridor, office or wards, areas where previously a hard floor covering would have been used. The majority of blankets produced are now by this fibre-to-fabric needling process.

(h) Stitch-bonding

Stitch-bonding is used for many furnishing fabrics and consists of a layer of staple fibres held together by rows of machined threads. This method of production is about ten times as fast as that of conventional knitting or weaving.

(i) Bonded-fibre fabrics

These fabrics are produced by using adhesive to bind together a web of fibres; the fibres are laid in parallels, crossed or completely at random and are either completely saturated by the adhesive or the adhesive is applied to the reverse. These fabrics are used for interlinings and many of the disposable cleaning cloths and other items.

(j) Flocking

Flocking is one of the older methods of producing a fabric and is used for wall coverings, carpets and furnishing materials. A base cloth, or paper, is coated with a pattern in an adhesive resin or latex and the surface then sprayed with a high concentration of short fibres. These fibres pass through an electrical field and are polarized so that they land and remain on the fabric at right-angles. The fibres used are usually nylon, viscose or cotton.

(k) Spin-bonding

This process produces a fabric formed from a mass of synthetic filaments, usually nylon or polyester, which are formed into a web as they are extruded and held together by heat or self-bonding to form a two-dimensional structure which becomes a firm 'mat' when set and dry. A similar process uses a filament which has an inner core and an outer mantle; the outer mantle has a lower melting point than the inner core so that when the mass of fibres are heated to a temperature between the melting points of the core and the mantle, only the outer part will melt. When cold, the *melt-weld* process will have formed strong bonds wherever the fibres crossed. Both methods produce a soft floor covering, strong and very serviceable for heavy-duty areas.

These later methods of production mean that the fabrics produced can only be self-coloured, multi-coloured and, occasionally, striped, as pattern cannot be introduced in the manufacturing stage. In some of the fabrics, pattern and colours are printed on in the finishing stage.

7.3 Factors to consider before buying

Fabrics must not only retain their appearance throughout their useful life but must also be serviceable, easy to maintain and, in most cases, long-lasting. The main factors to consider before buying are:

   1 Laundering and dry cleaning;
   2 Flame retardancy;
   3 Dimensional stability;

4 Strength;
5 Colour fastness;
6 Static electricity build-up;
7 Warmth and comfort;
8 Colour, pattern and texture.

7.3.1 Laundering and dry cleaning

After the costs for labour, the highest charge in a residential establishment is that for laundry and dry cleaning. From the cost point of view, any fabric which is soil- and crease-resistent, washes at a low temperature and requires no ironing is obviously going to be cheaper to maintain than a material which requires a high temperature wash, starching and ironing or one which must be dry-cleaned. This is important both for those items which require frequent laundering such as bed and table linen, net curtains, bedcovers and uniforms and for articles which are difficult to iron and finish, such as loose chair covers and fitted bedspreads.

For the Housekeeper, the laundering of fabrics falls into three main categories.

(1) Linen, cotton and union materials which require a high-wash temperature up to boiling point and need ironing to remove creases. Bleach may be necessary to maintain and colour and, in the case of table linen, starch to keep it crisp.

(2) The man-made synthetic fibres, acrylics, nylon and polyester used either on their own or blended with a natural fibre. These are washed at a hand-hot temperature of 50°C or lower, and most require no ironing. Temperatures higher than this will gradually remove the non-iron resinous finish and usually means that the material will have to be ironed in the future.

(3) Fabrics which have to be dry-cleaned. Many silks, acetates, brocades and light furnishing fabrics have to be dry-cleaned to avoid colour loss, water marking and shrinkage. Wool will not withstand frequent washing but may be dry-cleaned with safety – this may, indeed, be cheaper than having the articles washed as the fibres do not absorb the solvent as readily as they absorb water so that the drying time is considerably shorter. Fabrics will also have to be dry-cleaned if two or more different fibres are used in the construction as the shrinkage rates may be different. Some fabrics cannot be dry-cleaned, for instance, a P.V.C.-coated fabric or a rubberized cotton.

There have been numerous studies on the merits of providing

laundry facilities on the premises, linen hire or using a commercial laundry. These are discussed in Section 8.2.

7.3.2 Flame retardency

As far as possible, all fabrics used in a public building are expected to meet the standards set by the British Standards Institution (BSI). Curtains, textile wall coverings, upholstery fabrics and carpets should comply with BS 3120; the main requirements are that:

(1) The fabric has a flame rating of at least 150; that is, if it does burn, it will do so slowly and there is time either to escape from the area or to put the fire out. An untreated thin muslin or cotton material could have a fire rating as little as 25 or 30 which means that it will burn and flare rapidly whilst a treated material will shrink away from the heat and not burn or singe when out of contact with a flame.

(2) No toxic fumes are produced if the material is heated, smoulders or burns.

(3) The material retains its flame retardancy during washing or dry-cleaning – whichever is recommended – up to a minimum of 12 laundry processes. Hospital requirements for hygiene are such that the material must be capable of withstanding 50 washes before flame retardancy is lost.

The division between fibres which are flammable and those which are flame-retardant is somewhat arbitrary as it depends very much on:

(1) How the fabric is constructed;
(2) Whether the fibre is mixed or blended with another fibre;
(3) The weight per metre;
(4) The porosity;
(5) The surface texture.

Fabric made from glass will not burn but can be a problem to launder as it should not be spun-dried and must be hung carefully to avoid permanent creasing. Many materials made from nylon, polyester and acrylic do not flare but melt and bead which can cause severe burns to the body if they are used for uniforms.

Polyester and nylon both melt and shrink away from a flame but when blended with cotton or viscose, will blaze fiercely. In the same way, acrylic will burn rapidly when blended and used as curtaining, but will be safe when used in a heavy, tightly constructed carpet.

Wool, when used in a carpet or in a heavy-weight upholstery fabric will not burn easily and a cigarette end will usually extinguish itself. The great advantage in the use of wool for carpeting is that any charring of the pile is easily removed by brushing and rubbing in contrast to a burn in a synthetic fibre which beads, hardens, remains unsightly and is difficult to remove in any other way than to cut it out and patch.

To meet the requirements of the British Standards Insitute, many fibres are manufactured with a flame-retardent finish which is incorporated and baked into the chemical structure. These are inherently flame-retardant and are able to withstand innumerable washings.

The main fibres in general use which are inherently flame-retardant are the modified acrylics – modacrylic, and a modified viscose fibre such as Darelle. Both fibres can be used for blankets, bedcovers, furnishing materials and textile wall coverings.

A fabric which is *flame-proofed*, however, is one which has been treated with boric acid or a similar phosphorus-type compound; although this does not burn easily, the treatment is gradually removed when the material is washed or dry-cleaned. If the material is used under damp conditions, as it would be if hanging as a curtain by a window, the acid may crystallize and migrate to the surface of the cloth where it dries out to a white powder and makes the whole process ineffectual. The fabric is flame-proofed either by dipping or, in the case of a large article, it can be sprayed.

Flame-retardent fabrics are washed only in synthetic detergent and never in any soap or soap-flake product as this could cause a build-up of lime soap in the material in a hard-water area; this lime soap is inflammable.

7.3.3 Dimensional stability

(a) Shrinkage

The synthetic fibres shrink so little that it is hardly noticeable but some of the natural fibres such as cotton, linen, wool and viscose can shrink up to 6 or 8 per cent unless they have been specially treated.

Most shrinkage occurs when the fabric is wet. There are two main causes. *Relaxation shrinkage* is caused by the cloth being over-stretched on the looms during the weaving and finishing processes. In weaving, the warp and weft yarns are bent or 'crimped' over and under each other. Tensions develop at the crimp point; these are only released when the cloth is wet and rubbed or agitated in the washing machine. The result is a structural adjustment in the fabric and shrinkage occurs in both the warp and the weft. It is often difficult, if not impossible to impose enough pressure on the material to bring it back to its original shape.

Relaxation shrinkage can be controlled by the manufacturer using a 'compressive shrinkage' process. The material is washed to determine the shrinkage percentage and it is then brought to the required size on 'tenters' for the width and then compressed in the length-wise direction under controlled conditions. Finished in this way, cloth will shrink in use by under 1 per cent. The trade name for this process is 'Sanforised' or 'Rigmel-shrink'.

Cotton drill is usually sanforized before being made up into overalls and 'boiler-suits'; unfortunately, the making-up process stretches and extends the cloth. When it is washed it shrinks back to the original sanforized dimensions and leaves a fitted garment 2–3 per cent smaller.

A woollen fabric will shrink, harden, discolour and felt as the fibres entangle, when it is washed energetically in a warm, alkaline or acid solution. The property of felting only applies to wool and other animal hair and is caused by the hair being built from over-lapping scales the edges of which point towards the tip of the fibre; when wool is rubbed and agitated, the directional friction makes the scales overlap and shorten.

There are several ways or preventing this – overlapping can be prevented by a coating of a resinous polymer, the scales tips can be damaged by treating them with corrosive chemical, or a polymer can be applied to the cloth which binds the fibres together at the crimp point and prevents movement.

The specification for the material should give the percentage for shrinkage so that an allowance is made when buying.

(b) Fibre swelling

Fibre swelling caused by the absorption of water also creates problems. A highly absorbent fibre, such as cotton, linen or viscose, will swell in contact with water causing the length of the yarn to shorten as the diameter increases and a much greater crimp where the warp and weft yarns cross; unless tension is put on the cloth as it dries, it will not automatically return to its original length. This problem is greater with viscose cloth than with cotton. Fibre swelling is controlled by applying a synthetic resin finish to the cloth.

(c) Stretching

As has been mentioned, viscose is one of the fabrics which can stretch in use. The problem is normally only critical for upholstery material which should be firmly woven to resist the pushing, abrasive pressure of constant sitting and movement. The fabric must remain tight on the frame of the chair and the cushions.

7.3.4 Strength

It is difficult to compare accurately the different strengths of fibres and fabrics as this is dependent on the way in which the fibre is spun and on the construction of the cloth. A yarn which has a medium to high even twist will wear better than one which is loose and uneven. As a general guide, yarn spun from a filament or long fibres will be stronger than those made from short fibres; for instance, linen is a stronger fabric than cotton and Egyptian cotton stronger than American cotton, this is approximately equal in strength to silk. Wool is one of the weakest natural fibres. Both cotton and linen increase in strength by about 20 per cent when wet whilst silk loses 20 per cent of its strength.

Synthetic fibres are as strong or stronger than linen; the addition of a synthetic fibre to a natural fibre usually results in extending the life of the material by three or four times.

A fabric should be able to resist abrasive pressure so that threads do not break, snag or pull away from the weave. Some fabrics rub up into small 'pills' or balls; this can be unsightly on a synthetic material as the ball remains attached to the fabric and does not break away as it does with weaker fibres.

7.3.5 Colour fastness

Fading can make a fabric look dull, shabby and uninteresting so that it has to be replaced long before the material has lost its strength. The British Standard for Fade Resistency is BS 1006; the material is tested under a daylight fading lamp and the results compared and graded against a scale marked from 1–8. The higher the rating, the better will the material resist fading.

Unless the material is to be used in strong, direct sunlight, the minimum recommendation for curtain fabrics on the scale is 6 and, for upholstery materials, 5. Carpets and textile wall coverings, hessian, cotton, linen or silk weaves should also meet the British Standards specification particularly when used in a south-facing room. Washing and dry cleaning can also affect colour fastness.

7.3.6 Static electricity build-up

Static electricity is produced by the friction caused by the contact and separation of any pair of surfaces; for instance, when walking over a carpet, the sole of the shoe and the pile tufts have an electrical charge which is evenly distributed between both surfaces but as soon as the shoe is lifted one of the surfaces becomes positively charged and the other surface receives a negative charge. The amount of the charge received depends on whether the material has a high or a low resistence to electricity. Normally static electricity leaks away to earth through the building fabric; this is helped by wool, cotton and wood which are good conductors and cause few problems but many of the synthetic fibres are poor conductors and give trouble especially in a building which is centrally heated. Whether or not a material is a good conductor depends on its moisture content with most becoming more efficient as this content increases; no material creates much of a problem when the relative humidity of the air is above 50 per cent but in the winter with a cold, dry outside atmosphere, heating can produce an internal atmosphere in which the relative humidity can fall to about 20 per cent and the resultant lower moisture content makes fabrics and materials bad conductors and increases the static electricity in the building.

There are two main problems.

(1) The unpleasantness of the shocks and crackling experienced when a charged surface is touched – metal furniture, electric switches and equipment, and the handling of man-made fabrics such as acrylic blankets or nylon sheets.

(2) The risks of an explosion where inflammable gases, such as oxygen or ether, are used in a Hospital Operating Theatre or Intensive Care Unit. In these conditions, anti-static materials should be carefully considered as should the possible use of conductive clothing and shoes.

A smaller problem is that an electrically charged surface does attract dust.

There are several remedies.

(1) A conducting fibre can be woven into the fabric – this should

always be done with a nylon carpet. Both metallic and viscose fibres are good conductors and will carry static electricity to the back of the carpet and so to earth. Metal fibres used at a spacing of about 35 mm provide protection as does a blend of 5 per cent viscose: 95 per cent nylon, provided the relative humidity does not fall below 25 per cent.

(2) An anti-static finish can be sprayed onto a fabric. These are either oil or water-based and attract moisture from the atmosphere to the fibres. Most water-based anti-stats are not permanent and are removed by water.

(3) In a man-made fibre such as nylon or polyester, an anti-static additive is added at the melt stage before spinning; again, this increases the ability of the fibre to absorb moisture.

(4) Carbon molecules can be introduced into the surface of a fibre, in the same way that it can be added to a flooring material such as terrazzo.

7.3.7 Thermal insulation

The thermal insulation properties or *warmth* of a fabric is measured in units called 'togs'. A tog is equal to ten times the temperature difference between the two sides of the material.

The warmth of a material is determined by the thickness, the way in which it has been constructed and the weight and density of the fibres; as air is a poor conductor of heat, it follows that the more air that is trapped and held immobile within the fabric the better will be the insulation. Textile fibres are much better conductors of heat than air so an ideal material is one in which the structure is not so tight and dense that heat is lost through the fibres or is so open that it is lost through radiation and air movement. Wool is warm, not because of the way the fibre is constructed, but because of the amount of air trapped within the structure. In the same way, a fabric which has been brushed up or 'raised' will be warmer than if it had been left smooth. Average thermal resistance is as follows:

A sheet	0.2 togs;
An average weight bed-spread	0.5 togs;
A new, raised wool blanket	2.0 togs;
A blanket, washed several times	1.0–1.5 togs;
A continental quilt – these vary according to the filling	7.0–14.0 togs.

A bed, made up with a top sheet, two blankets and a bedspread has a tog value of about 4.7 and is quite warm enough for a hotel bedroom of 20°C whilst a continental quilt would be too warm. Bedding, to the value of between 9 and 10 togs is needed in a room with a temperature of 10°C.

Textiles also help to prevent the heat loss from a room.

Medium-weight curtains have an insulation value of	0.23–0.25 togs;
Wilton carpet, wool, heavy contract	1.62 togs;
The same carpet after one year in use	1.36 togs;
Axminster carpet, nylon pile	1.23 togs;
The same carpet with a foam underlay	2.73 togs;
Textile felt	2.89 togs;
compared with:	
P.V.C. tile	0.04 togs;
Linoleum	0.18 togs;
Cork tile	0.88 togs.

Thermal insulation can be increased by backing a fabric with a very fine layer of aluminium particles which reflect the heat. This fabric can be used as a curtain lining so that, in winter, the curtain reflects the internal heat back into the room and reduces the amount of heat lost through the window whilst, in summer, the principle operates in reverse and much of the sun's radiation is reflected away from the building. Metal particles can also be used on finer fabrics such as net so that, in addition to their role in providing privacy, net curtains can be used to control the amount of heat and light entering the building.

7.3.8 Comfort

What is comfortable in use is very subjective and dependent on what the individual considers important; it is affected by feel and texture, softness and the weight of the material. Any fabric which is in contact with the skin, such as that used for uniforms or bedding, should be absorbent; on average, a person will sweat approximately ¼ to ½ pint of water vapour each night, if this water is not absorbed quickly by sheets and blankets, a bed will feel cold and clammy which is why cotton or linen sheets are considered preferable to nylon – and wool to acrylic or polyester.

7.3.9 Colour, pattern and texture

Much thought has always gone towards the aesthetic use of colour and pattern when considering the way in which the atmosphere and attractiveness of an establishment is created (see Section 6.4) but often a decorative scheme is often introduced with no thought to the problems which can be created.

A dark colour will show dust, 'bits' and lighter marks, a light colour shows footmarks, dirt and stains all of which are less likely to be seen on a medium-toned colour.

A patterned or marbled surface tends to hide any marks or stains which become lost and hidden by the different colours and shapes. Furthermore, any patch or repair will be less noticeable. When hygiene requirements are important, white and pale colours are used.

A large pattern can be uneconomical if the material has to be matched or joined as the pattern 'drop' may not always coincide with the cutting line which means that material has to be discarded on each joined length. Plain colours, vertical stripes and small patterns are the most economical.

As a general rule, the rougher and more open the texture of a fabric, the more dust and dirt it will hold.

7.4 Bedding and table linen

7.4.1 Sheets

For comfort, the fabric used for sheets and pillowcases should be absorbent, warm and have a smooth, even texture.

Since the 15th century when *sheets* were first introduced, the traditional material has always been linen with cotton making its appearance in the 1830s; silk has been used for the most luxurious sheets for many years. Linen has become extremely expensive and is now used only in a very few establishments where it is considered that the cost is commensurate with the standard of service which is offered. The fibre is very strong, particularly when wet, and produces a cloth with a cool, very even, smooth, silky texture.

Cotton is slightly less durable. Egyptian cotton sheets are about half the cost of linen and are very smooth and fine; American cotton is coarser but is in general use as it is very much cheaper. Union cloth, a mixture of cotton and linen, combines the best qualities of both fibres.

Both cotton and linen are damaged by the amount of bleach used in the washing process. The service life of a sheet when washed at a commercial laundry, should be somewhere between 100 and 120 wash cycles although this can also be affected by the type of user — children being particularly heavy users. Shrinkage should not be more than 6 per cent. A viscose/cotton mixture has the same characteristics as cotton.

Polyester/cotton sheeting has the fibres blended at either a 67/33 or 50/50 ratio; by adding polyester, the service life of a sheet is extended to somewhere between 300 and 400 wash cycles and there is the added advantage that it is given a soil and crease-resistant finish so no ironing is needed. Any creases disappear when the sheet is stretched on the bed.

Most polyester/cotton fabrics are usually dyed or printed as polyester fibres attract and retain dirt and greasy deposits from the washing water (as do other synthetic fibres) so that a white material will become progressively greyer. Colour and pattern can add to the decorative features of a room and can be used to distinguish different sizes of sheets. Some hotels are reluctant to introduce polyester/cotton as it is felt that the customer expects crisp, white sheets and the use of a softer, coloured sheet would lower standards.

Because there is no shrinkage, sizes are smaller than for cotton, as is the weight, so that more sheets can be washed at a time — useful if there is an on-premises laundry.

Sheet sizes

	Single	Double
Cotton and linen	200 × 275 cm	230 × 275 cm
Polyester/cotton	175 × 260 cm	230 × 260 cm

Very few Housekeepers would buy fitted sheets; this is because the elastic at the corners needs frequent repair, they can only be used as a bottom sheet so that the total stocks have to be increased and it is questionable whether any time is saved when bed-making.

The choice between buying cotton or polyester/cotton can be affected by the laundry facilities. Cotton requires a high temperature wash and hot iron or flat-press finish and is usually processed through a commercial laundry whilst polyester/cotton is washed at hand-hot temperatures and is more suitable when an on-premises laundry is in use (Section 8.2).

With the need to sterilize all fabrics, a hospital will use a fabric which can be boiled and hot-ironed so that all bacteria and micro-organisms are killed.

7.4.2 Blankets

Traditionally, wool has always been used to make the thick cloth with the brushed, raised nap which we call a blanket. Merino-type, short staple wool is used for the lightest, softest, warmest and the most expensive, luxury blankets. Longer stapled wools from cross-bred sheep are used for less expensive blankets which are heavier, not so warm but more durable.

Wool has, however, two great disadvantages: it has to be very carefully washed to avoid shrinkage and felting and it is attractive to moth and their larvae; for all woollen materials, a shrink-resistent and moth proof finish should be considered. Any blanket which is stored for any period must be clean and, preferably, sprayed with a moth pesticide.

Partly to avoid the problem of shrinkage but mainly to reduce costs, other fibres are now used.

A 'union blanket' has cotton in the warp and woollen yarn used for the weft, it is this which is brushed to provide the pile. Viscose is often used to replace a percentage of the wool but as it does not have the same resilience as wool, the blankets tend to go flat and are not so warm. Cotton and cotton/rayon mixtures are used extensively in hospitals as these fibres will withstand frequent washing and sterilizing with little risk of building up a static electricity charge. They cannot be compared with wool having little resilience, and provide far less warmth for their weight.

Acrylic blankets are increasingly used as the appearance is very similar to wool, they are cheaper and there are not the same washing problems but they have a slight metallic feel and many develop static electricity. Modacrylics are flame-retardent and can be used for blanket and bed-covers where the risk of fire is great.

Woven blankets are still produced but, increasingly, a non-woven, needle-punch method is used; when the surface is brushed, it is difficult to tell the two methods apart. Cellular blankets are woven or knitted and are particularly light and warm – provided they are covered by a bedspread; this is necessary to prevent the displacement of air from the material caused by the movements of the sleeper or by air currents in the room.

Blanket-stitching or ribbon-binding are used to finish the ends whilst colours are introduced as part of the decorative scheme.

The efficiency of a blanket is often judged by the warmth-to-weight ratio. This is made by dividing the tog value of the blanket by its weight in g per cm^2; the higher the ratio, the more efficient the blanket. Raised wool blankets have a warmth-to-weight ratio of between 20 and 40; the ratio for a cellular blanket ranges from about 40 to 75 and produces the same warmth for about half the weight. A continental quilt has a warmth-to-weight ratio of between 80 and 200, depending on the fibre used in the filling.

The European Committee for Standardization gives eight sizes for blankets.

Size;	1	2	3	4	5	6	7	8
Width (cm)	75	100	150	180	200	220	280	300
Length (cm)	100	150	200	240	240	240	240	240

Quilting, as a means of providing a light-weight cover, is becoming much more popular.

7.4.3 Continental quilts or duvets

These quilts are used extensively on the continent but have been slow to be introduced in hotels and residential establishments in this country, the feeling being that, although young people like and use a quilt, the older generation and business travellers still expect the traditional top sheet and blankets. The A.A. classification requires that blankets should be available if requested.

By far the best, lightest, warmest and most expensive quilt is filled with down from the breast of the Eider Duck. Down consists of large numbers of filaments attached to a central point; commercially, a quilt filled with down can contain up to 15 per cent of very small, fluffy feathers mixed with either down from the farmyard duck or from geese – depending on the thickness, these quilts will have a tog value of between 11 and 14.

A down and feather quilt must contain 51 per cent down whilst a feather and down quilt contains 15 per cent down; these will be heavier than a down quilt with tog values of between 9 and 11. Polyester fibres are, to quote an advertisement, 'ideal for children because they are washable. They are also non-allergenic and therefore perfect for people who are allergic to natural fillings.' Tog values are between 8 and 11.

The casing should be a closely woven cotton cambric to prevent down or feathers working through and either has interior walls to hold the filling in place or is quilted with lines of stitching. Covers are usually made from a non-iron, polyester/cotton, fastened by 'poppers' or a zip fastener.

A quilt should be sufficiently large to settle over and cover the sleeper and go well over the sides of the mattress. Recommended sizes are:

Single bed	135 × 198 cm
Double bed	200 × 198 cm
King-size bed	220 × 198 cm

From the cost viewpoint and depending on the filling, there can be savings if quilts are used when compared with the cost for traditional bedding, in addition, the time required to remake or resheet a bed is very much reduced. There can also be the extra status in providing bedding which is 'up-to-date' and 'with it'.

In some of the larger London hotels, the practice has grown of using a third sheet to cover and protect the top blanket and offer an extra hygiene safeguard to the guest; if this custom spreads, it seems a short step to the introduction of the continental quilt.

7.4.4 Bedspreads

Bedspreads provide a large area of concentrated colour in a room so that the overall appearance is of great importance; they also receive a lot of misuse and it is essential to choose a fabric which is crease-resistant and easy to launder. A fitted bedspread is smart but expensive and needs more care than a flat bedspread; it is important that all fitted covers are shrink-resistant. Fringes are impractical as they can catch on the furniture and become entangled with the vacuum cleaner.

Candlewick, woven tweeds, and brocade or the same fabric which is used for curtaining are often used whilst a checked or tartan rug or blanket is practical and provides additional warmth.

7.4.5 Towels and bathmats

How quickly a towel removes moisture from the skin depends on the absorbency of the fibre, the density of the weave and the length of the pile loops. Terry or turkish towelling should have a strong base woven to form an interlacing with the loops, these should not snarl or pull out easily.

Cotton provides a soft towel and linen one which has a rough, coarser texture; which one prefers depends on whether a towel is used to dab dry or to rub vigorously. As linen is considerably more expensive, the bulk of towels are made from cotton or a cotton/linen mixture although polyester/cotton blends have now been introduced in the basic fabric to give extra strength.

It is important that selvedges are made from a heavier warp yarn to give extra strength or else they should be side-hemmed; bottom hems can be corded or coloured borders can be introduced. Many hotels have a monogram woven into the fabric. Sizes vary from one manufacturer to another but the most usual are:

Bath Sheet	147 × 200 cm;
Bath Towel	76 × 142 cm;
Large Hand Towel	56 × 112 cm;
Small Hand Towel	43 × 81 cm;
Flannel	28 × 28 cm.

For some years, towelling has also been produced by non-woven methods for lower quality goods using either tufting techniques or stitch knitting methods to produce cloth about fifteen times faster than it can be produced by weaving.

A huckaback weave produces a strong fabric which is also used for towels and is used extensively in the roller towel cabinets for cloakroom and kitchen use. This is approximately 45 yards in length.

Bathmats are usually made from turkish towelling, candlewick or from a heavy tufted fabric; those which have a rubberized backing should withstand washing at high temperatures. Disposable mats made from cellulose are quite attractive and often cheaper to buy than the cost of laundering a fabric mat, they are often used where hygiene factors are important.

7.4.6 Table linen

It is still accepted for silver-service standards that linen is the best material to use for table linen. Damask linen has a fine, lustrous appearance which drapes well on the table and, with cotton, is a fabric from which it is easy to remove stains by bleaching and boiling. Linen is expensive and used only by the luxury hotels and restaurants. A union of linen and cotton is about two-thirds of the cost, has a better appearance than a tablecloth made from cotton, but is noticeably different from pure linen; when the three fabrics are placed side by side, the differences become obvious. Polyester/cotton is used but some types of stain, such as that from red wine are difficult to remove.

The type of fabric used, the weave and the colour depends on the standard and type of the establishment and the atmosphere which is being created. At the cheaper end of the market, polythene which can be wiped over with a damp cloth or a disposable cloth can be used.

Tablecloth sizes are:
   137×137 cm (54×54 in) fits a table 76 cm^2 (2 ft 6 in)
   183×183 cm (72×72 in) fits a table 1 m^2 (3 ft^2)
   183×137 cm (72×54 in)
   183×244 cm (72×96 in) for rectangular tables
Buffetcloths $- 2 \times 4$ m (6×12 ft) These can be bought in longer lengths when required.
Serviettes 46 to 50 cm^2 (18 to 20 in^2)
Waiters and service cloths $\Big\}55 \times 76$ cm (21×30 in)
Tea and glass cloths
Slip cloths 1 m^2 (36 in^2) or a serviette are used to cover part of the tablecloth if only a small section has become stained; these, and the cloths used on a trolley or sideboard are often made in the linen-room from cloths which have become worn.

7.5 Curtaining and upholstery fabrics

When furnishing materials are bought, it is usually expected that they should last as long as possible; it is only in some of the prestige establishments that a material will be used for the limited time of one redecorating/refurbishing period to the next.

7.5.1 Curtains

The main purpose of *net curtains* is to provide privacy without obscuring the light but they are also used to partially hide an ugly view or outside feature; when one side of the net is coated with a thin coating of aluminium particles solar radiation is reflected away from a room and is one way of controlling the heat level, particularly in the summer.

Any fabric which hangs close to a window is affected by the photo-chemical effect of light which will cause loss of colour and strength, a loss which can be aggravated by an unsuitable choice of dye. Window glass absorbs ultra-violet wavelengths so the 'light-tendering' effect on materials depends on how close the curtain is to the window.

Research by the Shirley Institute for Textiles has found that a polyester net will retain its strength much better than a nylon net and is unaffected by the condensation and humidity found close to the glass; in similar conditions, a cotton net would be badly affected by mildew.

In a city hotel, net curtains need to be washed frequently so it is essential to choose a fabric which requires no ironing. Usually the curtains are washed on the premises, the surplus water removed in a towel and they are rehung slightly damp. Ironing is time-consuming and should be unnecessary.

Both *net curtains* and *heavy curtains* enhance the appearance of a room and must be carefully chosen as part of the decorative scheme.

Heavy curtains are usually *lined*; to protect the more expensive material from the damage caused by 'light-tendering', condensation, fading and the dirt blown in through the windows. The lining can be replaced much more cheaply than the whole curtain and is usually sewn into the curtain, but can also be attached at the top by means of a heading tape. This means that curtain and lining can be laundered separately (and at different frequencies) with no problem from differing shrinkage rates or washing processes. Separate linings can also be transferred to other curtains if an establishment is using different curtains in the summer and winter.

A lining also helps the material to hang and drape into folds over the window; some materials are too stiff to do this well and a length of fabric should be draped over a frame before buying. An important consideration when making-up is that the machining or blind-hemming should not show on the right side; this criteria is difficult to achieve if the material is very thin or if it is woven with a very smooth finish.

A bedroom curtain must be opaque as not everyone likes to be kept awake through a late summer evening or early sunrise and privacy is required when lights are used in the room; unless the material is very closely woven, a lining is necessary. Linings also give a better appearance to the building when it is viewed from the outside.

When drawn, curtains provide considerable heat-saving with a medium-weight curtain reducing the heat-loss by about 20 per cent at a single-glazed window; this is increased when an interlining such as Milium is used which has a reflective coating of aluminium. In public areas, curtains are used as an aid to reduce noise and sound reverberation so making the environment more comfortable.

As with all fabrics used in a public building, flame-retardancy should be an important factor to consider before buying as must fade-resistance and shrinkage (see Section 7.3).

Allowance has to be made for adequate gathers when the curtains are drawn, for hems and turnings, for pattern repeats and for shrinkage.

Curtain material requirements.

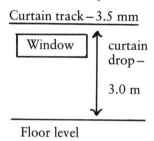

Curtain track – 3.5 mm

Window ↑ curtain drop –

3.0 m

Floor level

1. Measure length of curtain track.
2. Net or thin curtains – multiply by 2. Heavy curtains – multiply by 1½.
3. Divide the result by the width of the material.
   This gives the minimum number of widths of the material which have to be joined so that the curtains drape well when drawn.
4. Measure the required drop – from the curtain track to sill or floor.
5. Add an allowance for hems, usually 0.15 m. This gives the *cutting* measurement for *plain* or *vertically striped* materials.
6. For *patterned* materials – Divide the pattern repeat measurement into the cutting measurement. If this does not divide exactly, the cut has to be made at the end of the pattern repeat and some material will be wasted. The new cutting measurement would, therefore, be based on the pattern repeat.
7. Multiply the cutting measurement by the number of widths required.
8. Add the percentage (as stated in the specification) to allow for shrinkage.

1. Track length is 3.5 m
   (a) Multiply × 2 = 7 m
   (b) Multiply × 1½ = 5.25 m
3. Material width is 1.3 m
   (a) Divide 7 m by 1.3 = approx 5½ = 6 widths
   (b) Divide 5.25 m by 1.3 = approx 4 widths

4. Drop to floor is 3 m
5. Add 0.15 m for hem allowance = 3.15 m
6. Pattern repeat is 0.65 m Divide 0.65 into cutting measurement = 4.8. Allowance must be made for 5 pattern repeats = cutting measurement of 3.25 m

7. (a) Multiply 6 widths × 3.25 =   13.0 m
   19.5 m   8. Add 2 per cent for shrinkage.
   (b) Multiply 4 widths × 3.25 =   (a) 19.9 m (b) 13.25 m
If no allowance is made for pattern or shrinkage, the material required would be
   (a) 18.9 m   (b) 12.6 m

All materials must be laundered in accordance with the manufacturer's specifications. On average, curtains are laundered once or twice a year. To avoid rooms being 'off' for several days and the time-consuming task of removing and rehanging curtains, many Housekeepers have curtains cleaned *in situ* using similar equipment to the

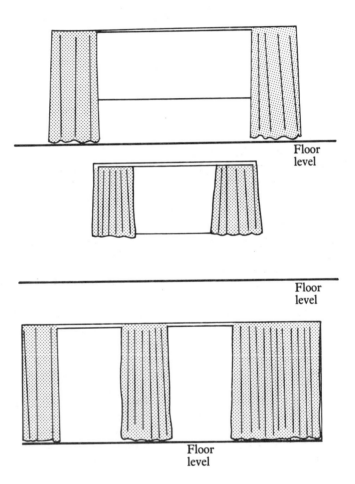

Floor
level

Floor
level

Floor
level

steam cleaning or hot water extraction processes which are used for carpets and upholstery; this is not as thorough as washing or dry-cleaning, so curtains are not left until they are really dirty but are cleaned when soiled.

Curtains made from a material of mixed fibres need special care and are more expensive to maintain, as do those with an open weave as these distort and pull out of shape so that the hems can become very uneven. Very large curtains have to be cleaned *in situ* as the size and the weight make them almost impossible to have washed or dry cleaned.

Pullcords are necessary to prevent the curtain being pulled, tugged and made dirty at the edge but they should be fairly conspicuous or they will not be noticed or used by the guest.

Pelmets, provided they are boxed in at the top, keep dust away from the fabric. A pelmet can look very attractive as they hide the track fittings and act as a decorative feature. They are usually made from wood, metal, plastics or plaster, if the curtain material is used there can be cleaning problems especially if fitted to padded boards.

The way in which curtains are hung can alter the look and appearance of a room by either covering or framing a window by drawing together different features. Curtains are also used to divide a room, as wall coverings and to hide doors, unsightly pipes, cupboards or other fittings.

In a modern building, louvred curtains are often used to provide privacy and to adjust light and heat levels in the summer, being vertical they attract less dust and are easier to maintain than a venetian blind.

7.5.2 Upholstery fabrics

Such fabrics are subjected to considerable stress from continual movement, rubbing and abrasion and can be caught and pulled easily. Over the years, some fabrics have proved their durability and ability to retain their appearance with hard use. A worsted yarn with a percentage of nylon made into a moquette cloth with either a cut or uncut pile is hard-wearing and easy to maintain. All materials must be closely woven and a smooth texture – other possible fabrics are velvets, tweeds, linen or laminated P.V.C. materials. The fabric must be:

(1) Flame-retardent;
(2) Firmly constructed so it will not pull or stretch;
(3) Able to resist abrasion;

(4) Colour-fast to both light and rubbing;

(5) Not 'pill';

(6) Easy to clean *in situ*;

(7) A medium-toned colour and patterned to hide spots and stains.

It is an advantage to have loose covers which 'zip' or hook on to the frame and can be removed for laundering. They have the added advantage of unifying a collection of different types of chairs and settees.

Arm-covers and head-rests or antimacassars help to prevent engrained dirt.

7.6 Uniforms

A uniform has two roles to play. The first is that a smart, well-fitting uniform with a good design does much to maintain staff morale and will give to the customer an immediate impression of the standard, efficiency and confidence of an establishment; so that there is a continuity in the impression that a customer receives, the colour and style of the uniforms should be planned to complement the decorative scheme. Information is provided by a uniform as it helps the visitor to identify each category and grade of staff so that he will know automatically from the colour and type whether he is talking to a receptionist, housekeeper, sister-in-charge or a nursing auxiliary; and the wearer will identify with the organization and be helped to establish a unity of purpose.

The second role is to give protection. The Health and Safety at Work Act, 1974, requires employers to issue protective clothing so that staff will be unaffected by any danger in their working environment, such as cleaning agents, equipment or hazards within the building. In many cases, there is also the need to protect food from the dust and dirt which could be transferred from an employee's clothing, and patients from dust and bacteria.

To be comfortable, a uniform must be sufficiently roomy and have a certain amount of 'give' to allow for active work. It should be made from a fabric which will absorb perspiration, it should not be too hot nor develop static electricity, should be available in many sizes, be of a design which suits all shapes and measurements, be acceptable to staff and must be able to withstand hard wear and constant laundering. Many fashion ranges in the 'ready-to-wear' domestic market are attractive and can look very suitable but they should be approached with care as they are not made or designed for constant use and frequent laundering.

A uniform can be marred by too flamboyant ties, too long hair, jewellery and cosmetics. Most women have definite and strong views about the length of a hem, shoes, the colour of tights and their personal adornment so that management must lay down the policy and standard that they expect.

Traditionally, working overalls have been made from *cotton* as it can be washed, scrubbed, boiled, bleached and starched to provide crisply ironed, white or coloured uniforms which are comfortable to wear. It is a fabric used extensively in hospitals as it can be sterilized in the wash process. Cotton drill is still the preferred material for kitchen 'whites' as it is highly absorbent and, where there is the risk of fire, will not cling to the skin as it burns. Cotton does, however, shrink and should be pre-shrunk before a garment is made. The cost of laundry is high and the wash temperature means that the uniform will not last as long as that made from another fibre.

A standard weight 4 oz *nylon* taffeta wears well, will drip-dry and needs little or no ironing so that washing can be done by the employee. It is inexpensive but is a fabric which is non-absorbent and becomes hot and clammy when worn – ventilation holes are needed under the arm. A knitted nylon is looser and more comfortable than woven nylon but does not keep its shape so well. Nylon should be treated to make it permanently anti-static to prevent the discomfort of it clinging.

Polyester fibre, when used on its own, is also uncomfortable to wear as it is non-absorbent and its easy-care, drip-dry properties are best utilized by combining it with another fibre.

For general use, a blend of *polyester/cotton* is more expensive but the life expectancy is about twice that of cotton so it is, in the long run, cheaper. The performance is better as it is crease-resistant and only requires a light iron.

A blend of *polyester and viscose* is used for smarter, dressier uniforms and is specially treated to prevent shrinkage, although with heavy use, the fabric can 'pill'. Both of these polyester blends can be permanently pleated.

Wool or a *wool and polyester* mixture is usually used for porter or reception staff uniforms.

A textured, pressed *polypropylene* can be made into overalls or boilersuits which are water-proof, unshrinkable, will resist chemicals, moulds and resins and are anti-static. The fabric is very light and porous so that garments do not become sweaty. It can be washed, boiled and ironed so is hygienic in use.

Most employers launder or dry-clean and repair uniforms as it is necessary; the minimum number needed for each employee is two but to maintain a high standard of cleanliness, a kitchen worker may require seven or eight sets of whites. To ensure that uniforms are returned at the end of the employment, all issues are recorded on the *Staff Record Card* and the cost is held against the last week of pay.

Increasingly, disposable clothing is being used; it is cheaper to throw away a chef's hat made from cellulose than to have a cotton hat washed and starched and, when hygiene standards are at stake, it is simpler to issue disposable uniforms, plastic bootees or gloves rather than to wash and sterilize the garments.

7.7 British textile standards

Many of these standards and tests are international and are used by the International Organization for Standardization (ISO) in order to promote world trade.

7.7.1 Dimensional stability of fabrics

BS 5807: Determination of dimensional change of textiles in domestic washing and drying which assesses shrinkage during washing, drying and finishing. This test takes into account the variations in the washing temperature, the times taken for both washing and rinsing and the method used for drying – whether it is drip dry, flat dry, line dry, tumble dry or a flat-bed press.
BS 4961: Determination of dimensional stability of textiles to dry cleaning in tetrachloroethylene. This is in two parts. The first part tests the results from a commercial-type dry cleaning machine, whilst the second part gives a laboratory method which can be used as the basis for a quality control procedure.

7.7.2 Colour fastness

BS 1006: Colour fastness of textiles and leather. This specifies the method of testing for the fastness of colour to light, water, washing and dry cleaning and other agents. As the fabric can be affected differently by these agents it may be that a fabric is fast to sunlight but not to dry-cleaning. The change in colour is measured against a scale of one to eight. The higher the number the better is the performance of the fabric. It is recommended that fabrics used for curtaining are not less than six on the scale and that fabrics used for upholstery have a minimum rating of five.

7.7.3 Crease recovery

BS 3086: Determination of recovery from creasing of textile fabrics by measuring the angle of recovery. This test is an indication of the speed at which a fabric recovers from creasing during the wear and tear of daily use and during washing. It is particularly important when buying fabrics for use in bedding and for covers.

7.7.4 Fabric stiffness and draping

BS 3356: Determination of stiffness in cloth. This tests the 'bending length' of stiffness inherent in the fabric and can be important when buying fabrics for curtaining.

7.7.5 Strength

BS 2576: Textiles, woven fabrics. The determination of breaking strength and elongation (strip method). In this test, the fabric is stretched until it breaks and the tensile strength recorded.

7.7.6 Fabric care

BS 2747: Textile Care Labelling Code. This specifies how the fabric should be washed and dried, dry cleaned, ironed or pressed. The symbols are international and are as follows.

O = Articles which can be dry-cleaned in any of the solvents normally used.

= The temperature for ironing.   o = cool iron at 110°C.

o o = warm iron.

o o o = hot iron.

= Do not iron.

= indicates bleach (chlorine-based) can be used.

= Indicates the temperature, type of spin at which the fabric has to be washed: i.e.

$$\frac{1}{95°C} =$$ a very hot to boil wash, the fabric can be spun dried. Suitable for white cotton and linen without a special finish.

or $\frac{4}{50°C} =$ a hand-hot wash at 50°C with a cold rinse followed by a short spin or drip dry. Suitable for coloured nylon, polyester, cotton and viscose fabrics with special finishes, acrylics, cotton/polyester fabrics.

= Indicates hand washing only.

If a process is not recommended, the symbol is crossed through.

= Do not dry-clean.

= Do not use a chlorine-based bleach.

This labelling system has one disadvantage; many manufacturers are cautious and specify that a fabric should be dry-cleaned so that they avoid any possible complaints for shrinkage or colour fastness even though, in many cases, the normal washing process would probably be safe.

7.7.7 Flame retardency

How a fabric burns depends on the type of fibre and on the way in which the material has been constructed; a blend of several fibres may mean that a melting fibre is held on a framework of a non-melting fibre so that instead of melting and dripping, it is unable to do so and may burn fiercely. Other factors which affect the degree of burning are the weight of the fabric, the backing such as upholstery materials or carpet underlays, the type of dye and finishing processes and the way in which the material is used and maintained.

BS 2963, 1958: Method of test for the flammability of fabrics.

BS 3121, 1959: Performance requirements of fabrics described as of low flammability.

These standards describe the methods of testing. BS 3121 specifies that the fabric must have a flame resistance rating of 150 or more if it is to be classified as of low flammability. This means that with a vertical strip of fabric, 100 inches or 2.54 m in length, a flame is applied to the bottom and the time it takes to spread from the bottom to the top is measured. The minimum time must be 150 seconds, a slow burning rate which will give the occupants of a room time to either put the fire out or to leave the building.

BS 5438, 1976: Method of test for flammability of vertically oriented textile fabrics and fabric assemblies subjected to a small igniting flame. This involves three methods of testing carried out either in sequence or individually, depending on the performance requirements. Test 1 determines the minimum flame application time that causes ignition. Test 2 determines the extent of the vertical and horizontal flame spread. The flaming debris behaviour, the duration of flaming and afterglow and the extent of the hole formation may be described. Test 3 determines the extent of vertical and horizontal flame spread when the fabric is too flammable for Test 2.

BS 5867, 1980: Fabrics for curtains and drapes:
   Part 1 – General requirements
   Part 2 – Flammability requirements

Part 2 specifies the flammability requirements for fabrics used for curtains, drapes and window-blinds when tested to BS 5438. It stresses that fabrics should be tested in the way in which they are to be used, including multi-layer constructions.

BS 5852, 1979: Fire Tests for furniture. There are two separate tests, the smouldering cigarette and the lighted match test, both designed to test for the ignitability by smoker's materials of upholstered furniture used for seating. The furniture fails if either of the two sources of ignition continues to smoulder or burn.

Fire is an ever-increasing risk so it is particularly important that all fabrics bought and used in large public buildings conform to the British Standard Specifications. The tests are specified by local authorities when authorizing fabrics for use in hotels, theatres or other large buildings but it is when these fabrics need to be replaced that emphasis is often placed more on the appearance than on the safety aspect.

7.8 Exercise and discussion

The Restaurant Manager has decided to buy curtains to cover the end wall of a small room which he often opens up for small functions. He wishes to make the room appear softer and more intimate and also to hide a door leading to a back corridor.

He cannot decide between two different materials, or whether a lining is necessary and has finally asked the Executive Housekeeper for advice.

The specifications for the material are:
(a) A polyester/silk mixture with a chinese bamboo and bird pattern with a repeat of 0.65 m. Width, 1300 mm: Colour Fastness, 4: Shrinkage, 4 per cent: Dry cleaning recommendation. Price: £7.25 per metre.
(b) A bonded velvet which requires no lining. Polyester and washable. Horizontal stripes with a pattern repeat of 0.35 m. Width, 825 mm: Colour fastness, 6: Shrinkage, 1 per cent. Price: £9.15 per metre.
(c) Lining material. Polyester and cotton. Width, 1050 mm: Shrinkage 7 per cent: Washable. Price: £1.45 per metre.

The size of the end wall is length, 6.42 m, and height, 2.7 m.

The Housekeeper contacts the Restaurant to ask whether the Manager wants curtains which are gathered or pleated and received the reply that he is not sure. She replies that pencil or pinch-pleating will mean that the amount of material needed to cover the walls will be increased and explains that, when the material is gathered, the track measurement is multiplied by either $1\frac{1}{2}$ or 2, depending on the weight of the fabric; but for both pencil or pinch-pleats it needs to be multiplied by $2\frac{1}{2}$ to obtain a good result. Gathering Tape costs 39p per metre, pencil and pinch-pleating tape, 89p per metre.

What would be the cost and the amount of material required for each material? What would be the difference if the curtains are pinch-pleated? Should she give any further advice regarding the material suggested? Write the report she would send to the Restaurant Manager.

8

The Linen Room and Laundry Facilities

8.1 The linen room

The task of the Linenkeeper is to control the supply of clean linen to all departments within the establishment. Other duties may include the issue and control of all staff uniforms, the control of guest and staff laundry and the responsibility for changing and washing all net curtains and the heavy curtains. During the off-peak season or in the vacation many small units will make both net and heavy curtains as they are needed and will do many of the repairs and renovations.

The *control* of linen stocks starts with the *security* of the linen room and of all linen cupboards; these should never be left unlocked and have access restricted by either a stable-type door or by an issue counter. All linen is expensive; the cost of a cotton sheet or a bath towel is often more than two or three times the cost of a bottle of wine or sherry so it is surprising how many establishments take such care of bar and wine stocks yet frequently accept that linen rooms and cupboards are left unlocked and unattended. There are many stories of loss which range from a hotel which received an invoice for £750 from its linen hire supplier to cover a three-month stock discrepancy to a Hospital Region which budgets for linen stock replacements of £100 000 each year.

The *linen stock* held depends on: the average length of stay by the customer; the re-sheeting frequency; laundry facilities (whether there is a 24 or 48-hour return of clean linen); occupancy levels; the allowance needed to cover laundry closures at weekends and bank holidays. A 5-star hotel, re-sheeting every day, will need about 14 sheets and other items for each occupied bed whilst a residence for student or staff accommodation, which re-sheets once a week, could manage on 4 to 5 sheets per bed. The amount of capital tied up in stock can be considerable: as an example of this, one small hotel group with about 900 rooms and large banqueting facilities has a stockholding of over one million pounds.

8.1.1 Issue of linen

There are several methods for issuing linen.

(a) Clean for dirty

The simplest is a straight exchange of clean for dirty. This is usual for most restaurant issues. The linen for any special function or banquet requirements would be issued on receipt of an indent from the restaurant. It is only a very small hotel which will exchange 'clean for dirty' in the linen room as it is so time-consuming. It is essential that work on the floors is not disrupted by lack of linen so it is usually sent up in advance of the time when it will be needed.

(b) Floor stocks

In a large establishment, most floors will have their own linen store which is designed to hold maximum stock for one day's usage i.e. to re-sheet 100 beds daily, there would be 200 sheets and pillowcases, 100 bath and hand towels and bathmats. This stock figure is maintained either by the supervisor indenting for new stock as it is required, the linen room porter checking and 'topping up' to stock level, or the linen room porter exchanging clean for dirty when the dirty linen is collected.

Complications set in when dirty linen is returned to the linen room via a linen chute as the linenkeeper has an overall total but no idea of the amount returned from each floor.

(c) Computer control

In a hotel, when a computer is used to programme arrivals and departures, the print-out can also be used to show linen issues with a copy being sent to the linen room (p. 208).

A *weekly control sheet* is used to control the circulating stock within the hotel. This gives the total of all clean linen which has been issued and dirty linen returned from all departments.

Weekly Control Sheet—Internal
Week ended..................

	Mon			Tues			Wed			Thur			Fri		
	Iss	R'td	Bal	Iss	R'td	Bal	Iss	R'td	Bal	Iss	R'td	Bal	Iss	R'td	Bal
Sheets	288	281	−7	256	261	−2	302	296	−8						
Pillowcases	278	278	−	260	258	−2	302	293	−11						
Bath towels	144	140	−4	125	123	−6	152	157	−1						
Hand towels	144	143	−1	125	125	−1	150	147	−4						
Bathmats	123	115	−8	125	129	−4	154	155	−3						

The running balance is carried forward from one week to the next and should not be allowed to become too large; discrepancies can occur when sheets are torn, stained or need changing or when there are alterations in the expected arrivals and departures. At one time, no linen was issued until it had been opened out and checked for stains or damage but this is time-consuming and most establishments rely on the maid to check the standard and replace the article when necessary.

A similar *Weekly Control Sheet* is used to control the movement of linen between the establishment and a commercial laundry or with a linen-hire supplier. A commercial laundry will often send back the linen 'short' rather than delay its return by waiting for items which may need to be rewashed or have become separated.

To avoid miscounts, a large establishment will use a push-button counter when checking, otherwise, staff are taught to count in batches of '10's or '20's. To avoid any risk of infection, a hospital will never count dirty linen either on the ward or in the laundry. It is counted when it is being packed ready for its return.

Other books kept in the linen room are for *Repairs* and the *Condemned stock book*. Many items can be remade into smaller articles, i.e. sheets into under pillowcases, tablecloths into slip cloths or sideboard covers. *Stock books* are altered when this happens or when an item is written off as a stock-taking discrepancy or when items are reported missing from a room.

Most establishments will spot-check vulnerable items every few weeks but only carry out a complete *stock-take* two or three times each year. The frequency depends on the amount lost. Stock-taking is time-consuming and care must be taken to avoid counting any item twice—such as a dirty sheet on an unchanged bed and later, the same sheet in the dirty linen bag.

To avoid loss and to identify one's own property, all linen must be marked. Stock bought direct from a manufacturer can have the name of the company woven into the fabric or the supplier will machine embroider each item before it is received for a small, extra charge;

otherwise, the linen room can either machine embroider, use a monogram machine or mark with an indelible pen. The date is often added as soon as the item is brought into use – this helps to establish the life of each item.

The average 'life' of a linen or cotton sheet or tablecloth depends to a large extent on the way it is laundered – the amount of bleach used, the alkalinity of the wash solution and the temperatures for wash and finishing. On average, cotton, union or linen should last up to about 150 washes.

When comparing prices the *depreciation cost* should be found; as an example a sheets costs £6.00 and it has a life expectancy of 150 washes then the depreciation cost will be 4p; this is added to the laundry charge of say, 19p, so the *cost-in-use* charge will be 23p (see Section 8.2).

The high cost-in-use charges are the reason why maids should not be allowed to use towels, napkins or pillowcases for cleaning purposes particularly as cleaning agents can affect and damage the fabric; it is cheaper to buy and issue cleaning cloths and sponges.

The costs also indicate when disposable items can be used profitably.

8.1.2 Staff uniforms

These should be signed out to the individual employee and the information recorded on the Staff Record Card. When the employee leaves, any uniform should be handed back. If this is not done, the value is deducted from the last payment of wages. It is usual for repairs and alterations to be done by the linen room staff and for the establishment to pay for laundry or dry cleaning costs. Uniform is replaced when necessary.

8.1.3 Guest laundry

Guest laundry is a facility offered by many hotels either on a 'return the same day' basis or it is returned the following day. Guests are asked to list their own laundry, place it in the bag provided and hand it to the maid as early in the day as is possible. To avoid any possible dispute, many linenkeepers will check that the list is accurate before the bags leave the hotel. When the laundry is returned, a record is taken of the cost and the amount either collected from the guest in person or it is added to the guest's account before he books out.

Many hotels offer a *Valet Service* so that shoes are cleaned and clothed pressed and any small stains removed. The valet's service room is usually next to the linen room. Again, charges are added to the guest's account.

8.1.4 Staff personal laundry

Staff personal laundry is often sent through the linen room with staff paying the cost when it is collected.

8.2 Laundry facilities

There have been numerous studies on the costs of the laundry services and many differing opinions on the best and cheapest solution available whilst maintaining good standards. There are three main options: buying linen which is then cleaned commercially, hiring linen and buying linen which is cleaned on the premises.

(a) Own linen stocks, commercially cleaned

This means that:

1 A considerable amount of capital can be tied up in stock;
2 Stock levels may be high if the laundry is unable to provide a 24-hour return service;
3 All repairs and replacements are the responsibility of the establishment;
4 It is easier to control the quality, size and standard of the linen used, distinctive linen can be used;
5 In many areas, there may only be one local laundry so that an establishment is unable to negotiate competitive prices. There may also be heavy transport charges included in the price;
6 The costs of checking linen in and out of the establishment can be high;
7 Washing methods cannot be controlled and there is the possibility that the laundry may use harsh washing products which can shorten the life of an article.

The most usual method of charging is at the 'flat' rate; that is, the same price is charged for all flat articles which are finished through the calendar or else require no ironing – such as a towel. Uniforms, chef's hats and starched items are charged on a separate price scale. Whether or not a discount can be negotiated depends on the size and status of the establishment and on whether there is any competition from an alternative laundry.

(b) Linen hire

All bed and table-linen, towels and uniforms can be hired. This means that:

(1) No capital expenditure is involved: all items are paid for as and when they are used, through revenue expenditure;

(2) Stock levels can be increased quickly for a sudden increase in occupancy;

(3) All repairs and replacement costs are borne by the supplier;

(4) The quality, sizes and standard of the linen is determined by the supplier and could vary over the period of the contract;

(5) Checking linen in and out of the establishment is still important – the supplier will stock-take at regular intervals and any discrepancy will be charged;

(6) The supplier buys in bulk so usually pays less for linen than would be possible for the individual buyer: laundry work may also be cheaper than is possible at a commercial laundry as a limited range of items are being washed;

(7) Hire companies prefer a regular, all-the-year-round business and for this reason, a seasonal hotel may find it difficult to negotiate a competitive price.

Charges are highly competitive and will compare favourably with those of a commercial laundry but must, obviously, take into account repair and depreciation costs. Discounts are usually available for bulk use. A number of firms will hire some linen for such items as roller towelling for the cloakrooms, uniforms or dust control mats. A linen-hire firm cannot deal with *guest laundry* which may still have to be sent to a commercial laundry.

(c) Own linen, cleaned on the premises

This means that:

(1) The establishment has full responsibility for all the problems

involved in operating a small laundry system and for all repairs and replacements for linen and equipment;

(2) Capital is required to pay for linen stocks, equipment and installation charges (all other charges are revenue expenditure). It is possible, however, for equipment and linen stocks to be hired;

(3) Stock levels can be reduced as the return of linen is usually either on a 12- or 24-hour basis which, in an an emergency, can be reduced to 3 to 4 hours;

(4) Control and security of stock is easier as nothing leaves the premises;

(5) The number of times an item is counted is reduced and usually takes place after it has been laundered;

(6) Greater control over the washing process extends the life of the linen;

(7) As in (a) the quality, size and standard of linen can be determined by the establishment and be distinctive;

(8) When an establishment is isolated many housekeepers prefer to be self-supporting, particularly during the winter.

The greatest advantage of operating an on-premises laundry (OPL) is in the reduction in costs with some installers talking of between 40 and 50 per cent savings. A recently quoted example concerns two London hotels which combined to open their own OPL. This produced savings as follows: in 1977, each hotel was reported as paying about £80 000 to a commercial laundry, a total of £160 000 a year. The combined OPL budget for 1980/81 was £120 000 which was, to quote the report 'a commendable figure in view of the last three year's inflation and considering that the new arrangement requires a van and driver'. Whether savings can be made and whether management wishes to take on further responsibilities will depend on local circumstances. The factors which have to be considered are listed in the basis of a report on *Laundry Facilities* (section 8.3).

There are two different systems for on-premises laundries; a small establishment is more likely to consider the type of equipment similar to (but larger) than that used in the home whilst a large concern will have enough laundry to merit the operation of commercial equipment.

A hospital group or large hotel would normally install and operate a laundry with washing machines, hydro-extractors, tumble-dryers, calendars and rotary-ironers and is able to handle all types of fabric and finish. This type of equipment is extremely expensive and only practical if the amount of work is sufficient for full-time working. It would be operated by an experienced Laundry Manager and requires skilled staff.

A small establishment can find it economical to use a washing-machine with a built-in spin-dryer and tumble-dryers and to use fabrics which are non-iron. This is necessary as the time needed to finish articles using a small rotary ironer or by hand-ironing is prohibitive. Ironing must be done with the fabric damp to remove creases; linen coming off a calender, which has three rollers, will be dry but items pressed on a single roller will have to be repassed two to three times before they are sufficiently dry to be stored.

This change in fabric means a departure from the traditional, crisp, white bed linen and starched tablecloths beloved by management to the patterns and colours of polyester/cotton and man-made fibres. Easy-care fabrics can be used for uniforms, covers, curtains and all bed and table-linen. To be successful, when non-iron fabrics are used, the following points should be remembered.

(1) Any badly soiled items should be soaked for several hours before washing.

(2) The right washing temperature must be used for each group of fabrics – so all articles must be sorted.

(3) When washing or drying polyester/cotton fabrics it is important not to overload the machines which should be at 75 per cent capacity to avoid creasing.

(4) When it is necessary to use a bleach, it should be added to the first rinse water and not added to the detergent used for washing as these agents can neutralize each other.

(5) All work should be folded as soon as it comes out from the dryer and not left – again to avoid creasing. Folded work should be allowed to 'rest' on the linen room shelves for about 24 hours to let any creases drop out slowly. Remaining creases should stretch out when the article is put into use.

This type of easy-care laundry is usually operated on a part-time basis using unskilled staff and in the charge of one of the housekeepers or of the linenkeeper. It should be located away from the linen room as any steam will affect clean stocks. There must always be duplicate machinery to avoid the problems caused by break-down. As a rough guide, the following equipment is considered suitable for an establishment with about 150 rooms:

Washing machines – 1 × 50 kg capacity;
                            1 × 20 kg capacity;
Tumbler dryers   2 × 22 kg capacity;
                            2 × 50 kg capacity.

This offers the greatest flexibility. Drying capacity is usually about twice that of the washing capacity as the work cycles differ.

There is a valid argument against the use of OPLs. This applies when non-iron fabrics are used and which are washed and ironed at low temperatures. There could be some risk of cross-infection as the temperature is not sufficient to destroy bacteria and other micro-organisms which may remain in the fabric.

The contrary argument is that the normal washing process will remove any bacteria with the dirt particles and that these will be rinsed away so that the fabric should be safe to use in low-risk areas such as in a hotel and for student and staff use. A hospital must, however, use high washing and finishing temperatures to sterilize all bedding.

There is a *fire-risk* in all laundry work. One risk is that the fluff arising from textile fabrics can ignite spontaneously especially if it has become impregnated with oil or grease and is near heat. This means that motors and heating coils, the areas under calenders and around the tumble-dryer ducts must be cleaned regularly.

Spontaneous combustion can also occur in finished work if it has been packed when still hot; instead of cooling, the temperature can continue to rise due to the slow oxidation of the fabric in the centre of the load and this risk increases if there is any residue of oil or soap left in the material. To avoid trouble, work should be cold before packing. In the same way, linen should not be left in a tumble dryer, but unloaded as soon as it is finished and the work separated and folded so that the heat is lost quickly.

8.3 Discussion

Suggested Headings for a Report on:
Laundry Facilities: A proposal to change from the use of either Commercial Laundry or Linen-hire to an On-premises Laundry.
1. *Present position*
    1.1 Analysis of costs – over the past 2 to 3 years.
    1.2 The number and type of items laundered – taken from a representative sample over the past two years for the low and high seasons.
    1.3 The average weight of laundry each week. The average weight for each occupied bed is 2 kg – 2 single sheets, 2 pillowcases, 1 bath towel, 1 hand towel and 1 bathmat.

1.4 Problem areas – 1.4.1 Guest laundry

                           1.4.2 Valeting and dry cleaning

                           1.4.3 Staff uniforms

                           1.4.5 Blankets and curtains

2. *The possible type of facilities*

    2.1 Installation of commercial laundry equipment – washing machines, hydro-extractors, tumble dryers, calender and rotary ironers.

    2.2 Installation of launderette type equipment – washing machine with spin-dryer, tumble dryers.

3. *Equipment*

    3.1 Types available – cost, size and capacity. The length of the operating wash cycle.

    3.2 Number required. This depends on the weight of the wash and the washing cycle.

       i.e.

$$\frac{\text{machine capacity}}{\substack{\text{total weight} \\ \text{of laundry}}} \times \text{washing cycle} = \substack{\text{the number of hours} \\ \text{machines have to operate.}}$$

    3.3 The need for 'back-up' equipment

4. *Location of laundry area*

    4.1 Size of room for 2.1

                    for 2.2

    4.2 Position – access

    4.3 Services and requirements 4.3.1 Plumbing and drainage

                                       4.3.2 Electricity and gas

                                       4.3.3 Floor – weight of machinery

                                       4.3.4 Ventilation

    4.4 Planning and legal requirements

               4.4.1 Building regulations

               4.4.2 Fire precautions

               4.4.3 Health and safety

               4.4.4 Hygiene regulations

    4.5 Noise and guest inconvenience

    4.6 Reduction in revenue from alternative use of area

5. *Staff*

    5.1 Estimated work-load in hours – for 2.1

                               for 2.2

    5.2 Number of staff required – for 2.1

                             for 2.2

    5.3 Need for skilled or unskilled staff

  5.4 Training of staff
  5.5 Staff Costs – for 2.1
                for 2.2
6. *Linen supplies and stock levels*
  6.1 Fabrics needed – for 2.1
                       for 2.2
  6.2 Advantages
  6.3 Disadvantages
  6.4 Stock levels
  6.5 Disposal of old stock – if stock is replaced for 2.2
  6.6 Stock security and control
7. *Costs*
  7.1 Machines – to buy
                  to hire
  7.2 Extra equipment – trollies, shelving, weighing machine.
  7.3 Installation charges
  7.4 Runnings costs – Staff
                        Power – electricity and gas
                        Detergents
                        Hot water and water softening
                        Maintenance
                        Insurance
8. *Conclusions*
  8.1 Cost savings with 2.1
  8.2 Cost savings with 2.2
9. *Recommendations*

9

Estimates and Control of the Budget

9.1 Estimates

Estimates for both revenue and capital expenditure are prepared some four to six months before the start of each financial year which usually begins on either the first of April or the first of January. *Revenue estimates* are for the money required to pay for the day-to-day running of the department – for staff wages, laundry, cleaning materials or guest supplies – whilst *capital estimates* relate to the equipment, furniture, and furnishings which need to be bought or replaced during the year. Whilst revenue estimates are usually completed for one year ahead, some organizations require capital estimates for one, two or even five years ahead.

An estimate is the amount of money that the *budget holder*, usually the Head of the Department, feels is necessary for the coming year. Money is always in short supply, however, and all the departmental estimates are collated and scrutinized by the Accountant who then allocates the money available as he sees the overall priorities with the result that, in many cases, the estimates may be reduced. When this happens, it should only be after consultation with the budget holder.

Estimates are based on detailed analysis. The Housekeeper will need the following information:

(1) The operating financial statements for the current year; from these can be found the cost of each unit of activity such as the cost for each room cleaned or the cost of servicing each 100 metres of the building.

(2) The financial statements for the past three years.

(3) The forecast of the level of activity for the forthcoming year. In a hospital there is little variation, in a hotel the occupancy can

fluctuate considerably whilst a college or university can be extremely busy during vacations with conferences, summer schools or tourist accommodation.

(4) Any proposed alteration in equipment used, the standard or the type of work which could affect the work-load. The heaviest expenditure is always for staff; as the number of hours allocated to the department are related to the work-load these may need revising. It is also worth considering the proportion of the work which is needed at weekends or at night and which has to be paid for at time and a half or at double time rates.

(5) The monthly consumption figures for all stores and linen supplies with an indication of the trend in price changes.

9.2 Budgets

Whereas an estimate is for the amount of money that one wants, the budget is what one gets and it is essential to see that this allocation of money is not exceeded. The budget holder is not entitled to use all the money allocated if the forecast level of activity is not achieved and the budget may have to be *updated* during the year. This usually happens where a high proportion of the work is *flexible* (see Section 1.1). As an example of this, a hotel estimates for its future level of activity of, say, 50 000 room lettings. It costs approximately £2.65 to clean and service a room so that the budget requirement for this will be £132 500. During the year it becomes apparent that this target will not be reached and only 42 000 room lettings will be made so that the budget figure must be reduced by £21 200; conversely, if occupancy increases to 53 000 lets, the budget should also increase proportionately by £7950 otherwise standards cannot be maintained.

Allowances for future *inflation* are normally added by the accountant and not by the budget holder, even so, the budget may still need to be updated to accommodate rising prices or increased wages which have not been anticipated.

A large group of firms or a large establishment will use a *coding system* to ensure that all spending is debited to the right budget. Each unit, hospital hotel will be numbered as will each department within the unit. As an example: There are 12 hotels in the group of which the Provost Hotel is numbered 4, each department is numbered consecutively so that the Restaurant would be –1, the bars –2, Housekeeping –3, Maintenance –4, etc. and within each department, the cost centres would be for Labour –1, Food supplies –2, Wines and spirits –3, Laundry –4, Guest supplies –5, Cleaning materials –6, etc., so that in Housekeeping, an invoice for cleaning materials would be coded as 4–3–6, and one for guest supplies as 4–3–5.

9.3 Budgetry control

Before panic sets in, it must be remembered that the rate of expenditure is not always constant throughout the year and that some cost centres could be fully spent within two or three months if advantage is taken of bulk-buying discounts and special offers or if the work-load is not spread evenly over the year.

There are two main areas for control – staff hours, overtime and weekend working which is discussed in Section 1.2 and the control of all stores and supplies which is discussed in Section 9.4.

Records of all expenditure must be kept. Most organizations print-out from the computer a statement of account which is sent regularly to each department and which will compare the level of expenditure against the budget figure and usually shows the percentage spent in each area. These figures are of little use if they are treated in isolation but must always be compared with the previous statements and an explanation found if there are any wide variations in spending (p. 172).

Weekly consumption sheets produced within the department for cleaning materials, guest supplies or linen issues will quickly show variations in use and the relationship to occupancy (p. 173).

Wages are controlled by the levels of staffing and are related to the work required. Where there is much flexible working, as in a hotel, a form similar to the Room-Maids Analysis Sheet would be used (Section 10.2.2). When pay is affected by overtime and varying payrates for weekend work, the control is through the duty rosters, clock-cards or the signing-in book and the Weekly Time Sheets. No overtime should be payable unless it has been previously agreed by the Supervisor. The standard time (see Section 1.1) should be sufficient so that any reason why a job is not going to be completed within the allotted time must be discussed; exceptions to this could be when there are late departures or if plumbers or carpenters have to complete emergency work before going off duty.

At the end of each financial year, the amount and value of all *stock* is sent to the accountant. This is needed before the yearly accounts are drawn up as he needs to know the difference between the cost of the

Monthly operating statement.

Department .... Month .... Year ....

Cost Centre	Code No.	Budget	Total amount spent	% of total	Amount spent last month	Amount spent this month	Balance

Weekly stock control sheet.

W/e 5 March ....

Product	Cost per unit (£p)	Total used	Cost (£p)
Detergent	0.38	14	6.08
Acid cleaner	0.63	8	5.04
Bleach	0.45	16	7.20
Liquid cream cleaner	0.45	12	5.40
Window cleaner	0.48	5	2.40
Metal polish — silver	0.83	—	—
Metal polish — brass	0.74	1	0.74
Furniture polish	0.62	7	4.34
Floor polish — solvent	0.90	—	—
Floor polish — emulsion	0.75	3	2.25
Spot-cleaner — carpets	1.65	3	4.95
Total cost			£36.90
Total number of rooms cleaned			1360
Cost per room			£0.028

Signed ...... R. Hurst ...... Head housekeeper

purchases and the amount of stock which has actually been used during the period. The figures are obtained by taking: the opening stock figure for the year, adding the amount spent during the accounting period and then subtracting the closing stock figure. This produces the value of the stock used – the closing stock figure does, of course, become the opening stock figure for the following year. It depends on the company policy how the stock is valued; it can be either at the price at which it has been bought or at the replacement value.

Accounts are produced for the completed year and should be compared with those from previous years for any variations in spending patterns. Many organizations subscribe to a Research Unit attached to one of the Universities or to a firm specializing in interfirm comparisons which compare the spending patterns in establishments similar in age, type of building and site. The cost per unit can then be compared to ensure that a department is not only operating efficiently by keeping within its budget, but is also providing the service at a price which is close to the average. A similar exercise is used in the National Health Service with hospitals being grouped on size, age and the type of patient such as in acute and general hospitals or long-term and geriatric units.

With all control systems, action must be taken to correct any discrepancy otherwise the whole procedure is a complete waste of time; the course of action needed will depend on the circumstances, but could take the form of increased supervision, better training and communication with staff by means of regular training 'half-hours', security and key control or revised working practices and frequencies.

9.4 Stock control

To prevent stock discrepancies and indiscriminate use, all stores, service rooms and cleaning cupboards must be kept locked with the keys held by the storekeeper or supervisor. Control starts with the placing of orders. The number of people authorized to place an order is usually limited to the Head Housekeeper or the Deputy and, occasionally, the storekeeper for routine orders. For preference the *Order Book* is in triplicate and the pages numbered; the top copy is sent to the supplier, the second copy is attached to the invoice or statement when it is passed for payment and the bottom copy retained in the department. When an order has been telephoned the order number must be given and the call should be followed up by the signed order.

Some suppliers send an *Advisory Note* as an advance warning that goods have been dispatched and when delivery may be expected; this is usually a carbon copy of the *Delivery Note* which is sent with the goods and lists the number and size of each item and is checked and signed to the effect that the supplies are as stated. A copy of this note is returned to the supplier; when it is not possible to check a delivery it is signed with the statement added that it is unchecked but so many containers have been received. The consignment must be checked as soon as possible after delivery and the supplier notified of any shortages or discrepancies.

Goods should be stacked in the store in such a way that they are used in rotation. In a large store, *bin cards* are used which record the date of all issues and receipts and the *re-order level*. The re-order level depends on the rate at which the commodity is used, the time-lag between the order being given and when the delivery is made and any advantages which are gained from bulk buying and trade discounts; it is calculated so that the new delivery arrives before stock runs out. The *value* of the *stock-holding* is usually a percentage of the yearly budget and is often somewhere between 5 and 10 per cent. The precise figure is a policy decision made to prevent too much money being used unprofitably.

Issues should be made at set times with entry to the store limited and the stores issued over a counter or a stable door. *Requisitions* or *indents* are completed either in duplicate or triplicate and signed by the supervisor needing the stores. When in duplicate, one copy is retained in the store and the second copy returned with the goods; when a third copy is used, this will be costed and debited to the section by the accountant. The second and third copy prevents a storeman covering up a discrepancy by marking it out on the store copy.

Issues can also be made directly from the store on a 'new for empty' or 'clean for dirty' basis or a *topping-up* system is used. By this method, the storekeeper or supervisor will load a trolley with the amount of stock which he expects to issue and will personally inspect all the cleaning or service rooms and 'top-up' the materials to the required level. This prevents over-issues and also checks that these service areas are kept in good order; it can also be quicker as there is no time lost by staff waiting to collect individual orders from the stores.

When goods are bought in bulk, they may need breaking down into smaller units for issue. When this happens, care must be taken in selecting and labelling the new containers so that there is no possibility that the contents can be mistaken for any food and drink; in the past, there have been too many cases of poisonous or corrosive cleaning materials, such as bleach or a descaler, being confused with something like lemonade and given to unsuspecting customers.

The balance on the bin-card is altered as the commodity is issued; *stock-sheets* are completed at the end of each day's issues. A separate stock-sheet is needed for each commodity and shows the cost, unit size, the receipts, issues and balance in addition to the maximum and minimum stock and re-order levels. There is usually a space for the monthly consumption figures at the bottom.

Year ending 19   Monthly consumption

	Jan.	Feb.	Mar.	Apr.	May	June	July	Aug.	Sept.	Oct.	Nov.	Dec.
Detergents — 5 litre	2	1	1	2	1	2						
Acid cleaner	25	21	30	26	25	22						
Bleach	48	52	47	50	52	46						

An *invoice* may be sent with the goods, or arrives later through the post, and shows the cost of each item; this is checked against the order and the delivery note and that all entries on the bin-cards and in the stock book have been made. When a discount is allowed for payment within 7 or 14 days, the invoice is passed for payment as soon as possible otherwise the invoices are generally kept until the *statement* arrives from the supplier, this is checked, the invoices are attached, the order number and the unit code is added and they are passed for payment.

Stock must be checked and costed at the end of each financial year and the figures passed to the accountant but it should also be checked much more frequently, often by spot-checking several items each week, or by taking a complete stock check every four or six weeks — depending on the value and on the accuracy of the storekeeper. Regular stock-taking discourages theft but also has the advantage of making the supervisor aware of the condition and turn-round of the stock. Stock should be checked and the results then compared with the stock-book figure; when possible, stock-taking should not be undertaken by the storekeeper to avoid any 'covering-up' of lost goods. One method of discouraging theft is to buy brands which are not available locally so they can be identified as coming from the establishment.

An *inventory* is a detailed list of the furniture and fittings which are in use in each room and should contain a brief description and the size of each article. This is necessary as, for instance, a rug could be a valuable Persian or it could be a cheap cotton or tufted mat and, unless, it is adequately described a substitution can be made without it being immediately obvious.

Many organizations arrange to buy 'under contract', that is, because of the size of the order they are able to negotiate a special price or discount rate often on the understanding that a certain quantity will be bought during the contract period and that the contractor will be the sole supplier. Contracts are usually renewed every year.

Buying under contract means that either the purchasing is done centrally with deliveries made to a central store from which each unit draws its stocks as they are needed, or it can mean that the unit continues to order stores direct from the supplier (quoting the contract number) and deliveries are made to the unit.

Records should be kept of all suppliers and prices – particularly for furniture, fabrics and fittings as considerable time can be wasted in trying to trace a supplier when replacements are required. Information is also often needed on the specification for fabrics or floor coverings such as shrinkage rates, fade resistancy or the methods for cleaning.

9.5 Exercise and discussion

1 In a comparatively rare afternoon when nothing seemed to be happening which demanded attention, the Executive Housekeeper decided to work out just how much money was contributed by her department towards the overhead costs of the hotel. The hotel has 240 twin-bedded rooms.

The cost of servicing a room is as follows:

Labour – for single occupancy,   25 minutes
        for double occupancy,   40 minutes
        for each cot or extra bed,   10 minutes
    Wages are £1.90 per hour.

Laundry – for each person, 2 sheets – laundry cost of   18p
                     2 pillowcases   8p
                     1 bath towel   16p
                     1 hand towel   10p
                     1 bathmat   10p

Cleaning materials – as per weekly issue sheet: the amount divided by the rooms cleaned – 3p per room.

Guest supplies—for each person: soap, toilet paper, matches, hair shampoo, advertising matter, stationery, etc. – 45p.

She turned up the records for the previous week and found that 1126 rooms had been let with double occupancy and 228 rooms with single occupancy. There had been 16 'extra' beds used.

The Hotel Tariff is: Double occupancy,   £44.25 per night.
                     Single occupancy,   £30.50 per night.
                     Extra beds charged at   £9.50 per night.

How much gross profit would the department have made during the week? And if the hotel had been running at 100 per cent occupancy.

The room-maids work a 40-hour week; if the staffing requirements are exact, how many should have been employed? (see p. 206).

What was the gross profit made by each maid?

After considering the results of her calculations for some time, the Housekeeper then started to wonder whether there might be a case for an all-round increase in pay?

2 The Auditor's Report states that there is £1250 stock discrepancy for linen and a small deficiency of £108 for Cleaning and Guest Supplies. Write the report that you send to your Manager stating your reaction to the report and what you intend to do about it.

10
Hotel Housekeeping

A chance customer will grade and judge a hotel as soon as he arrives at the entrance – is he attracted by the sign or impressed by the menu and the wine list – or is it the lights, the polished glass, the tubs of flowers and the cheerfulness and warmth of the staff? Given two hotels with similar prices and location, what is it that will draw the credit cards and cheque books to one building rather than to another – and keeps them there? What persuades a customer to return year after year?

A customer wants to know that he is welcome, that staff are courteous, attentive when needed, smart and well-dressed; he does not want to feel over-awed and out-of-place. The hotel should be warm and clean with the decor and furnishings reminding him of his own background whilst at the same time reflecting the characteristics of the country in which he is in and everyone should be able to find their way easily around the hotel without the embarrassment of asking 'where do I go for. . . ?'

By its appearance a hotel indicates the type of customer and the segment of the market in which it is interested – has it a brown leather, smoking club atmosphere, could it be a stately home or chintz and country, is it sedate and quiet for the older generation or full of bright lights, colour and excitement for the jet-set?

It is essential for Management to know what it is that makes a customer not come back and not recommend the hotel to his friends. It is often quite a small fault – a member of staff who has been too brusque, ashtrays left unemptied and the smell of stale smoke, messy toilets, fingermarks on the door-panels and dust in a corner. There is no complaint to the management but the guest does not return. A first impression is confirmed as soon as the customer crosses the threshold into Reception.

10.1 Accommodation

10.1.1 Reception

This is a prestige, area where appearance is important but, because it opens straight into the street and has the heaviest density of traffic in the building, it attracts the most dirt and needs constant attention to keep it looking fresh, tidy and attractive.

All floors should be protected. *Dust control mats* are the first line of defence and are designed to remove dust and dirt from shoes before it is carried into the building (Section 3.2.2).

(a) Floors

Both marble and terrazzo are very hard-wearing and functional, the appearance is good, they are difficult to damage and, although noisy and cold to the touch, if the colour is warm and the furnishings are bright, the impression is welcoming; both are easy to maintain with an emulsion floor dressing and should last as long as the building. When there is a seating area with chairs and coffee tables, a carpet is often fitted into the marble to provide comfort and a contrast of texture and colour. The carpet is not in the main traffic area and can be changed easily when required.

The most popular alternative to a hard floor is a heavy or medium-duty contract carpet with a wool/nylon pile – the weight of the carpet depending on the traffic-flow. A heavy contract tufted carpet or carpet squares are also suitable.

(b) Walls

The wall coverings must be durable and easy to clean. In addition, if the Reception area forms part of an escape route from the hotel under the Fire Precaution Act, it may have to conform with the Act's requirements and be finished with a flame-proof surface (Section 5.1.1).

(c) Lighting

Too high a level of lighting should be avoided, particularly at night as too great a contrast between interior and street lighting can be tiring and unpleasant. A level of between 150 and 350 lux is the normal recommendation but this is very dependent on the size of the area and on the colour scheme (Section 6.3).

(d) Furniture

The policy for buying furniture, carpets and fittings should be that the best possible quality is obtained so that all future maintenance and replacement costs are kept to the minimum.

Upholstered chairs and settees Chairs must be comfortable; not so low that an elderly person finds it difficult to get up nor so high that a guest will find it hard to cope with coffee and cake from a low lounge table. They must not take up too much space, be easy to carry and move, be hard-wearing and so constructed that damage is difficult. When buying, some hotel groups insist that, in addition to the finished product, a sample of the frame is also sent for inspection so that the constructional strength is clearly seen.

For comfort, the size and shape should meet the measurements of the average person; the majority of people will be comfortable when:

the seat height is 38–40 cm from the floor;
the seat depth is 42–44 cm;
the seat width is 50–52 cm;
the arm rest is 20 cm above the seat;
the backrest at a minimum height of 20 cm.

As with an upright chair for office or restaurant use, the seat should support the user so that he is not constantly flexing his muscles to stay in one place. The angle of the seat should be at about 7° from the horizontal and, as no one sits at a 90° angle, the most comfortable position for the backrest is at an angle of 105° from the horizontal.

Modern upholstered furniture is cushioned with latex or a synthetic plastic foam which is a fire hazard. As far as possible, this foam should be of flame-retardent quality and should be covered with a flame-retardent fabric in order to minimize the risk of fire from a smouldering cigarette end. All furniture sold after 1982 must carry a warning if there is any fire risk from the fabric.

The fabric chosen should be appropriate to the style of the building and should be easy to clean. Chairs with washable loose covers which can be zipped on and off make cleaning and repair easy and have the advantage that they provide uniformity to a variety of different chair and settee bases. Synthetic-fibred velvet, brocades, tweeds or vinyl 'leathercloths' are frequently used – but loose woven fabrics should be avoided. Wooden arms, rather than upholstered arms, are best for a heavy-duty area. To prevent stains and wear becoming too obvious, a medium-toned colour and a small pattern are used.

There is a nice description of a lounge and its chairs in *At Bertram's Hotel* by Agatha Christie (Collins; London, 1972) 'There was a general appearance of rich red velvet and plushy cosiness. The arm-chairs were not of this time and age. They were well above the level of the floor, so that rheumatic old ladies had not to struggle in an undignified manner in order to get to their feet. The seats of the chairs did not, as in so many modern high-priced arm-chairs, stop halfway between the thigh and the knee, thereby inflicting agony on those suffering from arthritis and sciatica; and they were not all of a pattern. There were straight backs and reclining backs, different widths to accommodate the slender and the obese. People of almost any dimension could find a comfortable chair at Bertram's.'

Lounge tables These are usually low between 30 and 38 cm high with the surface made from glass, marble, ceramic tiles or treated wood so that any damage is minimal. Large ashtrays are provided.

(e) Decorations

Flowers or an important collection of paintings, cartoons or sketches, tapestries or an antique are used as a focal point to attract the guest.

Lighting is subdued but in a lounge area, *secondary lighting* in the form of standard or side lights is usually placed for those customers who wish to read or write.

The *decorative schemes* used in all public and function rooms should be carefully chosen as these rooms are frequently hired by different organizations, not only for social gatherings but also for trade and fashion exhibitions where the colours and furnishings provide a backing for any displays and, as such, should show them and the guests off to the greatest advantage.

10.1.2 Guest rooms

The Guest room is the temporary home and refuge for travellers of many different nationalities and as such should offer privacy and quietness, warmth, security, and facilities for relaxation; it should provide a space to rest and to take stock of a new, and often strange, environment in clean and congenial surroundings.

To a certain extent, the standard of the accommodation is dependent on what the customer expects and what he considers is value for the price charged – and on what other, possibly better, facilities are offered by other hotels in the neighbourhood. What is acceptable for a one-night stopover may prove very cramped and irritating if used for several days when the customer finds there is absolutely no place to put anything and the lights are so shaded that it is impossible to read in bed.

The minimum recommended size for a single room is 9.9 m^2 and 13.5 m^2 for a twin-bedded room.

(a) Privacy and quietness

A guest's expectancy of an undisturbed occupancy of their room often conflicts with the housekeeping need to clean and service. To prevent disturbance, the guest must use the 'lock-out' button on the door-lock and should display the 'Do not Disturb' door-tag. Nevertheless, the Housekeeper will check daily to enquire when it is convenient to service the room and note the requirements on her Room Report.

Where a room could be overlooked, net curtains are always provided.

Quietness can be difficult to obtain. The Housekeeper should ensure that staff work quietly, doors are not constantly banged and that all trolleys, locks, doors and equipment are well-oiled and smooth-running. Vacuum cleaners and floor machines should be quiet and unobtrusive.

The transmission of noise and vibration can be reduced by sensible planning. Areas which generate noise, such as kitchens, incinerators, generators, boilerhouses, bars and discos should be grouped together and separated by doors to provide a quiet zone for the guest rooms, lounges and writing rooms. The problems caused by impact and vibration can be reduced when rooms are planned back-to-back so that bathroom and wardrobe areas are adjoining. Impact noise is also reduced by using heavy carpeting. All textiles are porous and are, therefore, sound absorbers so that all furnishings, carpets, lined curtains, wall coverings and acoustic ceiling tiles, play an important part in noise reduction.

It is at the planning stage that the main reductions can be made in external traffic noise by siting guest rooms at right angles to the road and by designing angled windows and balconies to form a sound barrier. Trees and shrubs also help to absorb traffic noise. Double glazing has a dual purpose; a distance of 150 mm between the panes of glass will both reduce noise and the loss of heat (see Section 6.1).

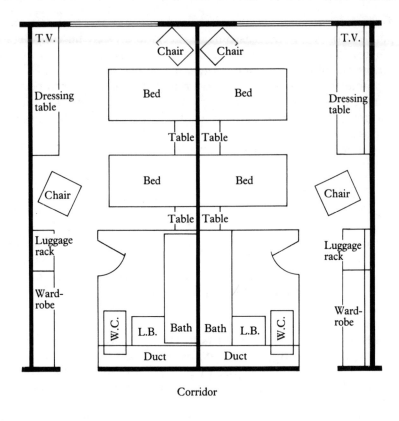

Typical layout for guest rooms.

(b) Warmth

It is a much-felt wish of many travellers that they can turn off or adjust the room temperature at will; whether heat (or coolness) is provided by air conditioning or conventional radiators, the control switch should work. A comfortable temperature for a guest room is between 18° and 21°C (65°–70°F).

There is no need to heat rooms to this level if they are unoccupied; it is sufficient to keep a room comfortably aired and free from dampness at a temperature of 13°C (55°C).

A new device, now being tested, is based on a heat control system which automatically turns off the heat when the room is empty. When the guest checks out, the key is handed to the Receptionist who returns it to a special micro-switch hook; the weight of the key is sufficient to cut the circuit and will switch off the radiator in that room. This system can be installed for both 'water' radiators and for electrically controlled heating, but not for any night storage units. During very cold weather, the key can be placed in the usual 'pigeon-hole' and the heating left on.

Alternatively, many hotels are instructing maids to turn the heating off when the room is serviced and the Hall Porter or the Receptionist will turn it on when the guest is shown to the room.

Much heat is lost through the window; by far the best method of reducing this loss is by installing double-glazing but a contribution is also made through the use of heavy curtains which can have an interlining of a flannelette material and are backed with an insulating fabric. These fabrics are coated on one side with aluminium particles which prevent most of the heat passing through the fabric and reflect it back into the room. South-facing rooms can become unpleasantly hot in the summer and the same principle is used to maintain an even temperature in the room. Net curtain fabric backed with metal particles will reflect a proportion of the sun's heat out from the room.

(c) Security

The problems of keys, their safekeeping and the responsibilities of the keyholders are discussed in Sections 5.3 and 10.2.3.

A guest should always use the lock-out button at night, a chain is usually provided and most doors now have a spyhole so that a guest can check before letting a stranger into the room. All guests should be encouraged to use the hotel safe deposit for the custody of money, jewellery or passport. Unless this is done, under the 1956 Hotel Proprietor's Act, the liability of a hotel for loss is limited to £50 for any one item and to a total of £100. This limit is very low and there have recently been discussions, instigated by the Department of Trade and by the Law Society, that this limit should be raised. The new levels suggested have been anything from £900 to £5000 or a sum related to the daily charge for the room.

It is only in rooms used for long-term residence that furniture would be fitted with a key.

(d) Furnishings

Beds It can be very difficult to sleep in strange surroundings or when overtired so it is essential that the bed is warm and comfortable.

Most hotel rooms are twin-bedded; the provision of two beds rather than one bed makes a basic difference in room size of 3.6 m² and increases the selling price for each square metre of room.

In a single room, the bed can be single but is often double-sized so that it could, if needed, be let to two people: a few hotels use double-sized beds in twin-bedded rooms so that the room can be let for family and multiple use; otherwise, folding or 'Vee' beds and cots are used when needed. The recommended standard size for a single bed is 100 × 200 cm, and for a double bed, 150 × 200 cm.

The majority of beds in use are of the *divan* type. These either have a padded base or a base made from wire-mesh, heavy webbing or slatted wooden boards – although these last are more suitable for staff or student accommodation. The divan is usually made from wood or metal or moulded from polypropylene foam. Whereas the divan has legs fitted or screwed to the base, a *bedstead* can be taken apart so that the headboard, endboard, base and mattress can be moved and stored separately.

A headboard is essential to make the guest comfortable when sitting up in bed, it ensures that the bedding stays in place and, will protect the wall from the damage arising from greasy hair or scratches from curlers and hairpins. The board is usually part of the bed but can be a fixed panel on the wall into which is incorporated the bedlight, electrical control switches, radio, television and call systems and fire detectors. The panel should be cushioned and easy to clean.

Endboards are not so necessary and can impede bed-making if they extend too far above the mattress. A good, compromise height for a bed is 60 cm to the top of the mattress; this gives a reasonable height for the guest and is not too low for bed-making and cleaning. Castors are essential to prevent damage to the floor as the bed is moved.

Studio beds are usually single-sized and so designed that they slide under a back fitment during the day so that the width is reduced to 43 cm which makes them comfortable to use as settees.

Mattresses fall into two types: those with springs and those made from latex, polyester or polyurethane. A sprung-interior mattress is generally considered the most comfortable and most luxurious. There are various grades. The cheapest have rows of narrow-diameter wire springs held together at top and bottom by strong helical wires, a more expensive mattress has each spring enclosed in its own pocket, 'pocket' springing, with each spring under tension so the mattress is firmer. A conventional mattress is padded with horse-hair, cotton wadding and covered with a cotton ticking but increasingly rubber or non-rubber foam is being used instead and some have the springs set horizontally inside a 'foam box'.

A foam mattress is lighter and slimmer, hygienic and vermin-free and are used extensively in hospitals, for student and staff accommodation and in the cheaper end of the market; because it is non-absorbent, it is better for use in a seasonal hotel where the bedding has to be stored during the winter. However, foam mattresses have two disadvantages – there have been cases of spontaneous combustion when foam mattresses have been stored tightly together in a warm room and they constitute a fire risk wherever there may be people smoking in bed. This does not mean they should not be used as a sprung-interior mattress will also burn. To quote a recent Information Paper from the Building Research Establishment on *Ignition and burning characteristics of continental quilts*, – 'The most rapid rates of burning and higher compartment temperatures were developed with polyester-filled quilts on beds with polyurethane foam mattresses with complete burn-out of the quilt/coverslip/bed assemblies in 10 to 20 minutes. Lower burning rates, but longer fire durations, 40 to 75 minutes, were observed with quilts/coverslips on beds with spring interior mattresses, which tended to produce the highest levels of smoke and toxic gases. Fire development depended to some extent on the quilt filling material but to a much greater extent on the composition of the mattress. Temperature measurements suggest that for polyurethane foam mattresses, polyester-filled quilts produced a more severe fire and feather-filled quilts a less severe fire than a similar bed with conventional bedclothes. . . .' Flame-retardent foam should specified and flame-retardent material used to cover both types of mattress.

For the sake of those customers who have back problems, the Housekeeper may be asked to provide bedboards. These are placed under the mattress.

Pillows have the same types of filling as those used for a continental quilt but in addition, polyurethane foam can be used. A luxury hotel will provide pillows with a down or a down and feather filling whilst a lower grade hotel will probably use feather or foam. Foam pillows are provided when a customer has asthma or bronchitis problems.

Other furniture All furniture should have a surface finish which is heat-, scratch-, water- and stain-resistant and, preferably, one which does not require any application of polish but merely needs rubbing up with a dry duster. The furniture should include the following items.

A *bedside table* should have sufficient space for an early-morning tea-tray, a book and such personal property as a watch, clock or glasses. Space may be needed for a *bedside lamp* although this is best as a fixture in the bedhead as it cannot then be knocked over or damaged so easily.

Hanging and storage space need not be extensive in a transient hotel where the guest is unlikely to unpack. The Design Council's publication on Hotel Furniture recommends that there should be space for 6 hangers for each person and a minimum drawer or shelf area of 0.7 m² for a single room and 1.2 m² for a double room; in luxury and longer-stay establishments, these areas can be doubled and trebled as most people find that there is never enough space when unpacking. It is easier for cleaning and there is less chance of a guest leaving property behind if shelves are provided for storage rather than drawers.

The *dressing table* top is also used for writing; the minimum recommendation for the surface area is 0.6 m² but, again, a larger area is desirable when possible. The *mirror* should be well-lit and sufficiently large for the guest to have a full-length view. A drawer is usually provided for the customer's cosmetics and small items – although many hotels have the distressing habit of filling this with the hotel folder and other advertising material.

A *luggage rack* is essential – in a transient hotel, this will be a permanent piece of furniture with a back to it to prevent suitcases damaging the wall, but a small, folding luggage rack is more likely in a luxury hotel where it is put away in the wardrobe when not in use.

An *easy chair* for each person, a *coffee table*, *television*, *radio* and *telephone* complete the furnishings in most function-built hotels.

A bedroom can get surprisingly dirty, particularly when families are accommodated, so it is advisable to have a wall covering which is washable. Silk and other fabrics can look beautiful, particularly if they match the curtains and covers, but can also be a Housekeeper's nightmare in the effort to keep them clean and unstained. Mirrors are often used to lighten a room, make it appear larger and give added sparkle but, when used as a wall finish, can also be a cleaning problem.

Most rooms have fitted carpets – a 'shaggy' carpet looks modern and introduces a different texture into the room but is difficult to clean and frequently needs raking to remove all footmarks.

10.1.3 The Bathroom

The amount of heat, steam and water generated in the bathroom and the assortment of chemicals used by the guest and the cleaning staff means that this is not an easy place to keep in good order.

The minimum recommended size for a bathroom is 3.5 m² which provides reasonable space for the bath and shower, wash basin and lavatory; if a bidet is installed, an extra $\frac{1}{2}$ m^2 is required. In most modern hotels, the bathroom is usually sited internally with the ducts for plumbing and electricity laid along the internal walls of the corridor for ease of maintenance but this can cause problems with ventilation and humidity unless the air conditioning or extraction fan systems are extremely efficient.

(a) Floors

As there is the risk of flooding, these floors should be solid with a floor drain – which also makes cleaning easier. Tiles fixed with adhesive are unsuitable anywhere where there is the risk of excess water on the floor so that the most practical and hygienic surface is marble, terrazzo or ceramic tiles laid in an impervious cement grouting. When a warm colour is used, the room will look warm but obviously will not feel warm to the bare feet so bathmats must always be supplied for each guest.

Some hotels use a fitted carpet, rubber or foam-backed to prevent shrinkage but even though a carpet has a silicone finish to prevent water being absorbed, the backing can gradually become wet and will smell or develop mildew and moulds if it cannot be dried quickly.

(b) Walls

With so much dampness and steam, it is important that walls should be non-absorbent and easy to wipe down. The most practical finish is ceramic tiles – coloured, patterned or textured; preferably, these should be fitted to ceiling height but for a cheaper, but less permanent finish, laminated melamine, oil paint or a washable vinyl is often used.

High humidity increases the likelihood of mould growing on the grouting between the tiles, even with daily cleaning. A mould inhibitor should either be mixed in with the grouting before the tiles are fixed or can be painted on afterwards.

At least one good-sized *mirror* is fitted above the washbasin. Mirrors are very useful to reflect light into a dark room and to create the illusion of space but they do have to be impeccably clean, a standard which is difficult to achieve quickly over large areas.

(c) Light fittings

All light fittings should be moisture-proof; there should be one to illuminate the mirror and a second central light. For safety, all switches are operated either by a pull-cord or are placed outside the bathroom. The only 'power' point which is allowed is a small 'universal' razor socket usually fitted close to the mirror; which is always double-insulated for safety.

All *fittings*, such as clothes hooks, holders, rails and screws should be rust-proof and made from chromium-plate or stainless steel.

(d) The bath

The most durable baths are still those made from cast iron with a porcelain enamel finish. Polyester/glass fibre and acrylic baths are much lighter but scratch easily and show cigarette burns – although some of these marks can be removed by rubbing with metal polish, a very fine abrasive or by burnishing with a nylon pad.

The normal bath size is 1700 mm but there is a lot to be said for installing one of the shorter bath-tubs found in America and Canada which will save many gallons of hot water. For the convenience of elderly guests, the base of the bath should be ridged or embossed at the tap end, to prevent slipping and a hand-rail provided. A rim height of 550 mm is a compromise between what is easiest for the guest to use and how far the maid has to stoop for cleaning.

It is simpler to fit taps to the wall rather than on the bath as plumbing costs will then be avoided when the bath has to be replaced. All taps should indicate 'hot' and 'cold' and be so designed that the valve does not overheat and become dangerous when turning the water off. Washers must be replaced as soon as possible – one hot tap dripping at the rate of 2 drops a second is wasting 380 litres a month and, particularly in a business concern where the water is metered and charged on the amount used, is expensive without even considering the cost of heating.

The soap-dish is fitted within reach on the wall as is the towel rail.

Even if a 'Guest Laundry Service' is provided, nothing seems to stop a guest doing a certain amount of washing so it saves trouble if a small rail, with or without hangers, is fitted above the bath so that the 'smalls' can drip-dry without the risk of causing damage to hotel property by the guest draping wet articles over the backs of chairs, radiators or even over the bedside lamp in an endeavour to dry and air.

The grouting or join between the bath and the wall should be carefully maintained as water seeping through can cause dry rot.

(c) Shower

Many hotels install a shower fitment in the bath; the shower head can be flexible or fixed, if it is fixed the most convenient height to avoid wet hair and for cleaning is 1660 mm. For preference, there should be a thermostatic mixing valve. As a shower only uses between 18 and 23 litres of hot water as opposed to 136 to 180 litres for a bath, it is obvious that, from the hotel point of view, showers should be encouraged. When space is at a premium, a shower, with a base container of 610 mm^2 or 760 mm^2 can often be installed when there is no room for a bath. The base is usually made from porcelain or terrazzo. Soap dishes, clothing and towel rails should be positioned out of reach of the water but in reach of the occupant.

Most shower curtains are made from non-absorbent plastic sheeting or nylon so that they can be regularly wiped down and dried to remove any trace of mould or soap scum and dirt deposits left by the steam. Alternatively, a perspex or glass shower-screen is fitted; this should be frosted or patterned as a clear finish shows every smear and needs prolonged polishing. The metal grooves holding the screen are also difficult to keep clean.

(f) Washbasin

Although washbasins are made from enamel, polyester/glass fibre or acrylic, porcelain is still the only material which does not scratch or burn. They come in a wide range of sizes but a basin which is approximately 560 × 410 mm installed at a height of 760 mm is suitable for a hotel. When it is fitted into a vanitory unit, a scratch- and burn-resistent material such as a laminated melamine or imitation marble-terrazzo finish is essential.

(g) Toilet or lavatory

Because they need to be impervious with a very smooth surface and extremely strong, fireclay, earthenware, vitreous china – and very occasionally, stainless steel, are used to make the lavatory bowls, urinals and bidets. The seat is usually made from plastic; this is more hygienic than wood and is easy to clean or replace when damaged. The standard height is 406 mm, plus the thickness of the seat, although it is possible to have a lower height for children or older people.

The most efficient cistern is the syphonic system rather than the flush type as it is important that the water should discharge in 5 seconds with a fast, quiet refill.

Most of the problems encountered in bathroom cleaning are caused by hard water. Hard water is alkaline and is either temporarily or permanently hard. Temporary hardness is caused by bicarbonates of magnesia and calcium dissolved in the water; when this water is left standing for any length of time, these salts are precipitated and form a crusty scale of 'fur' fixed to the surface of a lavatory bowl, the interior of pipes, or a kettle; the rate of precipitation increases with the temperature of the water. Sulphates of calcium and magnesia cause permanent hardness but, whilst these salts do not precipitate, their presence – and that of the bicarbonates – increases both the amount of soap needed and the resulting soap scum which is deposited as a tide-mark in the bath. Approximately, an additional 100 g. of soap is needed for every 500 litres of water if the water is hard.

The main problems caused by hard water are:

(1) Soap, body dirt and grease deposited as scum on baths, washbasins, tiles and surrounds by water and steam.

(2) Calcium and magnesium deposits forming an encrustation on taps, plugs and shower heads. The same deposits cause problems in the lavatory bowl and, if left, cause discoloration, roughness and a good breeding site for bacteria.

(3) Increased cleaning costs for staff time, soap and cleaning agents and the eventual replacement of fittings.

An added problem is caused by blue and brown stains from copper and iron salts in the water. The installation of a water-softening plant prevents most of these problems – otherwise, chemicals are needed to repair the damage but these, in their turn can affect the surfaces particularly chromium taps and shower heads (see Section 3.3.4).

10.1.3 Cleaning schedules

(a) Instructions for guest room cleaning

(1) Place trolley outside room in the corridor and wedge open the door using the rubber wedge provided.

(2) Pull back the heavy curtains. Open the window or adjust the air conditioning.

(3) Remove room service trolleys and trays and place in serviceroom.

(4) Empty ashtrays into metal ashbin and put them in the washbasin to wash, along with the bathroom glasses.

(5) Empty bathroom and guest room wastebins into container on trolley and clean.

(6) Flush toilet, put in disinfectant. Leave and continue guest room cleaning.

(7) Strip beds, place dirty linen on trolley and resheet. Check for underwear or pyjamas which could have been left behind. Check the condition of the blankets, mattress and covers.

Never leave dirty linen on the floor – it looks untidy and could cause an accident.

(8) Leave dust to settle in the room and clean the bathroom (see p. 194).

(9) Then, dust and polish all furniture. Start at the door and dust everything in contact with the wall, then all furniture in the centre of the room so nothing is missed. Don't forget pictures, mirrors, lamps, ledges, drawer handles and the back of the television. Check wardrobe for laundry bags (2) and hangers (6 for each person) placed the right way round. Check stationery drawer, telephone directories, Gideon's Bible.

(10) Close window or adjust air conditioning.

(11) Check and replace guest supplies.

(12) Check that all electrical fittings and television are working – if not, enter on section list and tell the Floor Housekeeper. Report anything missing or damaged.

(13) Replace ashtrays and wastebins.

(14) Vacuum floor, check upholstery.

(15) Before leaving, check the room appearance – curtains, pictures and covers straight? No smears on the mirror or furniture? Use air freshener if needed.

(16) Make sure the door is locked and cross off the room number from the section list.

If the room is occupied, check when it will be convenient for it to be serviced. Tidy but do not open drawers or the wardrobe and do not touch open handbags, wallets or suitcases as you might be blamed if anything is missing or broken. Do not throw away anything that is not in the wastebin, even a small scrap of paper could be important.

If you find a large sum of money in the room you must report this to the Floor Housekeeper, who will suggest to the guest that it is put in the safe deposit.

Usual Guest room Supplies
   Wardrobe –
      2 laundry bags and lists
      1 valet's bag
      Extra pillow and 1 blanket
      1 luggage rack

Dressing table –
on top
    1 service booklet
    1 tent card
    1 guest questionnaire
    1 ashtray with matches –
in top drawer
    Hotel folder containing: 3 sheets of notepaper, 3 envelopes, 2
        postcards, 1 security letter, 2 luggage labels
    1 sewing kit
    1 pen
Coffee table –
    Ashtray with matches
    Hotel magazine
By telephone –
    1 message pad
    1 pen
    1 ashtray with matches
– on bottom shelf
    2 telephone books, A–K and L–Z
    1 dialling code book
On handle inside door –
    Door-tag, 'Do Not Disturb' and 'Make-up Room' card
By bed –
    1 room service menu
    1 breakfast order door-tag.

(b) Instructions for bathroom cleaning

(1) Wash and dry ashtrays from guest room and bathroom. Empty and clean sanibin.

(2) Clean glasses and polish with the teatowel provided. Clean glass-shelf and replace glasses.

(3) Clean the bath paying attention to the waste-grid, overflow, plug, chain and taps. Wipe over the bath-panels, tiles, shower fitments and shower curtain, towel rail, soap-holder.

(4) Clean toilet using the toilet brush and wipe over the outside, both sides of the seat, cistern, flush-handle pipes and tiles. Use *red* cleaning cloth for this, then rinse and replace in polythene bag – this cloth is *only* to be used for toilet cleaning. At the end of the day, wash it and leave to dry.

(5) Wash your hands. Now clean the washbasin paying attention to

the waste-grid, overflow, plug and chain, taps, the underside of the bowl, vanitory unit, panels and mirror.

(6) Place clean towels on rail, bathmat on side of bath. Check toilet paper and replenish guest supplies.

(7) Wash floor using bucket from trolley and the sponge mop. Take care with corners and the area behind the door. Water must be changed when dirty.

(8) Replace sanibin.

(9) Leave bathroom door ajar and turn off lights.

Usual bathroom supplies

(1) *On bath* – large soap in holder. Bathmats over side of bath. Shower curtain pulled neatly to right and hanging inside bath.

(2) *Towel rail* – 2 bath towels and 2 hand towels neatly folded.

(3) *Shelf above washbasin* – on right, 2 soaps, 2 glasses and 2 face flannels – on left, ashtray with matches.

(4) *Box on wall* – tissues. Hair shampoo.

(5) *Toilet holder* – 2 toilet rolls, one with wrapper left on.

(6) *Floor* – sanibin, left-hand side by lavatory.

(7) *Shelf by lavatory* – 4 sanibags.

For V.I.P. rooms – flower in vase, right-hand side of washbasin.

Cleaning and drying cloths should be issued to maids; if this is not done, the maid will use the first item in sight which is probably a towel or a pillowcase. This should not be allowed as the cleaning chemicals will weaken and damage the fabric. It is extremely unhygienic if a dirty towel is used, even if it is clean there is then the cost of laundry and depreciation to be considered.

10.2 Staffing and organization

In a large hotel, the housekeeping department is under the control of the *Executive Housekeeper*. He or she is a member of the management team and will be fully responsible for the standard of cleaning and maintenance in the rooms, the staff, stock and equipment, the preparation of estimates and the control of the budget. She may also have responsibility for furnishings and the decorative schemes. A *Head Housekeeper* has not the same wide range of responsibilities; instead of reporting directly to the General Manager, the department may form part of the responsibilities of the Staff Manager or one of the Senior Assistant Managers who will then have the ultimate control of estimates and the budget, selection of staff and the refurbishing of rooms.

There will be a *Deputy* or *Senior Assistant Housekeeper*. The number of Assistant Housekeepers and Floor Housekeepers employed depends both on the number of staff and on the spread of hours through which the department is operating. In a small hotel, the department may only be staffed between the hours of 0700 and 1500 or 1600 hours but a city-centre hotel may bring early staff on duty at 0630 hours and provide cover until 2200 or 2300 hours at night whilst some of the Airport hotels have to provide a 24-hour service.

A *Floor Supervisor* will be responsible for the standard of cleanliness and maintenance of between fifty and one hundred rooms – perhaps two floors of 36 rooms or three floors of 30 rooms, the number being related to the layout of the hotel and to the standard expected. This means that she has the responsibility for the work of between five and seven room-maids and a houseporter. The supervisory ratio is high but the bulk of the work is concerned with room inspection. Usually, each room is checked twice, the first time, as soon as possible after the guest's departure to report damage, maintenance defects and lost property and again, after servicing to ensure that cleanliness, maintenance and the appearance of the room is at the required level and that the temperature and air freshness are acceptable. This helps to eliminate any subsequent dispute with customers or staff regarding the state of the room. When she is satisfied with the standard, the room is handed back to Reception for re-letting. In addition, most Floor Housekeepers work on a rota system for early, day or evening shifts.

When on early duty, the Supervisor is responsible for compiling both the housekeeper's report and the maids' worklist which show the departures, occupied and vacant rooms and whether they are of single, double or multiple occupancy; she will sign out the section keys to the maids and keys and bleeps to the housekeepers and re-allocate the work if there are any absentees (see pp. 197 and 198).

An evening-duty Housekeeper copes with any work left unfinished on the floors, late departures, guest requests, turning-down beds and must also ensure that all section keys are returned and checked (p. 204).

Each Housekeeper may also have some special responsibility for the issuing of stores, maintenance, equipment or training.

Both the Executive Housekeeper and the Hotel Manager will spot-check a percentage of rooms each week to ensure that the overall standard for the hotel is maintained.

A *room-maid* will have a section of between 12 and 15 rooms, each en suite with bathroom, to clean and service every day. The number

Maid's section list.

Maid ....   Date ....

Floor ....

Section ....

Extra rooms ....

....

....

....

Maid's Signature ....

....

Housekeeper's Signa-
ture ....

....

Room	Dep.	Occ.	Vac.	Remarks
01				
02				
03				
04				
04				
05				
06				
07				
08				
09				
10				
11				
12				
13				
14				
15				

will vary from one hotel to another as it depends on the standard of the hotel, the size of the rooms and the way in which they are furnished. The maid may also be asked to clean extra rooms or a 'split' section if there are staff shortages and for this she will receive additional payment.

As a means of reducing costs and of creating a more satisfying job, a number of hotels have introduced an intermediate grade of 'super' or 'key' maid. A key-maid is a maid who has consistently produced a high standard of work; she will have the responsibility of checking and handing back her own rooms to Reception. Spot checks will, of course, still be made by the Housekeeper and by the Manager so as to maintain a high, overall standard. She may also deputize for the housekeepers and so test her capability for promotion to this grade. Logically, however, this trend could lead to the abolition of the Floor Housekeeper.

Houseporters are employed to remove rubbish and dirty linen from the floors and may also restock the service rooms with clean linen and cleaning materials. They also help to move furniture, hang curtains,

Housekeeper's report.

Floor ....   Floor ....

Room	Dep.	Occ.	Vac.	Remarks	Room	Dep.	Occ.	Vac.	Remarks
01					01				
02					02				
03					03				
04					04				
05					05				
06					06				
07					07				
08					08				
09					09				
10					10				
11					11				
12					12				
13					13				
14					14				
15					15				
16					16				
17					17				
18					18				
19					19				
20					20				
21					21				
22					22				

Room	Dep.	Occ.	Vac.	Remarks	Room	Dep.	Occ.	Vac.	Remarks
23					23				
24					24				
25					25				
26					26				
27					27				
28					28				
29					29				
30					30				
31					31				
32					32				

Date ....

Signature ....

Maintenance request form.

Maintenance

Date 27 March ......   Job number 1608 ....

Location Room 404 ...

Fault Dripping Hot Water Tap ....

on wash basin ....

....

....

                              Signed J. Flowers FL H/kor .....

Job completed ....

                              Signed ....

---

put up beds and cots and may do some of the corridor and service area cleaning.

The *Linen room Staff*, headed by the Linenkeeper, control the supply of linen throughout the hotel and may also be responsible for staff uniforms, guest's laundry, the washing of net curtains and checking the condition of the heavy curtains and upholstery.

Organization Chart for a large Hotel

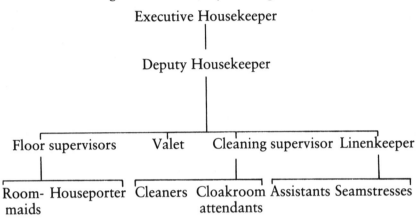

In a large 4- or 5-star hotel, a *valet* is usually available to look after the clothes and shoes of guests. He usually has a small room near the linen room where he can press, remove stains and polish shoes as required.

The Housekeeper may, or may not be responsible for cleaning the public and function rooms in the hotel and the staff areas. In many hotels, this can operate as a separate department. The work is done at night under the control of a *night cleaning supervisor* since the bulk of the work has to be completed before the guests start to use the hotel facilities and the Reception and Restaurant become busy. In a small hotel, this work is often done by the room-maids between 0630 and 0900 hours before they start room cleaning.

10.2.1 A routine day

To ensure smooth working, the Housekeeper depends on a very close liaison with the maintenance department and with Reception and the Advance Booking Office.

Arrival and departure lists are sent to the Housekeeping Office either last thing in the evening or they are compiled by the night staff and are available when the early-duty floor housekeeper arrives. This list shows the expected room status for that day with all departures, occupied, vacant, V.I.P. and special rooms and the details of single, double and multiple occupancy.

The floor housekeeper transfers this information to the *Section Lists* which are handed to each maid as she arrives on duty; with it, the maid receives the *pass key* for that section of rooms. The key is either on a chain which is worn around the waist as a belt or it is clipped on to a belt or pocket on her uniform so that there is no chance of her mislaying it or it being stolen. The floor housekeeper will also make out the housekeeper's reports for the floors (Figures 10.2 and 10.3).

In most hotels, *departure rooms* are inspected by the floor housekeeper as soon as they are vacated. They are checked for any damage or loss so that the guest can be charged for this before leaving the hotel. A check is also made for maintenance defects and the relevant maintenance request put through (Figure 10.4).

When the room has been serviced, it is again thoroughly checked to ensure that cleaning standards are correct, maintenance has been carried out, all guest supplies, stationery and advertising brochures are in place and the overall appearance and smell of the room is inviting.

A *departure* room is thoroughly cleaned by the maid – that is, it is daily and weekly cleaned; an *occupied* room is daily cleaned only and the maintenance is checked. All hotels have a strict rule that a maid does not touch any guest's property and no drawers or wardrobes are opened even to put away clothes and belongings. An *unoccupied* room is rechecked as soon as it is possible each day to ensure it is still up to standard, it is aired and dust-free. This is necessary as it is not unknown for maintenance or other staff to obtain a pass key and spend the afternoon watching sport on the colour television or for the room to have been let to a 'chance' customer without housekeeping being informed.

When a room is occupied for a longer period than the average of two or three days, a *key job* is added to the daily work. A key job could consist of cleaning the backs of the radiators, polishing furniture or the windows so that all parts of the room are cleaned in rotation.

Occupancy is checked against the Reception List to make sure that a single 'let' has not been used for double or triple occupancy. The housekeeper will also report any room where there is little or no luggage.

Hotel policy for V.I.P. lettings varies but it is usual to place in these rooms some of the special V.I.P. supplies such as flowers, fruit, a box of chocolates or a bottle of wine.

A room-maid has to be flexible and is expected to service a room as soon as possible after it has been vacated so that it can be re-let and arriving guests are not inconvenienced. To avoid too much disturbance, guests are asked to use a *Do Not Disturb* door-tag; however, if this is still in place in the afternoon, it is reported to the floor housekeeper and it is her responsibility to telephone the guest and enquire when it will be convenient for the room to be serviced and the maid is then informed. When no service is required, this is noted on her room report but if she gets no reply to her call she will notify either the Head Housekeeper or the Security Manager and the room will be entered and checked to make sure that nothing is wrong.

It is traditional that a maid works in a room with the door wedged open and her trolley outside; this protects the maid from any suspicion of too much curiosity or theft as the guest will automatically know that the room is being cleaned – and the housekeeper knows where to find the maid. Rooms must never be left unlocked.

At the end of her shift, the maid will tidy and replenish the contents of her trolley and clean and empty the vacuum cleaner. The section list is signed by the floor housekeeper to confirm that the work is completed and any 'extra' rooms serviced are recorded so that payment can be made, the pass key is returned and the maid is free to go off duty.

In a large hotel, the *evening shift* will complete the work not finished during the day and service late departure rooms (p. 204).

In a 4- or 5-star hotel, beds are turned down for the night. When this is done, the maid will pull the curtains, check and empty ash-trays and wastebins, tidy the bathroom and turn down the covers on the bed – if it has been used by the guest, she may need to re-sheet. Some hotels make the nice gesture of leaving a sweet or a small bar of chocolate on the pillow for each guest.

In a busy, transient hotel, the policy may be for the guest to turn down his own bed or it may be left 'turned down' when it is made in the morning.

Any article which a guest gives to a maid must be declared to the Housekeeper who will make out a *package pass*; this authorizes the maid to take the item from the building and should be shown to the door-keeper or to Security as she leaves (p. 199).

All *lost property* must be handed into the Housekeeping Office for safekeeping; there, it is *labelled* and its description entered into the *lost property book* so that it can be identified and returned to the owner – after the claimant has described it fully. If no claim is made, it is the usual practice either for the item to be returned to the finder or it is sold

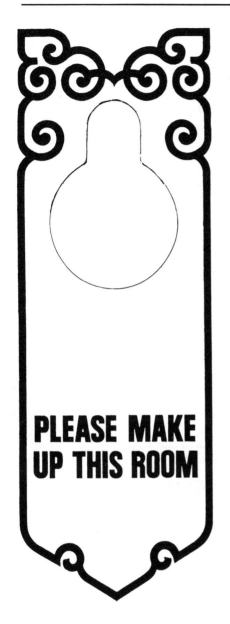

Hand-over from dayshift.

Supervisor .... Floor . Date .					
Rooms not checked		Dep. not left		Evening service	Day lets
Occ.	Dep.	Luggage	Not packed	What time	Late checkout
Flowers	Extra towels, beds or cots	Maintenance to check		Out of order rooms and why	Special requests
Rooms checked by evening housekeeper					
Occ.	Dep.	V.I.P.s	Stopovers	Discrepancies	
Signed .... Evening supervisor.					

Package pass

Department .Housekeeping..   Date 27 March..

   This is to certify that .Miss J. Flower.............

has permission to take .Bottle of Sherry - from.....
              Guest in Room 224
from the hotel.

       Signed R. Hurst.................
           Housekeeper .

---

and the proceeds paid into staff funds or into the hotel accounts. The Police should be notified if anything of value is found so that they can help in tracing the owner.

10.2.2 Staffing levels and control

Occupancy levels in a hotel vary from season to season and will also show differences for each day of the week; this means that the Housekeeping Department must maintain *flexible* staff levels if they are to operate economically. A hotel will maintain a nucleus of staff which is based on the average occupancy figure for the 'low' or 'off' season and which will be supplemented by seasonal, part-time or casual staff for the busier periods. It is, therefore, expected that the Housekeeping department will show a higher labour turnover figure than many others and could have a recruitment and training problem.

Due to the present heavy costs of employing staff – national insurance and superannuation payments, sickness, holidays, administration expenses, uniforms and training – it is often cheaper to pay overtime rates rather than increase the number of staff who may only be needed for a relatively short period. A housekeeper usually considers it better to remain under, rather than over-staffed and the maids asked to add extra rooms to their schedule as needed – for an additional payment.

As has been mentioned earlier, the Standard Time required to clean any area depends on its size, the type of furniture and the standard required; once these times have been agreed and the average occupancy and the length of stay for each guest is known, it is then possible to calculate the number of hours work required each week to maintain the department at an acceptable level – and to allocate the work amongst the staff so that it is fairly distributed (see Section 1.1).

As a guide, in a 5-star hotel with large rooms en suite with bathrooms, the Standard Cleaning Times could be as follows:

Departure room   45 min;
Occupied room   20 min;
Vacant room   5 min;
Corridor section 15 min.

Depending on the average ratio of occupied, vacant and departure rooms, a luxury hotel will require a maid to service from 10 to 12 rooms each day whilst in a purpose-built, transient hotel she will be responsible for 15 rooms in an 8-hour day; a productivity of between 50 and 75 rooms a week.

The staff to room ratio is controlled by the weekly *Room-maid Analysis Sheet*. A busy hotel will use this in two ways. When the forecast of future occupancy is received from Advance Bookings it is completed to show the numbers required on duty each day and at the end of the week it is filled in to show how closely the ratio of staff to rooms has been achieved.

Room maid analysis   Week ending 5 March

	Mon.	Tues.	Wed.	Thurs.	Fri.	Sat.	Sun.
Rooms cleaned	192	238	240	225	201	162	190
Maids on duty	11	14	15	15	14	11	13
Rooms per maid (av. 15)	17.4	17	16	15	14.3	14.7	14.6
Days off	9	6	4	4	5	7	5
Sick	—	—	1	1	Certificate 1	1	1
Absent	—	—	—	—		1 Holiday	1 Hol.
Total maids employed	20	20	20	20	20	20	20
Total rooms cleaned	1448	signed R. Hurst					
Av. per maid.	72.4	Executive housekeeper					

An alternative method of control, which is used in some hotel groups, is the 'points' system in which each point is equal to seven minutes of work and a maid is expected to complete 65 points each day, 325 points a week. In the 'points' system, the rating is as follows:

A single room   3 points;
A double room   4 points;
A bathroom   1 point;
A corridor section   2 points.

This system seems fairer than an arbitrary 15 rooms for each maid and is more closely related to the standard time for each job. An example of where this system can be linked to computer control is shown in the example of a computer print-out. This also shows the linen room requirements.

Computer print-out showing occupancy, linen requirements and 'points' allocated.

Name	Status	Sleeper	Room	Type	Points	Remarks
	vac		121	sb	0	
Mr Adams	occ	1	122	tb	4	VIP
Miss Berry	occ	1	123	tb	4	
Mr Cork	dep	2	124	tb	5	
Mr Dane	occ	2	125	tb	5	
	vac		126	tb	0	
Mrs Edmonds	dep	2	127	tb	5	
Mr Fetty	occ	2	128	db	5	VIP
Mr Gaites	occ	1	129	sb	4	
Mr Hann	dep	2	130	tb	5	
Mr Ivthes	occ	2	131	tb	5	
M/s Jones	dep	2	132	tb	5	
Mr Kingle	dep	2	133	tb	5	
	vac		134	tb	0	
Mr Longer	occ	2	135	tb	5	

Section 1   Total Points 58
Total Linen requirement

Single sheets	20
Double sheets	0
Pillowcases	20
Hand Towels	10
Bath Towels	10
Bath Mats	10

10.2.3 Computer control of room status and room access

At the beginning of 1978, there were only five or six hotels in the U.K. which were using computers for room status control and these were the larger tourist hotels with more than 500 bedrooms. Since then, with the advent of the micro-chip and micro-processor, electronic systems are providing many more hotels with services which free the staff from routine tasks and which greatly speeds the communication between departments.

Example of computer print-out.

A.   RE – Enter
       Housekeeping
       RE 406, 509
       Input correct.

B.   Housekeeping
       CO
       111   124   125
       201   222   224   231
       312
       422   423   424
       512   538   539   540
       603   605

C.   Housekeeping
       RP
       Total Rooms   240
       Out of Order   1
       Saleable Rooms   239
       Expected Arrivals   81
         Have Arrived   19
         To Arrive   62
       Unexpected Arrivals   12
       Expected Departures   82
         Have Departed   69
         To Depart   13
       Unexpected Checkouts   18
       Rooms Occupied   153
       Rooms Vacant   86
       Rooms Not Committed   37

CO = Check Out   RA = Recent Arrivals
ED = Expected Departure   RP = Registration Process
RE = Rooms Ready   VA = Vacant Areas

(a) Room status control

Liaison between Housekeeping and Reception is essential in a busy hotel so that the room status is constantly updated and rooms are serviced and relet as soon as they become available. Before computerization, this was done either by 'phone or by the Floor Housekeeper going in person to Reception; now, a terminal can be installed in Housekeeping which is linked to a terminal in Reception and the main computer in the control office. Data is fed into the computer as the guest and room details are received so that an accurate account is available at all times for guest arrivals and departures; the Housekeeper has either a visual reading on the terminal or receives a print-out which tells her which rooms are let, vacant or are waiting to be serviced. Alterations are fed into the computer by the Housekeepers so that, as soon as a room is serviced, Reception is informed; there is no time lost in transmitting information and the guest is provided with a faster service.

The computer is also programmed so that all *Advanced Booking* details can be obtained; this is usually for up to one year in advance, although a few computers are programmed for two to three years ahead so that the Housekeeper can plan the future staff levels.

The great disadvantage in the use of the computer seems to be the lack of social contact between departments as the process of communication becomes impersonal. There are problems if there is an electricity failure which is why computers are linked to an emergency power supply. Computer programes can be written in many different ways depending on what information is required. The example on page 208 shows at A that Housekeeping has entered the information that servicing has been completed in two rooms, 406 and 509. At B is shown the numbers of check-out rooms which have still to be serviced and C shows the exact state of rooms at that particular time. For example, at the time of the enquiry there were 86 rooms vacant, 17 of which are being serviced and there will be another 13 rooms to be added to this. There will be 62 more rooms let before the end of the day.

Page 207 shows a print-out for a section list for a maid which shows the occupancy for each room, the points allocated and the linen requirement. The number of points is below the normal 65 and she would expect to be asked to clean extra rooms or do some of the periodical cleaning to make up the difference.

In addition to room status control, electronics are also being used to control *room access*. Instead of keys, *computer-encoded plastic cards* are being increasingly introduced to improve room security.

When a guest books in, the Receptionist prints out plastic 'keycards' at the computer console so that all those using the room will have their own card – thus avoiding the problem of who has the key. The guest has to remember the room number as, for security reasons, this is not printed on the card.

The computer is programmed to print out a different number each time the room is let; the number is selected randomly and can be any number between one to several million. The door-lock is linked to the computer and will only open when the card with the new number is inserted in the slot. The new card automatically cancels all the previous cards. Most hotels are happy for the guest to keep these as a souvenir.

The door locks as soon as it is closed. Guests may still press an inner 'lock-out' on the door if they do not want to be disturbed which will exclude all other cards. When this happens and the Hotel finds that staff have to gain entry, a special *'security' card* on a one-off basis can be printed and is the only way of gaining access.

No-one can operate the console without an *authorization card*. There are usually three types of authorization cards; one, used by the Receptionist, is used to print out the guest's card whilst the other two authorizations are controlled by Management to print out the *sub-master keycards* for each maid and housekeeper section and the *master keycard*. No card can be printed without an authorization card first being inserted; as an added precaution the console has a security printer which automatically prints out the room number and the authorization card number so that a record is kept of all transactions.

Room-maids and housekeeping staff are issued with a *sub-master keycard* which is programmed for the number of rooms in each section and works in the same way as the guest card – when the new card is inserted in the slot, the previous Sub-master card is cancelled. This keycard can be changed at any time either daily or weekly.

There is usually only one *grand master keycard* for the entire hotel. To obtain this, a grandmaster authorization card along with a special code which is known only to a senior member of the management, are loaded into the console; this produces the master programme which has then to be inserted into every lock in the hotel before the change of master-code can be completed; for additional security, once this card has been programmed, a switch is turned to the 'off' position and the console will 'forget' the code which has been printed. The grandmaster card acts in the same way as the grandmaster key, that is, it will open every door in the hotel and will also double-lock so preventing the use of other cards. This may be necessary if valuables are stored in a room, if a crime has been committed or there has been a death and nothing is to be touched until the Police arrive or even if a guest has failed to contact Reception as requested so that he can be denied access until he does.

For a system such as this, it is essential that there is a link with an emergency power supply in case the main electricity fails.

10.3 Job descriptions

10.3.1 Example of a job description for an executive housekeeper

Job title: Executive Housekeeper
Responsible to: General Manager
Responsible for: All Housekeeping Staff
Scope of job: Responsible for cleaning, servicing and maintaining all guest and public areas to the standard acceptable to a 5-star hotel within the financial restraints as agreed with the General Manager and the Accountant.
Liaison with: The General Manager, the Accountant, the Duty Managers, Security, Reception, Maintenance, Night Cleaning Manager, Room Service and Laundry Manager.
Main Responsibilities:
A. *Finance*
   (1) The preparation of revenue estimates for: Staff, Laundry, Cleaning agents and equipment, Guest supplies and stationery.
   (2) The preparation of capital estimates for: Replacement Linen Stocks, Refurbishments, Redecorations, Equipment.
   (3) The control of all budgets so that they relate to occupancy levels.
B. *Staff*
   (1) The recruiting, selecting and training of staff – assisted by Personnel Department.
   (2) The welfare and supervision of staff, ensuring that they meet the required standard for smartness and courtesy.
   (3) Disciplinary and grievance procedures.
   (4) Ensuring that staff levels are consistent with the forecast for occupancy levels.
   (5) The supervision of 'sandwich'-course student trainees.
   (6) To advise management on Staff and Industrial Relations.

C. *Organization of Cleaning and Servicing*

(1) To establish standard work schedules for each work area.

(2) To ensure that periodical cleaning schedules are adhered to.

(3) To ensure that all maids and Housekeepers are trained to the same standard.

(4) To ensure that guest-rooms are serviced and handed back to Reception in as short a time as possible.

(5) To pay particular attention to V.I.P. guests, guest-rooms and V.I.P. supplies.

(6) To control the use and storage of cleaning agents, equipment and guest supplies.

(7) To arrange and control contracts for window cleaning, laundry and other services.

(8) To investigate and give advice on new cleaning agents, equipment, furnishings and fitments.

D. *Purchasing*

(1) To purchase cleaning agents, equipment, furnishings and fitments in accordance with the budget and the overall hotel policy.

E. *Maintenance and repairs*

(1) To ensure that service contracts for equipment are maintained.

(2) To ensure that all defects to the building fabric, furniture and fittings in the Accommodation Department are reported to Maintenance.

(3) To report all signs of infestation to Maintenance.

F. *Guests*

(1) To deal with guest welfare, minor sickness and to arrange for Doctor or Nursing Visits when necessary.

(2) To investigate all guest complaints.

(3) To arrange baby-minding and other services.

(4) To arrange for guest laundry services.

G. *Security*

(1) To control and safeguard all keys and 'bleeps'.

(2) To ensure that all staff are aware of security reporting procedures.

(3) To control all lost property.

H. *Health and Safety*

(1) To comply with all Fire Regulations and Health and Safety requirements.

(2) To ensure that all staff are practised in Emergency Procedures.

(3) To report and investigate all accidents within the department.

I. *Other Duties*

(1) Liaison with other departments as necessary.

(2) Attendance at Management Policy Meetings.

(3) Consultations as required with: Interior decorators, work study consultants.

(4) Other such duties relevant to the department.

10.3.2 Example of a job description for a floor supervisor

Job title: Floor Housekeeper – Guest Accommodation
Responsible to: Deputy Housekeeper
Responsible for: Maids and Houseporters in assigned section.
Scope of job: Responsible for arranging and supervising the work of the maids and houseporters to ensure that all guest rooms, corridors, fire exit stairways, service rooms and stores are clean, tidy, attractive and well-maintained.
Liaison with: Reception, Maintenance, Security, Room Service, Duty Manager, Linenkeeper and other housekeeping staff.
Duties
A. *Allocation of work*

(1) Take the duty turn in the opening of the Housekeeping Office as per rota. Prepare the worksheets for room-maids and supervisors.

(2) Control the signing out of keys and worksheets to maids, houseporters and supervisors.

(3) Allocate any special tasks such as V.I.P.s rooms, periodical cleaning or split sections.

B. *Room inspection*

(1) Check vacant rooms as soon as possible each morning and report any discrepancies.

(2) Check all rooms daily in section to ensure all have been cleaned, serviced and are of the standard required by the Hotel.

(3) Report any rooms not requiring service so that other rooms or duties can be allocated to the maids.

(4) Check state of all rooms before going off duty and prepare supervisor's report sheet and hand-over report for evening staff.

C. *Floor control*

(1) Supervise the work of the room-maids and houseporters and to take immediate corrective action if the work falls below the required standard. (a) Where a verbal warning needs to be given, to follow the laid-down disciplinary and grievance procedures. (b) All disciplinary and grievance problems to be reported in the Housekeeping Diary.

(2) Report any requirement or problem areas which could affect the standard in the section.

(3) Ensure that there are adequate supplies of linen, cleaning agents, equipment, and guest supplies available at all times. Requisition supplies as needed and ensure that there is no waste or damage; all storerooms and cupboards to be kept clean and tidy.

(4) Ensure that any guest requirements, such as hairdryers or electric blankets, are recorded and returned to the Housekeeping Office.

(5) Report any upholstery or soft furnishing in need of repair or cleaning; and supervise the changing of blankets, covers, pillows and mattress protectors as required.

(6) Pay special attention to V.I.P. rooms, the placing of V.I.P. supplies and attend to any plants or flowers placed in the rooms.

(7) Prepare, allocate and carry through the periodical cleaning schedules.

(8) Assist in checking inventories of linen, furniture and fittings as required.

(9) Liaise with room service in the event of trays and trollies not being cleared from the floors.

(10) Be responsible for seeing that a high standard of appearance, courtesy and conduct is adhered to by staff.

(11) Deal with all guest requests and complaints with courtesy and to exercise discretion.

D. *Maintenance*

(1) Ensure that all malfunctions are reported to Maintenance and that repairs are carried out.

(2) Ensure that all equipment is functioning correctly.

E. *Security*

(1) Report all lost and found articles and hand these in to the housekeeping office.

(2) Be responsible for all master, pass keys and 'bleeps' and their return to the housekeeping office at the end of each period of duty.

(3) Report any suspicious occurrence and any matters concerning the security of the hotel to the security office.

F. *Health and safety*

(1) Report anything which could be considered a hazard to health or safety.

(2) Report any accident, however minor, to the housekeeping office.

(3) Ensure that all staff know the hotel's policy on fire and bomb procedures.

(4) In the event of an emergency, assist in the checking of all rooms to ensure that guests are alerted and help in the evacuation of all guests and staff to the assembly point.

G. *Additional duties*
Carry out any further housekeeping duties as may be required by the
Executive Housekeeper.

10.3.3 Job description for a room-maid

Title: Room-maid – Guest Accommodation
Responsible to: Floor Housekeeper
Purpose of job: To be responsible for servicing and cleaning rooms
so that they are clean, tidy and in a well-maintained condition.
Duties
   (1) Clean and service all rooms according to their status of
departure, occupied or vacant to the standards required. Cleaning
includes such activities as:
(a) Removal of all rubbish in wastebins and ashtrays and any room
     service trays or trollies.
(b) Re-sheeting all beds with clean linen.
(c) Dusting all furniture, both inside and out, and all lamps, shades,
     pictures, skirtings and window sills.
(d) Vacuuming carpets and upholstered furniture.
(e) Cleaning all areas in bathroom by washing, drying and polishing.
(f) Replacing all guest supplies both in the bedroom and bathroom.
   (2) At all times, to respect guest's property and privacy and to
handle all guest's requests promptly and courteously. Any complaint
must be reported to the floor housekeeper immediately.
   (3) Carry out periodical cleaning as and when requested by the
floor housekeeper.
   (4) Report any stains or damage to the fabric of the room and to
report when blankets and covers require changing.
   (5) Be responsible for cleaning and restocking the maid's trolley
before going off duty.
   (6) Collect the section list each morning and return it before going
off duty.
   (7) Be responsible for the pass key.
   (8) Report to the floor housekeeper:
      (a) Any rooms which do not require servicing.
      (b) Rooms which have 'Do Not Disturb' notices on the door.
      (c) Any malfunctioning equipment.
      (d) Any suspicious person or incident.
      (e) Any lost or found articles.
      (f) Any personal gift from a guest – so that a 'package' pass can
          be completed.

(g) Anything which could constitute a health or safety hazard.

(9) When cleaning, to be responsible for wedging the door open when in guest's room and for locking the door when leaving. No room must be left open when the maid is not there.

(10) To perform the duties of other maids when necessary and to clean and service rooms extra to the normal requirement of 15 rooms each day. (If this does occur, an extra payment will be made for each room at a pro rata rate.)

10.4 Exercise and discussion

You have just been appointed Executive Housekeeper in a hotel which is owned and operated by one of the Airline Companies. There are 240 twin-bedded rooms, 2 bars, a coffee-shop seating 120 and an exclusive restaurant which seats 44. The function/reception area is 750 m². All the bedrooms are of basic design with identical bathrooms (Figure 10.1). Finishes throughout are mainly traditional with plaster on walls and ceiling areas – bedrooms and corridors are now wallpapered but a hessian fabric is used throughout the reception and function areas. The wet areas, bathrooms, toilets and kitchens have a tile finish. Terrazzo flooring is used in all bathrooms, vinyl-asbestos in the service areas, hardwood strip flooring in the function rooms, and carpeting in bedrooms, corridors and public areas.

Each floor has 48 rooms with one pantry/service room. Continental breakfasts are inclusive with the room tariff and are placed in the room each evening. Each room is provided with a small microwave oven and a kettle. There is no room service. The pantry/service room and the linen store are sited opposite the service lifts. There is a linen-chute for dirty linen.

The *Forecast* for occupancy is based on: The airline booking figures; a Forecast of tourist trends from the local Tourist Board and Present Bed Occupancy figures including the present rate for 'chance' bookings. Based on these figures, it is estimated that occupancy for next year is as follows:

Jan.	Feb.	Mar.	Apr.	May	June	July	Aug.	Sept.	Oct.	Nov.	Dec.
47%	41%	44%	58%	78%	89%	95%	92%	98%	81%	52%	78%

During the week, occupancy fluctuates as follows:

In the Spring

Mon.	Tues.	Wed.	Thur.	Fri.	Sat.	Sun.
45%	55%	70%	98%	82%	90%	42%

In the Autumn

Mon.	Tues.	Wed.	Thur.	Fri.	Sat.	Sun.
70%	80%	100%	100%	92%	100%	65%

Write a report to the Hotel Manager stating your proposed staff requirements for the guest rooms for the following year.

Prepare provisional estimates of staff costs (wages) for the Accountant.

Draw up a duty roster for the staff for either spring or autumn.

11

Hospital Domestic Services

In 1980/81, the cost of the Domestic Services in hospitals was £379 800 000 or 5.5 per cent of the total National Health Budget; a great deal of money by anyone's standards. For administrative purposes, hospitals are grouped into regions with the Regional Domestic Services Manager (RDSM) in an advisory capacity providing up-to-date information, technical knowledge and expertise on cleaning routines, cleaning agents and equipment, staffing levels and costs. He or she also maintains an even standard of performance in each of the hospitals in the region.

11.1 Responsibilities of the domestic services

Domestic Services have a dual responsibility. In addition to keeping premises clean and attractive, they also play a major and vital part in the control of infection and in the prevention of cross-infection from one person to another. Unlike most other housekeeping departments which clean and service rooms when the occupants are elsewhere, Domestic Assistants are working in ward and patient areas and have direct contact with people who are sick, with their visitors and with the nursing and medical staff.

Variations in patient levels do not affect staff levels as all areas have to be cleaned thoroughly whether the bed-state shows ten or twenty patients on a ward but training is essential as the standard of work required varies from one area to another. In a hospital or health care building the premises are divided into four main areas.

(a) Non-clinical

In staff, office and administrative accommodation standards would be at the socially acceptable level similar to that found in a hotel.

(b) Clinical

This includes all in-patient areas, wards, treatment rooms, sluices, stores, kitchens, equipment rooms and all corridors, stairs and landings within the patient area. It also includes out-patients and treatment departments such as X-ray or Physiotherapy.

(c) High-risk

This includes the operating theatres and special care units with the associated offices, corridors, stairs, kitchens, sluices and toilets.

(d) Special problem areas

Areas such as the Pathology Laboratories, Radiotherapy, X-ray, Pharmacy, Medical photography, Hydrotherapy pools and Computer Rooms.

In both the clinical and high-risk areas there is a need for the strict control of bacteria and other micro-organisms to avoid cross-infection. In problem areas there are very varied specific situations which can hinder the cleaning routine and are related to the need for security, limited access, chemical spillages, the control and safekeeping of drugs, delicate equipment or 24-hour manning.

11.2 Surfaces

All surfaces should be such that they are able to withstand constant cleaning without the need for frequent replacement or redecoration. Decorations are light in colour so that dirt is noticed immediately with joins and right-angles avoided as far as possible; this means that floors are curved up to form the skirting board and ceilings are coved to the walls so that dirt and bacteria cannot become engrained in the cracks.

Floors are usually laid in sheet form in ward areas with a covering, such as flexible P.V.C., which can be welded at the joins to make it impervious. Terrazzo is frequently used in theatres and treatment rooms, kitchens and toilets as it can be laid in one piece with no joins and can be made anti-static to prevent the danger of fire or explosion when gas cylinders are being used. Where there is the risk of slipping and as a covering to ramps and sloping corridors, an abrasive vinyl, which grips the sole of shoes, helps to prevent accidents.

There is a growing tendency to use soft floor coverings as these help to reduce the clinical, official, impression that patients and visitors receive as they enter the hospital and the wards and give a softer and friendlier appearance. They are quiet and warm and, in most areas, are quicker and easier to clean as they require to be vacuumed regularly but do not need to be damp-mopped and buffed daily or require the regular application of polish. In ward areas, the most usual soft covering is a fibre-bonded carpet with a very dense face-pile of nylon which is integrated with a waterproof P.V.C. base. Problems arise when this type of covering is used where there are incontinent patients, very young children or where liquids and chemicals are spilt as, although the carpet can be cleaned easily, it can remain damp for a time and may become smelly. Hygiene levels, in terms of the control of bacteria, are usually regarded as good.

Heavy-duty carpet tiles are suitable to use in out-patient areas as they can be removed for cleaning and changed around to even out the wear although, in a few cases, they have been found to be too mobile and some hospitals have found that carpet tiles can disappear overnight, particularly if they have been laid in an isolated corridor.

Most *walls* are tiled or have an oil or emulsion paint finish with metal or plastic protectors on the corners and with rails fitted at stretcher or trolley height to prevent wall damage.

Ward furniture must be simple, designed with no unnecessary ledges or joins and able to withstand very hard wear and constant cleaning; most tops have a melamine-type veneer finish which is impervious and can be cleaned quickly.

The Domestic Services provide a *Warden* or Supervisor in charge of the *Staff Accommodation* which provides long-term residence for all grades of staff. Here the conditions and needs are similar to those found in Halls of Residence for Colleges and Universities, that is, the room is home to the occupant and can become difficult to clean with personal property and impedimenta. Security can be a problem as many junior staff see no reason to keep outer doors locked at all times. In many hostels, basic furniture is provided with the occupants encouraged to provide their own personal 'finish'.

Flatlets and small houses can also be provided for more senior staff.

In these cases, the Domestic Services are generally responsible for the hand-over between one group of occupants and the next, that is, the inventory must be checked and the premises cleaned.

The Domestic Services Manager (DSM) is responsible for maintaining the standards of hygiene and cleanliness throughout the hospital, in the ancillary departments and in the staff accommodation. He or she may have sole responsibility for the preparation of estimates and the control of the budget or this may be done in conjunction with the RDSM; whether the DSM is also in charge of the linen supplies and laundry, the purchasing of domestic supplies, control of pests and infestation, ward housekeeping services or the porters depends on the organization and size of the unit. In many groups, the DSM assumes all the functions which are not medical or nursing and provides a comprehensive 'hotel' service.

Traditionally, a *maid* is responsible for the day-to-day cleaning on the ward; damp-dusting and mopping, floor buffing and kitchen, sluice, bathroom, toilet and office cleaning; she will also do the washing-up if there is no central washing-up unit. Heavy cleaning, for example, floor treatments such as scrubbing, stripping, the re-application of polish and carpet shampooing is the responsibility of a *Floor Cleaning Team* of two or three staff who operate on a rota so that all ward, corridor and ancillary areas are cleaned systematically.

Domestic staff work as an ancillary service on the wards, theatres and in departments where nursing and technical staff are in charge and, whereas the DSM is fully responsible for setting and maintaining standards, training and supervision, there is still an element of dual responsibility from the Sister or Officer-in-Charge so that the supervisory level is lower than that found in a hotel with approximately one supervisor to every twenty to twenty-four domestic staff. Each supervisor will be in charge of a section, either a group of wards, the operating theatres, staff accommodation or the ancillary areas and will enforce quality control standards. In addition some supervisors will be in charge of staff records, duty rosters, hours of work, stores or will specialize in staff training.

In the late 1960s, the 'Salmon' Report drew attention to the work of the nursing staff and stressed that it took three years to train a Nurse yet, in many cases, she spent a large proportion of her time doing routine work which could be done, more economically, by less highly trained staff. The report recommended the introduction of House-keeping Teams with a Ward Housekeeper and her Staff in charge of all the 'hotel' work on the ward and who would order food, diets and stores, receive and register patients, and deal with all queries,

A typical 'race-track' ward.

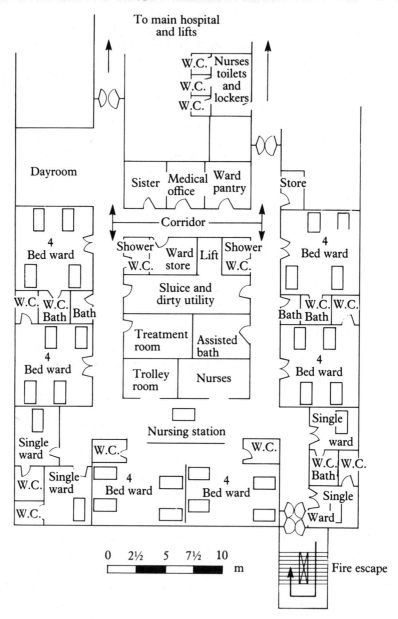

appointments and discharges in addition to the normal cleaning routines. This would leave the nurses to the specialist work in the operating theatre, intensive care, maternity and surgical wards and meant that there would be a considerable alteration in the levels and grades of staff with, on many wards, a decrease in the number of nurses and an increase in the numbers of domestic staff. The decision on whether the Salmon Report was implemented was left to the individual hospital and the vote of each member of staff with the result that some of the newer hospitals have Housekeeping Teams whilst many of the older hospitals have retained the traditional methods of organization.

In recent years, most new Hospitals have been built with the 'race-track' type of ward, which has been designed to offer every facility and maximum privacy to the patient but these have been found to be very expensive for both nursing and domestic staff so that there seems to be a trend back towards the older 'Nightingale' wards which are quicker and easier to maintain and simpler to supervise.'

11.3 Factors affecting work organization

11.3.1 Cross-infection

One of the main problems in a hospital is that bacteria and micro-organisms are very much more varied and tougher than they are anywhere else and patients who are already ill, and have lowered resistence to infection, can easily succumb to other infections found in a hospital ward or in the theatre. Hospitals have been using disinfectants and anti-septics for many years but, unfortunately, although 99.9 of micro-organisms will be destroyed by these methods, the bacteria and spores which remain develop. an immunity to disinfectants and so become much more dangerous than the bacteria found in the home.

Bacteria and micro-organisms are found everywhere; in dust, dirt and grease, in the air, on the skin, in the nose, throat and bowels—everywhere on the human body and on animals and insects as well as on clothes, bedding and furniture. Some bacteria are essential to the body processes and we could not live without them but some, the pathogens, are harmful; even so, a few bacteria will not usually harm either patients or staff. It is only when they have the right conditions to multiply that great harm can be done.

A single bacterium reproduces by dividing into two every ten to twenty minutes. This means that under ideal conditions one bacterium has multiplied to become sixty-four at the end of one hour; after two hours there are 4096 bacteria, 262 144 at the end of three hours and sixteen million bacteria at the end of the fourth hour. Bacteria multiply best at a body temperature of 37°C; as temperatures decrease towards 10°C the growing process becomes progressively slower until the organism becomes dormant; as the temperature increases to about 63°C they will also multiply more slowly until they are killed. Bacteria can also multiply by producing spores; these seed-like substances have particularly tough skins and can remain dormant for very long periods, they are frequently activated by medium heat but are destroyed by the very high temperatures of sterilization.

Bacteria also need time in which to multiply and sufficient food and moisture: the removal of one of the conditions of growth will not kill all the organisms but prevents them growing to such numbers that they become harmful.

There are three other ways in which bacteria are controlled – by good cleaning methods, by chemical means in the form of disinfectants and anti-septics and by sterilizing and autoclaving.

11.3.2 Cleaning methods

Thorough cleaning will not kill bacteria but it does remove them from the danger area. Bacteria exist in dust so it is important to control the movement of dust from one part of the hospital to another as it is transferred on shoes and on the wheels of trolleys and chairs. The first line of defence is in the use of *dust control mats* which should be placed at all entrances to the building and, internally, across main corridors and at doorways to prevent dust and bacteria being carried from one ward to another and into and from the operating and intensive care areas. These mats automatically remove and hold dust.

Care must also be taken in the collection of dust; the most efficient method is a *vacuum cleaner* with the exhaust filtered so that dust and bacteria are not blown back into the air and with the exhaust well above ground level so that dust is not disturbed before it can be collected. To meet the recommendations of the Medical Research Council, a vacuum should be fitted with three or four filters so that the maximum bacterial air count should not exceed the stated levels. For a casualty theatre, this is set at 20 per cu. ft; in a main theatre, 10 per cu. ft; and 0.1 to 2 per cu. ft. in a theatre used for special cases. When dust bags are full, they are incinerated and replaced with new bags. A *central vacuum system* provides suction outlets on each ward for the connection of cleaning tools so that the dust is drawn away from the ward and collected, where it can do no harm, in the basement area.

Sweeping and high-dusting mops are not quite so efficient as a vacuum in controlling dust, but have the advantage that they are quiet, fast, light to use, are considerably cheaper and can be used with disposable mop-heads which are thrown away after use. The alternative is to use a 'static' mop-head, made from nylon, which builds up sufficient static electricity to hold the dust and can then be washed when dirty and reused.

Any process which creates dust, such as bed-making or sweeping, should be completed at least one hour before dressings are changed to allow time for the dust in the air to settle. Brushes are not used as these flick particles into the air.

After vacuuming or mop-sweeping, a floor is *damp-mopped*. A two-bucket mopping system with a gear-press unit and a flat, long-tailed mop is fast and enables the mop to be rinsed in clear water before being re-used on the floor. The mopping water must be changed frequently otherwise dirt is re-distributed on the floor. All mop-heads should be detachable so that they can be washed and dried at the end of each day.

Furniture and ledges are damp-dusted using disposable cloths dampened with water or a little diluted vinegar – this holds the dust in the cloth. Away from the patient area, furniture polish is often used.

Cleaning frequencies increase in patient areas with floors vacuumed or swept and damp-mopped two to three times a day and treatment rooms and theatres cleaned after each patient.

Beds are an obvious source of infection; after a patient is discharged, all bedding is laundered and the bed, mattress and pillow cleaned with disinfectant, as is the locker and chair which the patient has used and the surrounding bedspace. Curtains may or may not be washed after each patient but they will be laundered frequently. Care is taken not to shake bedding or pillows when disposing of the dirty linen. To prevent infection, soiled articles are never checked but are placed directly into the linen-bag – and in the laundry, the linen is washed and only counted when it is clean and being returned to the ward.

Bedding from a patient suffering from an infectious disease is kept apart and placed in a special linen-bag (usually red) in which it is washed; the bag is stitched with an alginate thread which will melt in the high wash temperatures and the articles then become loose in the machine. The very high temperature during the wash process and the finish on the calender is sufficient to sterilize the bedding, even so, bedding from a highly infected patient is usually 'disposable' and will be burnt.

Cloths, cleaning sponges and equipment are *colour-coded* to indicate the areas in which they are to be used, for instance:

> *Red* – for 'danger' areas such as the sluice and toilets;
> *Blue* – for patient and ward areas;
> *White* – for kitchen areas.

Rubbish-bags are also colour-coded to indicate the contents and equipment marked clearly to ensure that it is used only in the designated area and not moved from one ward to another with the risk of transferring infection. Before equipment is put away, it must be cleaned and dried with particular attention paid to wheels, cables and flexes.

Staff must always wash their hands once they have finished working in one area before moving on to the next job and *rubber gloves* should be worn when a dirty area is being cleaned – these must also be washed after use.

Infected or contagious patients are nursed in single rooms. Staff are protected by using *barrier nursing and cleaning* procedures and disposable equipment, utensils and cloths. The maid wears special protective clothing – mask, overalls, cap and gloves which are cleaned or disposed of after use.

11.3.3 Standard times

These are based on detailed work study observations and have been used to determine the numbers and grades of staff in the larger hospitals for some years. They also form the basis for bonus schemes. This is discussed in detail in Chapter 1.

11.3.4 Disinfectants

Disinfectants are used with care and discrimination in a hospital and, to quote from a Hospital Cleaning Manual, 'it is difficult to justify the routine use of disinfectants'. When they are used correctly, disinfectants will kill some 99.9 per cent of bacteria but will have little effect on spores which remain to develop and multiply.

The general rules for using a disinfectant are as follows:

(1) They must be used in the *right concentration*, if over-diluted, bacteria will not be killed but can develop an immunity. Periodically, the Pathologist or the Control of Infection Officer will take swabs and test these to see how effective the disinfectant is against the local bacteria. The result of the tests indicate whether the disinfectant should be used or changed and the Domestic Services Manager will be informed accordingly. There is, as yet, no means of testing the efficiency of a disinfectant for killing viruses.

(2) A disinfectant does not work on a dry surface and is very inefficient when there is dirt or grease present; before applying, all surfaces must be *clean*.

(3) The *contact time* before the bacteria is killed varies from two minutes to thirty minutes or more – depending on the type of bacteria and the strength of the disinfectant. Sodium hypochloride (bleach) on a previously cleaned surface needs two minutes; a phenolic, such as Jeyes Fluid, Izzal or Dettol, requires eight minutes when used on a clean surface but thirty minutes if the surface is at all dirty or greasy. The surface must remain *wet* for the disinfectant to be effective.

(4) Generally, disinfectants perform better in *hot water* than in cold and when diluted with *soft water* rather than hard water.

(5) Many disinfectants, particularly bleach, have a self-life and, when diluted, deteriorate quickly. There was a recent case in New York when a cleaning assistant, rather than 'waste' disinfectant, decided to top-up the remaining liquid with new solution; this was used to spray the theatre after each operating session and the practice only discovered when the disinfectant had deteriorated, some bacteria had become immune, and several patients had developed gangrene poisoning.

The smell is no indication of strength and can, indeed, be very unpleasant to a patient. A strong-smelling disinfectant – such as some of the phenols – should be kept well away from food and food stores as the smell can be readily absorbed making some foodstuffs useless. In general use, sodium hypochloride is considered safe – when diluted – to use in kitchens and disinfectants of the phenol group are kept for outside drains and gulleys and in areas where pus, urine or faeces have been present.

Many disinfectants are corrosive and toxic and, in common with other cleaning agents, should be kept locked in the cleaning cupboards to prevent misuse and the risk of children or older people spilling or drinking them in mistake for some other fluid.

11.3.5 Heat treatment

The only way to be totally certain that all bacteria, spores, viruses and micro-organisms are killed is to use *heat treatment*. A *sterilizer* operates under pressure. Items are placed inside and the temperature is raised to and held at 121°C for 15 minutes; this renders them completely safe provided they are not re-contaminated by careless handling. Obviously, while this process is needed for all surgical instruments, dressings and equipment, it is expensive and is not necessary for cleaning equipment and materials unless they are to be used in highly specialized areas where the environment has to be kept as sterile as possible. An autoclave operates at 73°C for 15 minutes and disinfects but it will not kill spores. If cleaning equipment is to be autoclaved it must withstand high temperatures.

When washing-up is done on the ward, it accounts for between 30 and 35 per cent of the ward-maid's work so that, in order to reduce costs and to improve hygiene standards, many hospitals have installed a central dish-washing unit with machines which operate at high temperatures.

One talks, loosely, of a *sterilizing unit for washing-up crockery* and cutlery. This means that two sinks are used for *manual washing-up*. Plates are stripped of debris and rinsed. They are then washed in the first sink in detergent and water at a temperature of 40°C, placed in racks and immersed in clean water in the second sink which is at a temperature of between 77°C and 82°C (170°F–180°F). The articles must be so placed that all surfaces are in contact with the water and left until the body of the plate or cup is of the water temperature – for one minute; this is sufficient to destroy any bacteria remaining on the crockery but spores will not be killed. Each item should be hot enough to steam-dry so that there is no need to dry with a clean or – more often, not-so-clean – tea towel and crockery is put away clean and 'sterile'.

11.3.6 Radiation

All staff must be told of the dangers which can arise from X-ray equipment and radio-active materials and never touch any object or open a door where the Radiation Symbol is displayed or when there is a warning light. Permanent staff, working in any area where radioactive material is used, will be given a badge to wear which is checked regularly for contact with radiation.

This symbol shows that radiation is present. It is usually shown black on yellow.

Alternatively, a notice stating – RADIATION – is displayed.

11.3.7 Anti-static or conductive floors

Any friction or movement will produce a build-up of static electricity but usually, with natural materials, no problem is created as the electricity discharges slowly through the fabric of the building to earth; it is, however, dangerous when flammable gases, such as oxygen or ether, are being used in a dry atmosphere and when there is a risk of a spark caused by instruments or equipment which could ignite the gas and cause fire or an explosion. Where there is this type of risk in operating theatres or intensive care units, anti-static floors are installed. Many floor materials can be given anti-static properties. Some are laid over a galvanized wire mesh, carbon black is added to the cement used in Terrazzo and carbon can also be added to linoleum, rubber and flexible P.V.C.; copper salts are added to magnesite. As far as possible the humidity of a room should not drop below 55° or the anti-static properties are affected.

These floors are expensive to install and are sensitive to even slight changes in the environment and the methods of cleaning. The floor should be washed frequently using either a mild neutral detergent or a bactericidal detergent and the minimum of water (preferably soft) – no seal, polish or other floor dressing should ever be used as this upsets the anti-static properties.

The floor is usually tested every three months to ensure that the resistance properties are being maintained and have not deteriorated. Once the properties have been lost, the floor is replaced.

Many man-made materials are poor conductors and some carpets made from nylon may also need earthing for general use. This prevents the electricity being earthed unintentionally by someone or something touching metal, such as a typewriter, furniture or a door knob, and creating an electric current, the shock of which can be most unpleasant.

11.3.8 Patients

A patient is not part of the furniture and must be treated with care, consideration and courtesy, and all staff must avoid making too much noise, knocking beds or jolting medical equipment. They must be cheerful and are expected to pause and talk a little with a patient – although obviously not too much – to ask how they are or to mention some of the local gossip.

11.3.9 Staff

Personal hygiene and tidiness is important and staff must remember to be particular about their personal cleanliness and clothing and to wash after cleaning each area. Heavy colds and infections must be reported. A medical examination is a necessity before staff are employed. Staff must be flexible and able to adapt to the changing pressures and schedules of the ward and hospital organization.

11.4 Job descriptions

11.4.1 Job description for a domestic services manager

Job title: Domestic Services Manager Hospital Administrator
Responsible to: Regional Domestic Services Manager
Overall purpose of job: To be responsible for maintaining the required standard of hygiene and cleanliness throughout the hospital and ancillary areas.
Main responsibilities may include:

(1) To prepare estimates for the department and to control the budget allocated.

(2) To prepare and implement work schedules in accordance with work study reports and ward, floor maintenance, carpet and other cleaning programmes.

(3) To ensure that all infection control, fire and safety procedures are adhered to and to make recommendations for improvements to the services.

(4) To control the receipt, issue and use of all cleaning agents and equipment and to maintain stock records.

(5) To make regular weekly visits to all wards and departments and maintain close liaison with nursing and other staff. To attend Domestic Department Meetings, Study Days and Interdepartmental Meetings.

(6) To recruit, interview and select all grades of staff employed within the department in accordance with the agreed establishment.

(7) To be responsible for staff induction and training, welfare, counselling and discipline.

(8) To maintain and complete record forms for each employee, all administration documents, training records, monthly returns, duty rosters and time-sheets.

(9) To supervise in-service training for supervisors, monitor performance and to allocate to each a specific work area.

(10) To ensure that annual leave and time in lieu is organized with the least disruption to the department.

(11) To ensure that a member of the supervisory team is on duty to cover the hours which the department is open.

(12) To carry out such tasks as may be required and which may be regarded as being within the scope of the Domestic Services.

11.4.2 Job descriptions – for a domestic supervisor

Job title: Domestic Supervisor
Responsible to: Domestic Services Manager
Responsible for: Domestic Assistants
Purpose of job: To supervise cleaning and domestic duties in all parts of the Hospital to the required standard.
Main duties will include:

(1) The training and supervision, welfare and discipline of staff.

(2) Allocation of work and quality control.

(3) Arrangement of duty rotas.

(4) The checking of work schedules and making any temporary adjustments.

(5) Ensuring that the cleanliness and hygiene standards of the area of the Hospital which has been allocated to the Supervisor, is maintained to the required standard.

(6) The control and usage of cleaning materials.

(7) The control, use and safety checking of all equipment and machinery and the reporting of any malfunction.

(8) To report the need for any structural and fabric repair and any sign of pest infestation.

(9) To report all accidents to Domestic Staff and to ensure that all staff are familiar with the requirements of the Health and Safety at Work Act and carry out their duties without hazard to others.

(10) To be aware of the security problems of the Hospital and to report any suspicious occurrence to the Security Officer.

(11) To liaise with Sister on each ward or the Departmental Head, discuss any problems and report back to the Domestic Services Manager.

(12) To carry out such other supervisory duties as may be requested, as defined by the Whitley Council.

I UNDERSTAND AND AGREE THAT I MAY BE REQUIRED TO CARRY OUT ALL THE TASKS CONTAINED IN THIS JOB DESCRIPTION.

Signed ....

Date ....

11.4.3 Job description of a domestic assistant

Job title: Domestic Assistant
Responsible to: Domestic Services Manager
Reports to: Domestic Supervisor
Purpose of job: To perform cleaning and domestic duties in all parts of the Hospital.
Duties may include:

(1) Daily cleaning of areas, including wards, ward kitchens, offices, restrooms, corridors and stairs, floors, beds and cots, furniture and fittings, sinks, the emptying and replacement of refuse bags and waste bins, and the replenishment of paper towels, toilet rolls. etc.

(2) The daily cleaning of sanitary areas – baths, wash-basins, sluices, sinks and toilets, floors and all furniture and fittings.

(3) The periodical cleaning of walls and paintwork, skirting boards, gullies and covings, radiators, floors, windows (internal) and glass, curtain rails and high dusting areas, and the cleaning and polishing of furniture and fittings and kitchen cupboards and refrigerators.

(4) To follow the laid-down cleaning methods and schedules as instructed.

(5) To look after and clean daily all equipment, machinery and the domestic storage areas and leave tidy.

(6) To report any faults in equipment or machinery to the Domestic Supervisor.

(7) To wash (either by hand or machine) crockery, cutlery and kitchen utensils used on the ward or in the residences.

(8) To clean the heated food trolleys at the end of each meal service.

(9) To report immediately any accident and to perform all duties in accordance with the Hospital Policy on Health and Safety.

(10) To co-operate with all ward and departmental staff so that work is carried out as a team.

(11) At all times, to be courteous to patients and to visitors to the hospital, to respect their property and privacy and to maintain a high standard of appearance and conduct as required by the standards and status of the Domestic Services Department and the Hospital.

(12) Any other duties, as defined by the Whitley Council, as may be required by the Domestic Services Department.

I UNDERSTAND AND AGREE THAT I MAY BE REQUIRED TO CARRY OUT ALL THE TASKS CONTAINED IN THIS JOB DESCRIPTION.

Signed ....

Date ....

11.4.4 Job description for a domestic assistant in a floor cleaning team

Job title: Domestic Assistant – Floor Cleaning Team
Responsible to: Domestic Services Manager
Reports to: Domestic Supervisor
Purpose of job: To perform cleaning and domestic duties in all parts of the Hospital as required.
Main duties:

(1) To clean all floor surfaces using scrubbing machines, polishing machines, vacuum cleaners, high-speed cleaning machines and wet pick-ups.

(2) Vacuuming and shampooing of carpet surfaces.

(3) Use and care of vacuum, floor and polishing machines – this to include the cleaning of all equipment before it is put away and to report any malfunctioning to the Domestic Supervisor.

(4) Use and care of impregnated or static mops to carry out high dusting and dust control.

(5) Use and care of damp-dusting techniques.

(6) Use and care of damp-mopping equipment and using all such equipment on floor surfaces.

(7) The emptying of all litter bins on corridors as required.

(8) Reporting all repairs, obstructions or any unusual incidents on corridors.

(9) Wall washing as required.

(10) To perform all tasks so as to safeguard the health and safety of all users of the hospital.

(11) To undertake such other jobs as may be required.

I UNDERSTAND AND AGREE THAT I MAY BE REQUIRED TO CARRY OUT ALL THE TASKS CONTAINED IN THIS JOB DESCRIPTION.

Signed ....

Date ....

11.4.5 Job description for a ward housekeeper

Job title: Ward Housekeeper
Responsible to: Domestic Services Manager
Responsible for: Housekeeping Aides
Purpose of job: Responsibility for the domestic services of a ward area of approx. 60 patients and the maintenance of the required standards of cleanliness and hygiene by the housekeeping staff under her control. Responsibility for the ward clerical duties and for liaison with patients and relatives.
Main duties:

(1) The supervision, training, discipline and welfare of the ward housekeeping staff; this includes the adherence to rotas, reporting of absence and sickness. To ensure that the standards of courteousness, appearance and conduct are maintained.

(2) To ensure the correct use and care of cleaning agents and equipment.

(3) To ensure the observance of safe working methods and of all Fire and Safety regulations.

(4) To liaise with the Floor Cleaning Team Supervisor.

(5) To ensure the ordering, collection, storage and control of all cleaning materials, crockery, hardware, food supplies, stationery, and linen.

(6) To arrange for visits from the Hospital Chaplain, hairdresser, beautician, chiropodists, etc.

(7) To escort patients and visitors to a location off the ward when no Nursing attendance is needed.

(8) To assist patients on arrival and on discharge or transfer to another ward.

(9) To order and arrange diets with the Sister/Dietician and to assist with the service of meals and beverages.

(10) The filing of medical reports in patient's casenotes.

(11) The clerical work involved in the admittance of patients – completing name cards, preparing charts, ordering meals.

(12) The clerical work involved in the discharge of patients – ordering transport, informing next-of-kin, making follow-up appointments.

(13) Arrange transport to other departments, hospitals, home.

(14) Make appointments as required with X-ray, physiotherapy, etc.

(15) Update bed state with Admissions Unit twice daily.

(16) Receive telephone calls, locate recipient or take and pass-on messages.

(17) Check ward equipment, services and stock levels. Make out requisitions for repairs and stocks.

(18) Issue and collection of menu cards and assisting patients in completing the cards.

(19) Attending to relatives, friends and visitors and arranging overnight accommodation when needed.

(20) Carrying out the specified procedures for the control of patients' property.

(21) The sorting, distribution and redirection of mail.

(22) Liaison with the Ward Sister, maintenance, laundry and portering departments.

(23) And any such duties which may be required.

I UNDERSTAND AND AGREE THAT I MAY BE REQUIRED TO CARRY OUT ALL THE TASKS CONTAINED IN THIS JOB DESCRIPTION.

Signed ....

Date ....

11.4.6 Job description for a housekeeping aide

Job title: Housekeeping Aide
Responsible to: Domestic Services Manager

Reports to: Ward Housekeeper

Purpose of job: The general cleaning and domestic duties in the wards and such other rooms associated with them and undertaking other domestic duties as instructed in order to relieve nursing staff of non-nursing duties. Doing such other patient-orientated tasks under the supervision of the nursing staff as may be required.

Main duties:

(1) Prepare for and assist the serving of meals and beverages.

(2) Washing of crockery, cutlery and kitchen utensils as required.

(3) Clean and tidy all areas at specified times. This includes:

    (a) Vacuum clean all floors.

    (b) Damp-dust furniture, fittings, ledges, shelves, bedhead lights, bedrails and supports.

    (c) Remove patient's rubbish.

    (d) Mop spillages from floor or damp-mop as required.

    (e) Empty and clean ashtrays and wastebins.

    (f) Clean soiled dressing bins and replace liners.

    (g) Clean W.C.s in the prescribed manner.

    (h) Clean washbasins, sinks, baths and showers.

    (i) Clean internal glass – partitions, mirrors, pictures, doors.

    (j) Clean dirty marks from paintwork.

    (k) Clean and replenish store cupboards.

    (l) High level dusting.

    (m) Clean and make vacant beds; clean vacant lockers on discharge of patients.

(4) Replenish toilet soap, paper towels, toilet rolls, rubbish bags.

(5) Remove bags of soiled linen from stands, tie the top of the bags and place ready for collection. Re-equip stands with empty bags. Check that clean linen has been delivered.

(6) Seal rubbish bags and place ready for collection. Re-equip sack holders.

(7) Attend to patient's fruit and flowers. Clean vases and fruit bowls.

(8) Change curtains as required.

(9) Strip and make unoccupied beds.

(10) Maintain all equipment in a clean and safe condition. Report any malfunctioning.

(11) To perform all duties in such a manner as to protect the health and safety of everyone using the premises.

(12) At all times, to respect patient's property and privacy and to treat patients and visitors with courtesy and patience. To maintain a

high standard of appearance and conduct as required by the standards and status of the Domestic Services Department and the Hospital.

(13) To perform such other duties as may, from time to time, occur. I UNDERSTAND AND AGREE THAT I MAY BE REQUIRED TO CARRY OUT ALL THE TASKS CONTAINED IN THIS JOB DESCRIPTION.

Signed ....

Date ....

11.5 Exercise and discussion

1 The cleaning requirements for a typical ward are as follows:

		Material	Task	Frequency	Time
Floors	Corridors Wards Stores	P.V.C.	Vacuum, sweep Damp-mop Buff	Twice a day	
	Offices Dayroom	Nylon carpet	Vacuum Shampoo	Twice a day Every 4 months	
	Sluice Bathrooms Toilets Pantry Treatment room	Terrazzo	Vacuum, sweep Damp-mop	Three times a day	
Walls	All except for	Emulsion paint	Wash	Every 2 weeks	
	Sluice Bathrooms Toilets Pantry Treatment room	Ceramic tiles	Wash and polish	Daily	
Furniture and ledges	All areas	Wood and melamine	Damp-dust	Twice a day	
Internal windows between corridors and wards	All areas	Glass	Clean	Daily	
Baths Toilets Showers Sluice			Clean	Three times a day	
Waste-containers			Remove and replace	As necessary	

Using the plan of a typical ward (p. 222) as a guide, the examples of Standard Cleaning Times (p. 9), the relevant information in the text and your own practical knowledge and ability, complete the above specification adding to it the cleaning areas you feel may have been omitted. There is no ward washing-up.

How many Domestic Assistants would be employed to cover this work?

2 Many hospital staff belong to a trade union. As a newly appointed Domestic Services Manager, what action would you take to ensure that there are good relationships between you and the union representatives? What part do you feel the unions have to play in the organization?

12

University and College Residences

There is much more variation in the job structure of a Domestic Bursar working in a university or college than there is for those in Hospitals or Hotels. In many cases, the Domestic Bursar is required to be resident and can be responsible for all household affairs ranging from the accommodation and catering to the student welfare (and often discipline) and the upkeep of any surrounding gardens.

The difficulty in providing student accommodation at an economical price is long-standing. The problem is that most students are in residence for between thirty and thirty-six weeks of the year whilst the buildings have to be insured, staffed and maintained for the entire year. A traditional way of reducing costs was to keep staff either on a 'retainer' or on half pay during the vacations – but while this may be convenient for the housewife with children, it does nothing to attract professional, trained staff. As a means of fully utilizing the resources of both staff and buildings, many residences are now actively marketing their accommodation and offering facilities for conferences, summer schools, functions and basic hotel services for tourists. The extra revenue is used to reduce the level of charges made to the student, but it also makes for a much more interesting job for the Bursar and his staff who may then be working at two different standards during the year – that of the student and that of the hotelier.

The Bursar will be supported by several Assistants each with specific responsibilities such as catering, housekeeping or student welfare. Supervisory levels are governed by the need to provide 24-hour cover with one member of staff always on-call. Academic staff are often provided with residential accommodation at a reduced charge on the understanding that they take their turn with supervision.

There can be much controversy in running a residence and clear-cut rules are essential. The Bursar, supported by both catering and housekeeping supervisors, will have regular meetings with the Student's committee which is elected by all those in residence. The committee should be used to discuss and decide on all matters which affect the students such as general entertainments and the thorny problems of noise, behaviour or damage, and visitors.

As regards damage, it is usual for all students to contribute to a Damage Fund when they first come into residence and any payment for individual damage or an apportionment for general damage is met through this fund. At the end of the year any money remaining is returned to the student.

Visitors are always a bone of contention and many halls now compromise on over-night accommodation for friends and allow this on a temporary basis of two or three nights only, but stipulate that it is a concession, not a right, and will not be allowed as a permanent arrangement. Other Halls consider that this is too much of a security risk, that it will lead to over-use of the student facilities and they will do their utmost to prevent friends stopping-over; as far as possible, all visitors should be signed in by their student friend. Many Halls require students to sign out if they are going to be away at the weekend and to leave an address of their whereabouts so they can be contacted if needed. Signing-out for meals is also needed when there is an all-in charge made for food and accommodation – particularly at weekends to prevent wastage.

12.1 Systems of cleaning

The cleaning of any room used by a student – or any other long-term resident – is particularly difficult as a considerable volume of personal possessions can be accumulated in a surprisingly short time; storage space is limited and there is a great aversion to having college work moved or touched. Many students also acquire food, make late-night drinks and forget to wash and tidy away dirty plates and cups with the (occasional) interesting smell and the risk of attracting mice and other pests. Other students can be so tidy that one hardly knows that the room has been used.

Whereas at one time, all rooms were serviced daily, now the majority of Halls clean thoroughly once a week on a rota basis with the occupants expected to make their own beds and tidy the room on the other days of the week – much as they would be expected to do at home, and the room left clear for the weekly turn-out by the domestic staff.

Most Halls do, however, maintain a daily 'right of access' with the maid emptying the rubbish or cleaning the washbasin; this may seem unnecessary but it ensures that the room is checked regularly for damage and, more important, for any unreported student sickness or absence. In this way, a maid can be responsible for cleaning between 30 and 40 rooms each week.

Many Residences budget for a total cleaning time of one hour per week for each student so that if there are 300 students, there will be 300 cleaning hours; at one time, this allowance would have been double. In the endeavour to reduce costs many Residences are replacing blankets and covers with duvets whilst some of the Northern Halls have been known to use sleeping bags. Many are talking of asking students to provide their own linen.

Periodic or special cleaning is always done during the vacations. *Block* cleaning systems are sometimes used in this type of accommodation when all the rooms are empty during the day. This method means that in a block of, say, 10 or 15 rooms all the tasks are carried out in rotation, that is, all the beds are made, then all the washbasins cleaned, etc. It means that the maid is not always changing from one set of equipment to another but it also means that none of the rooms are finished until shortly before the maid goes off duty. It is a method unsuited to a hotel or staff residence when people are coming and going during the day.

If many rooms are let during the vacation, it is especially important that they are kept in good condition and the ruling that nothing must be pinned or attached to the wall must be enforced – a cork or peg-board section is, however, usually provided so that posters, family pictures and notices can be displayed.

12.2 Extra facilities

It is essential to provide a large *luggage-room* to store trunks during term time and for the storage of the student's possessions if the room is going to be let during the vacation.

To avoid the heavy expense of formal kitchen and dining facilities, the future trend is towards self-catering with vending-machines and a bar installed to increase profits; these are usually operated by the Student's Union and, obviously, need careful control.

Each group of students is usually provided with a *utility-room* where they can make snacks, tea or coffee and also wash and iron.

Students can have accidents or fall sick and, particularly when they are from overseas, some basic nursing may have to be provided by the Bursar's staff – for convenience, most sick-rooms are situated fairly close to the kitchens and refectory.

12.3 Budget and stock control

The Bursar will have the same responsibilities as other Managers for producing estimates for the budget, the purchase, control and issue of all stocks and furniture inventories, staff, maintenance and, in addition, usually has some joint responsibility with the academic staff and tutors, for student welfare and discipline.

12.4 Vacation and flatlet letting

Many Bursars have full responsibility for *vacation lettings* or are required to assist in these arrangements with the College Registrar or Administrator. This adds an extra dimension to an already interesting job and includes advertising, pricing the accommodation and making booking arrangements with groups or individuals. The internal arrangements may mean a different type of menu, a committment to an early morning tea service or turning down the beds at night: extra staff may have to be recruited as basic hotel services are usually offered, in that beds are made each day and all bedrooms are daily cleaned.

The design of a Residence does affect the type of letting; for instance, if students are self-catering and there is no refectory, it is very difficult (although not impossible) to accommodate conferences or summer schools but it would be quite suitable for tourists who would take advantage of any local restaurants in the neighbourhood.

In an endeavour to reduce costs for students, some colleges have bought large houses and converted these into self-contained flatlet accommodation which is let to second or third-year students. Basic furniture, such as beds, tables and chairs are provided, but the student is expected to provide linen and all the smaller items. The room is inspected at the beginning of the academic year and the student signs the inventory; he is then responsible for the cleaning and upkeep and for returning the room to the college at the end of the year in the same condition (subject to reasonable wear and tear) as he received it. Heating can be included in the charge or may be provided through a meter so that the student pays only for what is used. This type of accommodation is much cheaper as no staff are required apart from the need for annual servicing at the end of the year. Many Bursars are also responsible for controlling this flatlet letting.

12.5 Job descriptions

12.5.1 Example of a job description for an accommodation officer or senior bursar in charge of halls of residence for colleges or university

Job title: Accommodation Officer/Senior Domestic Bursar
Responsible to: The Administrator
Responsible for: All Housekeeping and Cleaning Staff
Scope of job: To maintain all accommodation in a clean and attractive condition during term-time and in the vacations when the premises are heavily used by a wide range of visitors such as holiday makers and tourists, summer school students and conference delegates.
Main duties
(1) To supervise the work of the housekeeping staff of each Hall and to give guidance on work schedules and methods of work.
(2) To prepare estimates and budgets in accordance with the policies agreed with the Management Services Committee and the Administrator.
(3) To control all revenue expenditure for laundry, electricity consumption and cleaning equipment and materials.
(4) To prepare and arrange redecoration schedules.
(5) To ensure that furniture, furnishings and equipment are maintained in good repair and are replaced in accordance with purchasing policy.
(6) To maintain close liaison with the Estates Manager in connection with the day-to-day routine maintenance and with the Annual Maintenance Schedules.
(7) To maintain close liaison with the Catering Manager and the Conference Manager in connection with the organization for functions during term-time and the reception and accommodation of all visitors during the vacations.

(8) To ensure that all problems, disputes and complaints in relation to the Halls are dealt with and to alert Senior Management when a serious matter arises. Maintain a close liaison with the Student's Union Executive Officers.

(9) To advise Senior Management on the most economic utilization of the Hall's resources and to review all procedures and operations with the objective of maintaining standards whilst reducing costs.

(10) To undertake such other duties as may be determined by the Administrator.

12.5.2 Example of a job description for a domestic bursar or housekeeper in a hall of residence

Job title: Domestic Bursar/Housekeeper
Responsible to: The Accommodation Officer/Senior Domestic Bursar
Responsible for: All Domestic and Cleaning Staff
Scope of job: To be responsible for the management of all household affairs and to ensure that the Hall is maintained to a high standard.
Main duties

(1) The employment, supervision, training and welfare of all domestic staff.

(2) The supervision of all cleaning.

(3) The control and issue of linen and staff uniforms.

(4) The control and issue of cleaning equipment and materials within budget limits.

(5) The location and distribution of furniture and furnishings and responsibility for repairs and replacements as required.

(6) To liaise with the Student's Committee and the Student's Counsellor in all matters connected with student functions, discipline and welfare.

(7) To ensure that the Hall is staffed at all times with a Supervisor in accordance with the rota.

(8) To ensure that all procedures for security, safety, health and fire precautions are adhered to in accordance with the safety policy.

(9) To make arrangements for all vacation accommodation requirements.

(10) To undertake any other such duties which may be considered relevant to the position.

12.5.3 Example of a job description for an assistant domestic bursar

Job title: Asst. Domestic Bursar
Responsible to: The Domestic Bursar
Responsible for: Domestic Cleaning Staff
Scope of job: To deputize for the Domestic Bursar in his absence and to have responsibility for the day-to-day housekeeping in the Hall.
Main duties

(1) The supervision and control of the Domestic Cleaning Staff and the maintenance of cleaning standards.

(2) The control and issue of all housekeeping stores.

(3) Supervision of the linen room.

(4) The reporting of all maintenance defects for furniture and the building fabric.

(5) The arrangements for the care and welfare of sick residents.

(6) The keeping of all relevant housekeeping records.

(7) The preparation and authorization of time cards for the payment of wages.

(8) To assist with the administration for conferences, holiday visitors, and special funcitons.

(9) To assist in the safety policy for the Hall and in all security measures.

(10) To perform such other duties as may be reasonably required by the Domestic Bursar.

12.6 Exercise and discussion

1 You have been asked to form a committee with the Administrator, the Architect and the Accountant in order to design a new accommodation block. The accommodation required is for:

A self-contained flatlet for the Assistant Domestic Bursar;
A suite for sick-bay use with 4 beds and bathroom facilities;
24 study-bedrooms with toilet facilities, 2 utility service rooms,
2 lounges and storage for linen, cleaners and luggage.

There is to be a ground and first floor. No lifts.

In order to put forward logical and constructive recommendations you spend your spare time at the weekend to:

(a) Make a sketch plan of the layout and approximate sizes for the new block;
(b) Make notes for floor, wall and ceiling finishes taking into account cleaning routines and safety;
(c) The type of furniture and furnishings required with an estimation of the cost.

2 You are the newly appointed Accommodation Officer for a small University situated near a well-known beauty spot. Apart from two 5-day Conferences and a Sports Weekend, the premises are not used during the vacations and you have been asked to consider all means to increase revenue from this source. You are aksed to produce an advertising brochure to be distributed to colleges and clubs in other parts of the country, aimed at holiday-makers and tourists staying for a minimum period of 3 or 5 days.

The Domestic Bursars (3) and their staff are concerned if the Halls are fully occupied for 48 weeks of the year. Make notes for the talk you will have to have with them on how they will be affected, possible staffing alterations and any differences in standards. What information will you give to the Executive of the Student's Union?

13
Offices and other Public Buildings

In offices and other buildings open to the public, cleaning is a continuous operation of which the occupants and the public are usually unaware. Cleaning and services are varied and relate to the particular organization but, as a general rule, most large office blocks have a Resident Caretaker or House Manager who has overall charge of the building for security, fire prevention, heating and ventilation and who will either liaise with the tenants for their cleaning arrangements, supervise contractors or organize his own staff. All the main cleaning has to be completed before offices are opened or the public are admitted and work may be going on in the evening, overnight or early in the morning with, in most cases, a small back-up staff employed during the day to cope with the toilet areas, dust and debris and for any emergency.

To quote the Building Services Manager of the National Theatre, the Public Areas are a headache and take 'a lot of hammer' from the continually heavy foot traffic and from food and drink spillages in the buffet and restaurants. Many of these buildings have vast areas for workshops, rehearsals, dressing-rooms and offices which are almost continuously in use and make cleaning difficult. A museum or a stately home has the problem of maintaining valuable and very old furniture and furnishings which is highly skilled and expert work.

13.1 Job descriptions

13.1.1 Job description of an office housekeeping manager

Job title: Offices Housekeeping Manager
Responsible to: Offices Administrator

Responsible for: Cleaners, the supervision of contractors, boiler-house attendant.

Purpose of job: To supervise and control the cleaning, maintenance and heating of the property and to liaise with the individual tenants.

Main duties

(1) Supervision of the daily cleaning and the organization and supervision of the periodical cleaning.

(2) Supervision of contractors—for windows, boilers and lifts, floral displays, specialist cleaners.

(3) The recruitment and selection of cleaners within the offices establishment.

(4) Training, organization and welfare of all cleaning staff.

(5) The purchase and stock control of all cleaning supplies and equipment within the budget limits.

(6) Maintaining regular inspections of the building fabric, furniture, fittings plant and equipment and arranging routine repairs. Reporting any major faults to the Offices Administrator.

(7) Liaising with tenants and users of the establishment on cleaning and housekeeping requirements.

(8) The disposal of confidential waste by shredder and incinerator and the control and disposal of rubbish.

(9) Any security measures as determined by the tenants and the Offices Administrator.

(10) The statutory requirements for the building under the Health and Safety at Work Act, 1974, local by-laws for Fire Precautions, the Hygiene Regulations.

(11) Any other duties which can be considered part of the Housekeeping Services.

13.1.2 Example of a job description for a house supervisor in a theatre or arts centre

Job title: House Supervisor

Responsible to: House Manager

Responsible for: House staff and supervision of cleaning contractors

Scope of job: On a rota basis, to be responsible for the cleaning and maintenance of the building and to participate in the management at a supervisory level.

Main duties

(1) The training, organization and supervision of the house staff.

(2) The supervision of the daily cleaning, periodical cleaning and reporting all maintenance defects.

(3) The supervision of all cleaning contractors as needed.

(4) The control and issue of all cleaning stores.

(5) To liaise with all users of the establishment on cleaning and housekeeping requirements.

(6) To ensure that all safety, fire and health procedures are adhered to as laid down in the Safety Policies. To report to the House Manager all safety hazards.

(7) As and when necessary, to help in the control of the public particularly in the prevention of vandalism and in preventing 'nuisance'.

(8) To assist management in such other ways as may be considered relevant to the job.

References and Bibliography

Building Research Establishment:

Maintenance — Maintenance and Running Costs of School Buildings (1968)

Maintenance Standards and Costs (55/74)

Occupancy Costs of Offices (44/77)

Collection and Use of Building Maintenance Data (3/78)

Building Better Houses, BRE News (Winter 1982)

Energy — Energy Research — BRE News (Winter 1978 and 1981)

Low Energy Houses — BRE News (Spring 1982)

Lighting — Studies in the use of Artificial Lighting in Offices (47/78)

Water — Saving Water in the Home (BRE News, Winter 1976)

Research on Water Supply (BRE News, Winter 1982)

Noise — BRE News (Spring 1982 and Summer 1983)

Fire — The Dublin Disco Fire, BRE News (Spring 1982)

Nurses' Home Fire, BRE News (Winter 1982).

The Electricity Council:
  Lighting in Hotels and Restaurants.
The Shirley Institute of Textiles — articles on: Textiles in Buildings — Acoustics, Thermal insulation, Static and flammability, Continental quilts, blankets and sheeting.
British Wood Preserving Association
  Timber Preservation.

The Architect's Journal Handbook of Building Structure (The Architectural Press: London, 1980).
Hospital Hygiene, I. M. Maurer (Edward Arnold: London, 1974).

Index